Guiding Students from Cheating and Plagiarism to Honesty and Integrity

Guiding Students from Cheating and Plagiarism to Honesty and Integrity

Strategies for Change

Ann Lathrop and Kathleen Foss

2005

A Member of the Greenwood Publishing Group

Westport, Connecticut • London

Library of Congress Cataloging-in-Publication Data

Lathrop, Ann.
    Guiding students from cheating and plagiarism to honesty and integrity :
strategies for change / Ann Lathrop and Kathleen Foss.
        p. cm.
    Includes bibliographical references and index.
    ISBN 1-59158-275-X (alk. paper)
    1. Cheating (Education) 2. Students—Conduct of life. I. Foss, Kathleen.
II. Title.
    LB3609.L27 2005
    371.5'8—dc22   2005018010

British Library Cataloguing in Publication Data is available.

Library of Congress Catalog Card Number: 2005018010
ISBN: 1–59158–275–X

First published in 2005

Libraries Unlimited, 88 Post Road West, Westport, CT 06881
A Member of the Greenwood Publishing Group, Inc.
www.lu.com

Printed in the United States of America

The paper used in this book complies with the
Permanent Paper Standard issued by the National
Information Standards Organization (Z39.48–1984).

10 9 8 7 6 5 4 3

Dedication

Now, more than ever,

This book is dedicated to honest students.

Their integrity and hard work need to be recognized, supported, and protected by parents, teachers, administrators, and all concerned members of society.

This new book is dedicated also to the growing numbers of parents and educators whose efforts are building a culture that supports honest students in our schools and homes. They will help our honest students to remain so.

Contents

COPY ME Pages

Preface

David Callahan

Nobody goes into teaching to be a cop. And for many teachers, at high schools and universities alike, cheating by students stands as the most odious fact of professional life. Who wants to police and discipline the very students you are supposed to inspire? Who wants the confrontations, the denials, the tears and—too often—the administrative battles? Nobody, which is one reason why research shows that a great many teachers are often aware of cheating and yet take no action.

But like it not, enforcing standards of academic integrity is a central responsibility of teachers. This is especially true now, when surveys show pervasive cheating at both the high school and university level. The good news is that we now have more insights than ever before about ways to foster an environment of academic integrity. This excellent book shares some of the best thinking available and will stand as a major contribution to the field.

Faculty who confront cheating are not alone. They now can find help and support in a growing network of researchers and activists. Nothing less than a national movement is under way to advance the principle of honesty in academic life.

Yet even as we cheer all the strides that have been made—the new studies with new insights, the new policies and procedures, the new engagement by administrators, faculty, students, and parents—we have to be crystal clear about just what we are up against. The problems of academic dishonesty are symptoms of larger problems in American society. Many sectors of our society—sports, business, law, medicine, accounting—face a crisis of ethics, a crisis rooted in changes over the past few decades in our economy, culture, government, and personal values.

To make a long story short, America has become a far more cut-throat society in recent decades. We are a society that bestows ever larger rewards on the winners, whatever field they may be in, while leaving ordinary people feeling more insecure about their economic prospects. We are a society that has grown more materialistic, where a greater number of people judge their self-worth by their net worth, and where our cultural icons are people like Donald Trump and Paris Hilton. Meanwhile, inequities in our democracy and the criminal justice system enable those with more money and power to bend society's rules to suit their own interests and to go unpunished when they break the rules.

All of this is a formula for anxiety and cynicism. A great many Americans—young and old alike—worry about being left behind, or have lost sight of any other aspiration beyond winning the money chase. And a great many Americans understand that the rules of life aren't fair these days and that honesty is not necessarily the best policy.

What happens when people don't believe that the rules are fair? They make up their own rules. Better that than to be the honest chump in a culture of cheating. Surveys of young people show that this understanding informs student cheating. Many students believe they need to cheat to succeed in life, because that is the way the world works. Even students determined to be honest may feel they must cheat to be competitive with cheaters.

Honor codes and other strategies for academic integrity are a vital part of any solution to the cheating culture. At the very least, faculty and administrators must create a climate where honest students don't feel they are at a disadvantage. Just as cheating can become normalized at a school, so too can academic integrity efforts move the pendulum in the other direction and create a climate where cheating is not cool. Youth culture, as we know, can so often turn on a dime.

But the challenge for institutions of learning is much larger: These institutions must help reverse the broader societal forces that create so much anxiety and cynicism. This can include any number of things, such as encouraging students to engage in civic life and become active stakeholders in our democracy, or requiring community service from students so they learn to think of others and not just themselves.

Perhaps of most importance, schools must reaffirm the humanist ideal of learning as an end in and of itself and as a means of becoming a whole person. If education is nothing more than a market activity—part of a large trend toward the commodification of everything—then widespread cheating is inevitable. School is just another hoop to jump through on the path to making money. But if education is something deeper and more meaningful, then cheating makes no sense. You are just hurting yourself.

Dismantling the culture of cheating won't happen overnight. But books like this one will help us to achieve this goal sooner rather than later.

[David Callahan is the author of *The Cheating Culture: Why More Americans Are Doing Wrong to Get Ahead* (Harcourt, 2004) online at www.cheatingculture.com and is Director of Research for Demos (220 Fifth Ave. FL5, New York, NY 10001). His e-mail address is dcallahan@demos.org.]

Introduction

We need to create a new social contract in America that gives people faith in a few simple principles: Anyone who plays by the rules can get ahead. Everyone has some say in how the rules get made. Everyone who breaks the rules suffers the same penalties. And all of us are in the same boat, living in the same "moral community" and striving together to build a society that confers respect on people based on a wide variety of accomplishments. . . . If the next generations of Americans are to help build a more ethical society and sustain it, they must come of age within institutions that are far less tolerant of cheating than today's high schools and universities. They also must learn early on to commit themselves to principles beyond their own individual self-interest. (Callahan 263, 286)

We believe, with David Callahan, that we must create "institutions that are far less tolerant of cheating than today's high schools and universities." We have developed this book as a practical guide to successful policies, programs, and resources that can help students move toward honesty and integrity.

This new book is a companion to our earlier book, *Student Cheating and Plagiarism in the Internet Era: A Wake-Up Call,* an in-depth examination of electronic and traditional cheating and plagiarism. It is *not* a revision; with the exception of one COPY ME page, all of the material is new.

Students' voices speak to us throughout the book. They tell us why they cheat and why they don't. In response, we offer first-person accounts written by educators, parents, and students who have approached the problem of cheating and plagiarism in a variety of effective ways.

COPY ME pages to help you move students toward honesty and integrity

Almost every chapter has one or more COPY ME pages. Many of these are short articles written by experts in the field. There are lists of resources on specific topics, selected carefully from the many available in print and online. Other pages share practical suggestions from our own experiences or compilations of suggestions from brainstorming sessions with students and teachers.

Any page with COPY ME at the top may be reproduced for class instruction, discussion groups, workshop or conference handouts, newsletter articles, or other educational uses. Permission is granted to make print copies of these pages, but they may not be put on a Web site or distributed in any digital format. The content of the COPY ME page must not be changed and the following credit statement must be included whenever the page is reproduced:

Reprinted with permission of the authors: Guiding Students from Cheating and Plagiarism to Honesty and Integrity: Strategies for Change, *by Ann Lathrop and Kathleen Foss (Libraries Unlimited, 2005). Permission is granted to make print copies for class instruction, discussion groups, workshops, conferences, or newsletters. This material must not be placed on a Web site or distributed in any digital format. This statement must appear in its entirety on each print copy.*

Some of the guest articles are clearly marked as COPY ME pages; the others may not be copied without written permission from the original author and publisher.

What you won't find

We do not address plagiarism of computer code, cheating on the SAT and other standardized tests administered nationally, or dishonesty by administrators and teachers who allow cheating on standardized tests or report false test data to improve the ratings of their school or district. Three books that cover these issues effectively, and that we recommend highly, are:

- *The Cheating Culture: Why More Americans Are Doing Wrong to Get Ahead,* by David Callahan (Harcourt, 2004), is a comprehensive review of cheating in all areas of American life. See related material and updates at www.cheatingculture.com.
- *Cheating on Tests: How to Do It, Detect It, and Prevent It,* by Gregory Cizek (Lawrence Erlbaum, 1999), provides specific information about teachers and principals who cheat, examines legal issues, describes methods of statistical analysis of answers on objective tests, and so on.
- *Detecting and Preventing Classroom Cheating: Promoting Integrity in Assessment*, also by Gregory Cizek (Corwin, 2003), is a thorough over-

view of cheating in our schools with an emphasis on ways to reduce cheating by changes in student testing.

A COPY ME page listing these and other books on student cheating, and books dealing with ethical issues, is in Chapter 1. COPY ME pages listing books and online resources for teaching about plagiarism are in Chapters 9 and 10.

A word of appreciation

We deeply appreciate our many contributors who took time from busy lives to tell their stories. Their voices speak with deep commitment from our pages. Thank you, each of you, for sharing your experiences and your wisdom.

We also appreciate the many helpful comments and suggestions received from readers of our earlier book. Again, we look forward to hearing from *you*.

Ann Lathrop	Kathleen Foss
alathrop@csulb.edu	k_foss@losal.org

References

Callahan, David. *The Cheating Culture: Why More Americans Are Doing Wrong to Get Ahead*. New York: Harcourt, 2004.

Part I

FOCUS ON HONESTY
AND INTEGRITY

CHAPTER ONE

Creating a School Culture of Honesty and Integrity

Interview question: What can you tell me about cheating at your school?

Cheating is no big deal. You just do it—you don't think about it. It's just too easy. Teachers don't watch students during tests, they sit at their desks and grade papers. Students can do anything they want to cheat. It goes on so much, none of the kids think much about it. I don't know of anyone who ever turned anyone in for cheating. No one tells because they're all cheating too. They ignore cheaters because there's so much cheating going on. I think you can stop the cheating—if the teacher cooperates with administrators to stop the cheating. Teachers could stop the cheating if they wanted to. Our principal, I don't know if he had cheating on his mind. He was worried about other stuff besides cheating. 10th grade boy

Student acceptance of cheating is a fact of life in a school where "everybody cheats." Honest students know their own grades are lowered when cheaters get higher scores, but they refuse to "rat out" the cheaters. If "everybody cheats" and teachers cannot possibly catch all the cheaters or identify all the plagiarized papers, then it is time for us to find new ways to tackle the problem.

Five years ago we wrote *Student Cheating and Plagiarism in the Internet Era: A Wake-Up Call*. The vast amount of information on cheating and plagiarism in print and online today is enough to have awakened anyone interested in the issue.

In this new book, we challenge you as educators and parents to work together to change your own school culture from one that tolerates cheating and plagiarism to one that values and encourages honesty and integrity. The programs, policies, and resources in this book can support your efforts.

Four important and encouraging changes have occurred since the first book was published in 2000:

- Schools are taking the problem more seriously.
- Students are playing a leadership role in seeking and implementing solutions.
- Many more schools now have some form of Academic Integrity Policy.
- Many more Web sites and journal articles focus on ways to prevent student cheating and plagiarism.

Teachers, administrators, parents, and students are demanding change, and positive changes are being made.

The hidden barrier to honesty and integrity

These programs and policies all provide a foundation for change. Sadly, their potential effectiveness is destroyed in many schools and districts by a hidden barrier. To date there has been little open discussion of this barrier, yet it is the one most difficult to overcome in truly changing school culture. This barrier is the sometimes public, but more often hidden, reluctance of parents, teachers, administrators, and School Board members to enforce an Academic Integrity Policy fairly and impartially.

It is always difficult for a teacher to accuse a student of cheating or plagiarism, to prove it, and to assign an effective penalty. This takes a great deal of a teacher's time and can create severe emotional stress. A teacher who identifies and tries to penalize cheaters may be criticized by other teachers or administrators. In reality, many teachers do not report student cheating because they do not want to deal with the problem; they ignore it by assuming that all of their students are honest. Students know who these teachers are and continue to cheat without penalty in their classes.

Worse, there are many administrators and School Board members who fail to support a teacher who does identify and penalize a student for cheating or plagiarism. They make excuses, choose to avoid negative publicity, or yield to parental demands for leniency. Parents add to the problem when they shield students from the consequences of their dishonesty; some even threaten lawsuits.

It is important that we each accept individual responsibility for the destruction of this hidden barrier. We must model honesty and integrity for all of our students by creating and enforcing an Academic Integrity Policy consistently and fairly. We must accept the challenge to create a true culture of honesty and integrity in our schools and for our students. Only in this way can we support our honest students and give them the level playing field they want and deserve.

How this book is organized

Part I: Focus on Honesty and Integrity

We surveyed students to learn more about why some refuse to cheat, some cheat whenever they can, and some cheat in many classes but not in all. Student comments from our surveys and interviews, and a summary of the results, are in Chapter 2. They are summarized as COPY ME pages and can be effective discussion starters with students, faculty, and parents. If you use the surveys with your own students, their comments can provide an effective starting point for efforts to change your own school culture. Chapter 3 is a reflection on the students' comments. Chapter 4 turns the focus to the parents' role in developing student honesty and integrity.

Part II: Leadership in Action

Students and educators who are working together for change describe their programs. Several schools implemented an Academic Integrity Policy as an important first step toward change; three were initiated in response to students' requests for help to combat cheating. Teachers and students suggest ways to reduce cheating by changing tests and homework assignments. Librarians describe their leadership roles and urge us to shift our emphasis from the *research paper* to the *research process* as one way to reduce plagiarism. Athletic directors and administrators tell how they encourage young athletes to *Pursue Victory With Honor.*

Part III: Integrity in the Writing Process

Noted educators offer a variety of approaches to discouraging plagiarism in student writing. Sample lessons and COPY ME pages support these efforts.

Part IV: Using Technology with Integrity

Chapter 11 explores ways to maintain honesty and integrity in online education. Mentioned only briefly in our first book, the increasing importance of online education now demands this added attention.

Chapter 12 updates the information on high-tech cheating in our first book and suggests prevention strategies. Much more extensive and specific information on the prevention of both high-tech and traditional cheating and plagiarism is in *Student Cheating and Plagiarism in the Internet Era: A Wake-Up Call,* and that material is not repeated here.

Part V: Appendices

Updated statistics on student cheating and plagiarism are included as background information in Appendix A. Appendix B includes all student survey forms used for this book, with permission to use and adapt them for your school.

Appendix C summarizes the topics, related articles, and COPY ME pages covered in each chapter of *Student Cheating and Plagiarism in the Internet Era: A Wake-Up Call* (Libraries Unlimited, 2000).

Resources

Article:

Thomas G. Layton: "The Digital Child"

COPY ME pages:

Michael Josephson: "Cheating Isn't the Problem"
Books and ERIC Documents: Ethical Issues, Student Cheating

See Appendix C for related information in *Student Cheating and Plagiarism in the Internet Era: A Wake-Up Call:* Chapter 7, Integrity, Ethics, and Character Education.

The Digital Child

Thomas G. Layton

The "digital child" is the boy or girl who came into existence and has lived his or her whole life in a digital world. This child has never known a time when computers were not an ordinary part of day-to-day life, or a time when constant change in the world was not the norm, or a time when it was difficult to access information or to communicate with other human beings with little regard to their actual geographical location.

Time and location

For the digital child, life is a balance between working, learning, playing, and tending to physical and spiritual needs. Life is not broken up into concrete and nearly immobile blocks of time as it was for most twentieth-century children. Instead, all activities are interspersed throughout the day and throughout the year. Just as time is fitted to the child, so is the location of life's activities. Learning does not always take place in the same building or even at the same longitude and latitude. Learning is something that is a constant throughout the day and can occur anywhere in the virtual world.

Activities

In fact, the lines between learning, work, and play are difficult to distinguish. Activities are no longer compartmentalized according to time and place—the time for recess, the place where the computers are housed—and that has tended to blur the lines. Of course, there are times when the digital child is clearly at play or clearly at work, but there are also many times when these activities are inseparable.

Relationships

Family relationships, personal relationships, community relationships, working relationships, and learning relationships form the fabric of the digital child's existence. These relationships are much less subject to time and place than were the relationships forged by the twentieth-century child. Digital children learn and play with people whose age, religion, culture, economic status, and first language are quite different from their own or those of their parents. And, most likely, a significant number of these relationships are with people who live thousands of miles away. This is important because, when they grow up, digital children will be expected to work with people of any age, religion, culture, economic status, and first language at any workplace, anywhere.

Technology

An old proverb says, "Fish can't see water." Likewise, our digital child swims in an ocean of changing technologies. The ebb and flow of new gizmos and scientific discoveries are merely punctuated by occasional technological typhoons reminiscent of the Y2K storm. Quite at home in this swirling sea, the digital student learns to take advantage of each new technological advancement, confidently awaiting the next new breakthrough.

Learning style

Digital children do not learn in isolation. They might work alone, but they learn in groups, and some group members may live in other countries. For them, knowledge is like dropping a pebble in a pond. Waves of understanding wash over the digital classroom. Working out an answer and sharing it with your digital classmate is no longer considered cheating. Cheating is keeping the answer to yourself. Learning is collaborative and social, not solitary and competitive.

Digital children seek relevance. They want to solve real problems. They want what they do to make a genuine contribution to the world. They instinctively understand that today's knowledge might turn out to be useless tomorrow. They do not accept the proposition that they must learn something now because it will be useful 10 years from now. They know better.

Curriculum

The digital school must prepare students for life in a time of explosive social change driven by explosive advances in technology. Digital children must learn to read critically, write effectively, listen intently, and speak fluently. They must be able to find information, understand the information they locate, evaluate the reliability of that information, and see how to apply it to answer a pressing question or to take advantage of a new opportunity. They must be able to communicate their ideas to diverse groups using a variety of media. They must also be able to understand the ideas of others and see how their own concepts might blend with those of their work-mates to solve problems and create new things.

Quality

The digital community demands quality in education above everything else. Its members know that an excellent education is the key to thriving in the digital world. They are not misled by the educational/political trends of the analog twentieth century: Standards will be replaced by choice; test scores will be replaced by products and solutions; and diplomas will be replaced by the flow from data to information to insight to wisdom.

[Adapted and reprinted with permission from the author and from *Electronic School,* an editorially independent publication of the National School Boards Association.

Thomas G. Layton, a self-professed online learning evangelist, is the originator of CyberSchool (now COOLSchool), coolschool.k12.or.us, the first Internet-based public high school distance learning program. He is a consultant with Clarity Innovations, Inc., in Portland, OR.]

Cheating Isn't the Problem

Michael Josephson

Though rising cheating rates in schools have signaled for a decade that the hole in our moral ozone is getting bigger, the media seem to have just discovered that there's a problem. But the new hook they've seized upon concerns the use of high-tech tools from the Internet to cell phones.

This drives me crazy because the more we focus on all the clever ways young-sters can cheat, the more likely we are to ignore the fact that the biggest single factor in escalating academic dishonesty is the failure of parents and teachers to diligently teach, enforce, advocate and model personal integrity. It's the adults, not the kids, who have the greatest responsibility to create an ethical culture that nurtures the virtues of honor, honesty and fairness.

One part of that responsibility is to demonstrate a commitment to the integrity of exams and grades. Thus, we can solve the problem of high-tech exam cheating by old-fashioned low-tech methods: Don't let students bring anything into the exam room that isn't essential to the test! And if calculators are really necessary, adopt a procedure that assures that students empty the device of any improper information.

There are many well-established procedures that eliminate or reduce cheating, such as having alternative forms of exams, not giving the same test at different times in the day, and assuring that the exam is proctored by an attentive adult who continuously walks among the test takers. What message do you think schools send when these simple procedures are ignored?

The truth is we will never solve the cheating problem until those who have the opportunity to instill values and shape attitudes of young people engage in thoughtful, systematic and comprehensive efforts to promote integrity and prevent cheating.

This is Michael Josephson reminding you that **CHARACTER COUNTS!** [May 13, 2004]

COPY ME

Books and ERIC Documents

Ethical Issues

American Association of School Librarians. *Information Power: Building Partnerships for Learning.* Chicago: American Library Association, 1998.

International Society for Technology in Education (ISTE). *National Educational Technology Standards Project: for Students* (2000); *for Teachers* (2002); *for Administrators* (2002). Eugene, OR: International Society for Technology in Education, 2000–2002.

Johnson, Doug. *Learning Right from Wrong in the Digital Age: An Ethics Guide for Parents, Teachers, Librarians, and Others Who Care About Computer-Using Young People.* Worthington, OH: Linworth, 2003.

Josephson, Michael, and Melissa Mertz. *Honor Above All.* Los Angeles, CA: Josephson Institute of Ethics, 2004.

Lee, David L., et al. *How to Deal Effectively with Lying, Stealing, and Cheating.* Austin, TX: Pro Ed, 2003.

Satterlee, Anita G. "Academic Dishonesty among Students: Consequences and Interventions." July 2002. ERIC (ED 469 468).

Simpson, Carol, ed. *Ethics In School Librarianship: A Reader.* Worthington, OH: Linworth, 2003.

Willard, Nancy E. *Computer Ethics, Etiquette, & Safety for the 21st Century Student.* Eugene, OR: International Society for Technology in Education, 2002.

Student Cheating

Bopp, Mary, et al. *Reducing Incidents of Cheating in Adolescence.* Master of Arts Action Research Project. Chicago: Saint Xavier U. 2001. (ED 456127)

Callahan, David. *The Cheating Culture: Why More Americans Are Doing Wrong to Get Ahead.* New York: Harcourt, 2004. www.cheatingculture.com/davidcallahaninterview.htm

Cizek, Gregory J. *Cheating on Tests: How to Do It, Detect It, and Prevent It.* Mahwah, NJ: Lawrence Erlbaum, 1999.

Cizek, Gregory J. *Detecting and Preventing Classroom Cheating: Promoting Integrity in Assessment.* Thousand Oaks, CA: Corwin, 2003.

Lathrop, Ann, and Kathleen E. Foss. *Student Cheating and Plagiarism in the Internet Era: A Wake-Up Call.* Libraries Unlimited, 2000.

Whitley, Bernard E., Jr., and Patricia Keith-Spiegel. *Academic Dishonesty: An Educator's Guide.* Mahwah, NJ: Lawrence Erlbaum, 2002.

CHAPTER TWO

Student Voices

I Don't Cheat

I would never cheat in any class because of integrity. Most people my age don't have that, but I do. I want to know that I did the work and I'm really that smart by my grades. I don't cheat because I did the thinking. My knowledge, not someone else's, is golden to me. "I think, therefore I am"—some famous dude, I forget his name. 7th grade boy

I Cheat

Cheating is the "cool" thing to do. It's like having the latest designer shoes or the "hip" haircut. It's an accepted fact among students that we all cheat, and it's considered a sin to turn someone in. Since so many students cheat, no one really considers how immoral it is. It's as habitual as inhaling and exhaling, or brushing one's teeth. 11th grade girl

Many students do not cheat. *Why not?* Others cheat at every opportunity. *Why?* What makes students cheat in some classes but not in others? Student responses to these questions, as reported to us in a 2004 survey, are summarized in this chapter.

We received comments from more than 600 students, grades 7–12, from schools in five states. The schools were selected because we knew a librarian there who was willing to help. The box indicates what we asked the students to tell us. All four questions were placed at the top of the page so someone glancing at a student's paper would not know which question was being answered.

Please choose ONE question to write about. Circle the question you choose:
1   2   3   4

1. If you cheat in all or most all of your classes, why do you cheat?
2. Describe one time when you could have cheated in school but you didn't. Why did you decide not to cheat?
3. Why would you never cheat, even when other students are cheating?
4. If you cheat in some classes, but there is one class you absolutely would never cheat in, why don't you cheat in that class?

We tabulated a total of 906 comments after eliminating those that were illegible, too short, or too general. Of these, 676 comments were responses to "Why I Don't Cheat" and 230 comments were responses to "Why I Cheat." Some students wrote only one or two sentences; others filled the page, and a few even wrote on the back.

There is no statistical analysis of these surveys and we draw no scientific conclusions. We found the comments interesting and you may wish to survey your own students for a comparison.

These surveys, and others that we used in our first book, are in Appendix B. Permission is granted to use them "as is" or to adapt them. We suggest that you clear any survey with your administration before asking students to complete it. The results can provide interesting material for discussion in class or at faculty and parent meetings.

Three COPY ME pages summarize the responses, followed by additional COPY ME pages with selected student comments. We organized responses into three categories:

1. Why I don't cheat
2. Why I cheat
3. Why I cheat in some classes but not in others

We use [Teacher] to replace any teacher's name in a response. Some spelling errors were corrected automatically by our word processor; the other errors remain. The grammar and underlining are all theirs. We are especially fond of the first statement at the beginning of this chapter.

Discussion

Far and away the most disturbing student comments were those identifying teacher behaviors that make cheating easy, or even encourage cheating. When "Teacher makes cheating easy" is combined with "I don't like / respect the teacher," this category becomes the most frequent survey response. It also may be the category we can change most easily to make cheating more difficult.

One unexpected result was that only 23 of the 906 student comments mentioned parents' attitudes or moral standards. This may indicate that parents are failing to give moral direction to their children.

The statements were written anonymously and there is no way to determine the degree of honesty in the survey. However, many statements have the ring of truth and they target student and teacher practices that need to be changed if we are to reach our goal of creating a culture of honesty and integrity in our schools.

Resources

Article:

Jason M. Stephens: "Justice or Just Us? What to Do About Cheating"

COPY ME pages:

Student Voices
Student Comments / Discussion

See survey forms in Appendix B.

See Appendix C for related information in *Student Cheating and Plagiarism in the Internet Era: A Wake-Up Call*: Chapter 4, Why We Are Alarmed.

COPY ME

Student Voices: Why I Don't Cheat

This tabulation summarizes the relative frequency of student responses.

responses (%)

A. Pride in work / desire to learn   **194 (21%)**
- I studied, know the material / I'm smart / I don't need to cheat (70)
- I want to earn my grades / challenge myself / reach my potential (52)
- I need to learn the material for my career, for college, for athletics (51)
- A test should show what I know, not what someone else knows (21)

B. Consequences and penalties   **165 (18%)**
- Afraid to get caught (113)
- Severe consequences / expulsion / poor college referrals (52)

C. Moral beliefs and values   **164 (18%)**
- Cheating is bad / I'd feel guilty / conscience bothers me (106)
- Religious beliefs / moral values / want to respect myself (28)
- Cheating is a bad habit / can't cheat through life, in real world (15)
- Cheating only hurts myself / cheating myself of an education (15)

D. Peers   **46 (5%)**
- The student I'm copying from may not know any more than I do (22)
- Cheating isn't fair to students who worked hard for their grade (21)
- I want my friends to respect me (3)

E. Parents   **13 (1%)**
- Would be disappointed in me / punish me (10)
- Say "don't cheat" (3)

F. Academic Integrity Policy / Honor Code at school   **8 (1%)**
- An Academic Integrity Policy / Honor Code is helpful (8)

Student Voices: Why I Cheat

responses (%)

G. Cheating is easier than studying   **65 (7%)**
- I'm lazy / didn't study (29)
- Studying takes too much time / have a job / have better things to do (26)
- Cheating is fun / it's easy / it's a challenge (10)

H. Grades   57 (6%)
- Need to pass the class / I'm failing / need a better grade (31)
- Need good grades for college entry or sports (18)
- Class or test is too hard / can't get good grades even if I study (8)

I. Peers   11 (1%)
- Friends help me to cheat / expect me to help them cheat (11)

J. Parents   10 (1%)
- Expect / demand good grades (10)

Student Voices: Why I Cheat In Some Classes But Not In Others

responses (%)

K. Classroom management / "some teachers make cheating easy" 59 (7%)
- Teacher leaves room during tests (22)
- Teacher works at desk during tests / doesn't pay attention to class (6)
- Teacher doesn't care if we cheat / doesn't try to prevent cheating (7)
- Substitute teachers make it really easy to cheat (3)
- Tests / answer keys are left out on desk during or before test (7)
- Desks / chairs at table are close together so it's easy to copy (6)
- Teacher lets us correct our own papers or correct a friend's paper (3)
- Students take make-up tests in a room without supervision (2)
- Students from earlier periods tell us test questions for later in day (3)

L. Teacher's positive relationship with student   46 (5%)
- Teacher trusts me / would feel bad, lose respect for me if I cheat (23)
- I like or respect the teacher / like the class (23)

M. Classroom management / "some teachers make cheating hard" 40 (4%)
- Teacher watches us / checks everything so we won't cheat / is strict (38)
- Teacher tries hard to be sure we learn everything / really cares (2)

N. Negative attitude toward learning / toward teacher   14 (2%)
- Class isn't important to me / not useful for college / is a joke (7)
- I don't like / respect the teacher (7)

O. Homework   14 (2%)
- Too much homework / it's just busywork (9)
- Friends help me / expect me to share homework (5)

COPY ME

Student Comments / Discussion: Why I Don't Cheat

A. Pride in work / desire to learn: 194 total comments

Discussion: This category has the largest number of responses. It also has some of the most indignant ones, made by students who were offended by the mere idea that they might need to cheat.

I studied / know the material / I'm smart / I don't need to cheat (70)

- *I had stayed up till 1 o'clock a.m. studying because it was going to be the last grade of the quarter. [Teacher] went out of the classroom and some people started sharing answers. I was about to because I couldn't think straight and I needed a lot of help on some questions. I didn't cheat though because I felt very confident about my grade on the test. The next day, I got my test back and found out that I only missed one question, but I still got an A. I am a very good guy!!!!! 8th grade boy*
- This one time I was going to cheat for my Spanish final. I stayed up making a cheatsheet. But when I came to it writing all that stuff down helped me to study and I knew the material when the time came so I ripped up the cheatsheet. 12th grade boy
- *I am smart enough to get a good grade without the help of other people. When other people are cheating I just do my work and then sit back and hope they get caught. 8th grade boy*

Want to earn my grades / challenge myself / reach my potential (52)

- *I would never cheat because I like the satisfactory of getting good grades on my own. When a hard test comes up and I've been studying like crazy, it feels good to get a good grade. I also get the satisfaction of knowing I learned something. 9th grade boy*
- If you cheat what grade you got on that assignment really isn't yours so you can't have pride in it. It is a cheap imitation of the real thing. 12th grade girl
- *There's no better feeling than aceing the test and knowing that you did it on your own! 9th grade girl*
- It is about keeping your dignity and challenging yourself. 10th grade boy

Need to learn the material for my career / for college / for athletics (51)

- *I definately don't cheat in math because I really need to know that stuff for the future. 10th grade girl*
- I wouldn't cheat in Spanish because I actually want to learn that language. 10th grade boy

- *If I were to never cheat in a class it would be math. I think that math is the only class we will need in life so I take it a little more serious then other classes. 12th grade boy*
- If I am cheating, I'm not learning anything and if I want to be a Physical Therapist then I can't cheat. I'll never get through pre-med and med school. 9th grade boy

Test should show what I know, not what someone else knows (21)

- *I always want to earn my grades. If I get an A I want to do it on my own, or if I get an "F" I want to do it on my own so I know what I did wrong. 8th grade girl*
- My grades are reflective of my work habits and effort, not of my ability to glance sneakily at a paper. 8th grade girl
- *I would never cheat because I want to learn. I feel that the whole point of taking a test is so your teacher can see if you understand the material that he or she has taught you. It is also a test so you can understand too. 11th grade boy*

B. Consequences and penalties: 165 total comments

Discussion: Students are concerned by the possibility of being caught and the penalties they might face. Important factors are whether the teacher would "actually do anything about it" and if there would, in fact, be any penalty enforced.

Afraid to get caught (113)

- *I know many students who cheat but for me the risk of getting caught is too great. Cheating might get me an A on a test but if I got caught I would get a zero. 11th grade girl*
- I'm afraid of being embarrassed by getting caught. 12th grade boy

Severe consequences / expulsion / poor college referrals (52)

- *I wouldn't cheat in Physics because I think that's the only class where the teacher would actually do anything about it. 12th grade boy*
- To me it is not worth cheating in math. If you are caught you are given a zero on the test and a referral. 12th grade boy
- *The reason why I wouldn't cheat is because of the consequences. You could get your test taking away. You could get detention. You could also be sent to the office. You could even be suspended for a day or two. 7th grade boy*

C. Moral beliefs and values: 164 total comments

Discussion: Statements indicate that many students do hold strong moral and religious values. Yet only 18 percent of student responses mentioned these values as an important reason not to cheat.

Cheating is bad / I'd feel guilty / conscience bothers me (106)

- *It is dishonest, lazy, and contrary to the principle of self-reliance. 12th grade girl*
- If I only got a good grade because I copied someone else's paper or plagirized, I would feel guilty about receiving a good grade. 11th grade girl
- *I personally have a guilty conscience if I do something wrong, I feel physically ill, so cheating is not really a possibility when it comes to my own health and welfare. 12th grade girl*
- Whenever I feel like I'm going to do something bad I always ask myself, "What would I tell my children." Like, "Yeah, I used to always cheat." That would just be stupid and I'd rather not lie to my children and feel bad about myself. 9th grade girl

Religious beliefs / moral values / want to respect myself (28)

- *I never cheat because its wrong and very bad for your karma. God does not approve. 12th grade boy*
- I was brought up in a Christian household. It is wrong for someone to get the fruits of another's labor. 10th grade girl
- *I don't cheat because on the first day of school, [Teacher] told us that a truly honest person means being honest even when no one is there to witness it. Whenever I have the urge to cheat because I don't know an answer, I always remember [Teacher's] words. After that, all I can do is try my hardest and I get whichever grade I get, my conscience is clean, and that's what is most important to me. 7th grade girl*
- I'd never cheat. Ever! It's morally wrong and I want to go to heaven. 11th grade boy
- *I never cheat because I know it is not right and God would not want me to. 9th grade boy*

Cheating is a bad habit / can't cheat through life, in real world (15)

- *Cheating now doesn't help you in the long run, eventually there won't be anyone to cheat off of and you'll be, for lack of a better word, screwed. 12th grade girl*
- I have thought of cheating before. However, I do not do it, because I know the consequences. Even if I don't get caught, I can't develop a habit of cheating throughout life. 10th grade girl
- *You will never get anywhere by cheating. You may get good grades from it now but when you get older you will fail right out. Then your life is ruined. 7th grade boy*

- I want to be able to get into a good college, and if I cheat now, I might never stop, and if I get caught there, I can only look forward to flipping burgers my whole life. I don't cheat for my future. 8th grade boy

Cheating only hurts myself / cheating myself of an education (15)

- *If you cheat, your not cheating against anyone but yourself. You will never understand the questions on the test and you will probably have problems in the future. 7th grade girl*
- If I don't know the material that I am supposed to, it makes it harder for me to progress into a higher level. 8th grade boy
- *What's the point of cheating? It's like lying on your resume to get a hard job then when you get there you can't perform up to expectation. In the end you just screw yourself. 12th grade girl*

D. Peers: 46 total comments

Discussion: The responses were refreshingly frank in recognizing that another student's answers could be wrong and commenting on how unfair cheating is to the student who actually studied for the test or did the homework assignment.

The student I'm copying from may not know any more than I do (22)

- *Cheating is pointless and useless. First off why should I trust other people's answers over mine? That's an insult to my own intelligence. 11th grade boy*
- I would never cheat because you never know if the people you are cheating off of even have the right answers. 7th grade girl
- *The person could be easily lying to me and purposely be giving me incorrect answers or the person could be un-intelligent and have wrong answers. 9th grade girl*

Cheating isn't fair to other students who worked hard for their grade (21)

- *I never cheat because it isn't fair to your classmates and peers. If my friend was in my class and I cheated, and the teacher graded on a curve, and his/her grade dropped because of guys like me, I would feel horrible. 9th grade boy*
- From an ethical standpoint, cheating is a horrible thing to do; the student that studies is taken advantage of, and the student that cheats gains nothing but a grade. 12th grade girl
- *Someone worked hard and figured out the answers and then you just copy. I think that that is a very rude thing to do. This is why I never cheat. 8th grade girl*

- None of the kids try to cheat in Honors Biology. One tried to cheat on a test but no one would help him. Everyone in that class works hard and no one wants to help someone who doesn't work. 10th grade boy

I want my friends to respect me (3)

- *People always respect individuals for doing well or trying their hardest, they don't respect cheaters and eventually everyone will find out if you cheated. The risks are too big, your credibility is shot, so is your reputation as a student. 12th grade girl*
- I can't think of any of my friends who cheat in class. I try to surround myself with peers who try to achieve similar goals as myself, such as work hard and get good grades. 8th grade girl

E. Parents: 13 total comments

Discussion: Only 13 students mentioned their parents. This small number was our most unexpected result and may indicate that parents are failing to give moral direction to their children.

Would be disappointed in me / punish me (10)

- *Why I didn't cheat was because of my mom. She often reminds me that she'd rather me fail a test rather than to lie and cheat on one. 8th grade girl*
- Just because other students are imature and don't study doesn't mean you should follow their example. Besides, my mom and dad would kill me if they ever found out. 9th grade girl
- *I don't cheat 'cause my parents work at school and my life would be a living hell if I did. It's not worth it anyway. 9th grade girl*
- My mother would be heartbroken if I got in trouble for cheating. 11th grade girl
- *My parents, my teachers and my friends all trust me. To cheat, if I got caught, I would lose all of that trust. I want to keep that trust. 7th grade girl*

Say "don't cheat" (3)

- *My parents have instilled into me that cheating is wrong and I feel guilty as hell if I think of cheating. I don't know but it's like betraying them or something. To tell the truth parent trust is quite difficult to get. 10th grade girl*
- My parents raised me with enough pride in myself and my abilities that I don't usually feel tempted. 11th grade girl

F. Academic Integrity Policy / Honor Code at school: 8 total comments

Discussion: One school had an Honor Council in place and another had recently implemented an Academic Integrity Policy at the time of the survey, yet only eight student comments mentioned the policies.

- *I am on Honor Council and I know the consequences and I have a conscience. 10th grade girl*
- Teachers often leave the room and I've been tempted to cheat. But then I remember [Teacher] and his honor council speeches so I don't. 9th grade girl

Author's note: Student comments are unedited except for the use of [Teacher] to replace any teacher's name in a response and some spelling errors corrected automatically by our word processor.

Friends help me to cheat / expect me to help them cheat (11)

- *If I'm very good and a friend is not good at that class, I would let her cheat off me. 10th grade girl*
- There are people who help others cheat, either because they are friends or they feel some kind of pity for them, seeing them struggle where they themselves are excelling. 12th grade boy

J. Parents: 10 total comments

Discussion: The very few students who mentioned parents was our most unexpected result. Parents may be, by omission, responsible for their children's cheating.

Expect / demand good grades (10)

- *Students these days have so much on them that in some cases if they don't do well they will be punished, so they feel that is their only option. 11th grade girl*
- I don't usually study. And if I got a bad grade, I would die a horrible death by my mom. 9th grade boy
- *My parents lately have become obsessed with my grades and I feel that if I don't cheat and I do bad that I will be a failure in my parents eyes. 11th grade girl*
- I cheat because I want to get good grades to make my parents proud. 7th grade boy

Author's note: Student comments are unedited except for the use of [Teacher] to replace any teacher's name in a response and some spelling errors corrected automatically by our word processor.

COPY ME

Student Comments / Discussion: Why I Cheat
In Some Classes But Not In Others

K. Classroom management / "some teachers make cheating easy": 59 total comments

Discussion: These comments were the most disturbing ones in the survey. They identify teacher behaviors that can and should be changed. It is unrealistic to expect students to value honesty when "teachers make it so easy to cheat."

Teacher leaves room during tests (22)

- *Teachers that leave the room during testing, it's like a Chinese fire drill. 9th grade boy*
- A while back, our teacher had basically given up on teaching because he knew he was to retire anyways, so we figured that he would probably end up leaving the room while we were taking the test, and he did. 12th grade girl
- *The teacher left for a moment and everyone started sharing answers. 10th grade boy*
- I cheat in all of my classes because the teachers make it so easy to cheat. When I cheat I get good grades. 8th grade girl
- *The teacher had left the room and many of the other students decided to take advantage of this opportunity and ask their neighbors for help. 11th grade boy*

Teacher works at desk during tests, doesn't pay attention to class (6)

- *Some teachers notice everything so I'm too afraid to cheat in those classes, but other teachers leave the classroom or don't pay attention so then I cheat. 10th grade girl*
- Some classes are easier to cheat in because the teacher doesn't walk around and scan the room to see who's cheating or talking, etc. 11th grade girl
- *My English teacher always sits behind her computer doing other things. 8th grade girl*

Teacher doesn't care if we cheat, doesn't try to prevent cheating (7)

- *I cheat in some of my classes because my teachers are really clueless and they would never know. 10th grade girl*
- Some teachers are good at catching but most are bad. 9th grade boy
- *He of course forgot about all the maps showing the 13 colonys on his walls. And I saw many of the kids looking at these maps but I didn't need them so I just took my test got an A and told the teacher about the maps. 9th grade boy*

- Some teachers see cheating and neglect to act. 11th grade girl

Substitute teachers make it really easy to cheat (3)

- *If there is a sub that's the best time to cheat because they don't know what's going on. 12th grade boy*

Tests / answer keys are left out on desk during or before test (7)

- *One time in math we were taking a test and I sat by the teachers desk and the answers were on his desk. 8th grade girl*
- Our chemistry teacher left the class and a student went on his computer to play a game as our teacher allowed us to do. He found the final on the computer so he saved it on a disk and offered to give it to people at a later date. 12th grade girl

Desks / chairs at table are close together so it's easy to copy (6)

- *Our class is set up in rows, so it's easy to look. 8th grade boy*
- We just sit scattered all over the room and we all have our backpacks next to us so it's crowded and it's easy to look at a paper with answers. 9th grade girl

Teacher lets us correct our own papers or correct a friend's paper (3)

- *We have a quiz every day and switch papers to grade. We can keep our own paper or switch with a buddy. So we get most of the answers right. 12th grade girl*

Students take make-up tests in a room without supervision (2)

- *I was taking a final in the library by myself with no supervision. 12th grade girl*
- My teacher let me go in an empty room, with my backpack, to take a test. 12th grade boy

Students from earlier periods tell us test questions for later in day (3)

- *Someone tells someone in a later period what is on the test, most people do it. 12th grade girl*
- People like me, we ask our friends, who've taken the test in an earlier class, what's on the test. Some people might not even consider this cheating, but deep down I know its wrong. 12th grade girl

L. Teacher's positive relationship with student: 46 total comments

Discussion: These statements reaffirm the value of a positive teacher-student relationship and the important influence a teacher has on student behavior.

Teacher trusts me / would feel bad, lose respect for me if I cheat (23)

- *I would never cheat in my Honors U.S. history class because the teacher is extremely strict. I know how extremely disappointed she would be and I don't think I could carry the stigmatizm of being a cheater in her class. 12th grade girl*
- I would never cheat in my English class because I had a personal relationship with my teacher. He took cheating very personally and I didn't want my coach to be disappointed in me. 12th grade boy
- *One of my goals every year is to impress my teacher. I wouldn't cheat because I would get into trouble which is not impressing my teacher. 9th grade girl*
- I simply respect that teacher too much to cheat. 8th grade boy

I like or respect the teacher / like the class (23)

- *I wouldn't cheat in that one class because I respected the teacher and actually cared about what they thought of me. When a teacher shows respect to you it is a lot harder to cheat than if the teacher isn't respectful. 11th grade girl*
- The reason why I wouldn't cheat would be out of respect for a certain teacher I liked very much. I think that if you respect the teacher you should respect them with honesty. [Teacher] let us grade our own tests and by respecting us, he made us want to respect ourselfs and him by not cheating. 12th grade boy
- *[Teacher] is not a teacher who favors a smart student over a lesser one. Even when I don't do as good as I wanted on something I know she won't hold it against me. I know she will help me to do better next time. 10th grade girl*

M. Classroom management / "some teachers make cheating hard": 40 total comments

Discussion: Students are very aware of teacher attitudes and behaviors that strongly discourage cheating. For many, a personal relationship with the teacher is an important factor in their "cheat–don't cheat" decision.

Teacher watches us, checks everything so we won't cheat, is strict (38)

- *I would never cheat in my history class. My teacher is incredibly precautious and checks everything, even every little thing on the Works Cited. I think she is a very good teacher. 10th grade girl*
- Some teachers make us roll up our sleeves and check our arms for notes. Our math teacher checks our calculators. 12th grade boy
- *The teacher always is looking around the room and checking backpacks and people who are hiding things, so it is not worth it. 10th grade boy*
- There are some classes where you would just never cheat in. Those are usually the classes with the *strictest and most careful* teachers. 10th grade girl

- *I don't know the teacher well and he has a crazy policy against cheating. 12th grade boy*

Teacher tries hard to be sure we learn everything / really cares (2)

- *I would never cheat in U.S. history with [Teacher]. She makes us take notes every day and makes sure we understand the material by playing review games. It is easier to study than cheat in that class. 10th grade girl*
- There was a time in [Teacher's] U.S. History class. We had a test coming up, but his tests were different from any other. The day before, he would give us the essay questions and we had the whole period to look them up, and bring them up to him to find out if it was wrong or right. 12th grade boy

N. Negative Attitude Toward Learning / Toward Teacher: 14 total comments

Discussion: Positive changes in teacher behavior can lead to more positive student attitudes toward learning and toward the class. Efforts also can be made to help students understand the value of any given class and why it can be important to their lives.

Class isn't important to me, not useful for college, is a joke (7)

- *I would cheat in history class on a final exam because in the real world, nobody cares who led the 54th cavalry in the Civil war. 8th grade boy*
- I definitely don't cheat in math because I'm going to really need to know that stuff for the future, but when it's something I don't need why not cheat? 11th grade girl
- *The curriculum is BS and I spend time on more relevant things. 10th grade boy*

I don't like / respect the teacher (7)

- *I know that if I get a teacher who is a jerk, I don't feel like trying for them or caring much about their class so I will cheat. 12th grade boy*
- Why do we cheat? For two reasons: 1) We don't like the teacher and/or the class. 2) We feel we can get away with something we haven't earned. 10th grade girl
- *If the teacher is mean or does unfair things, then I don't feel bad about cheating. 11th grade girl*

O. Homework: 14 total comments

Discussion: The challenge here is to create homework assignments that students regard as meaningful and important to their own learning. It also could be helpful for teachers in academic departments to cooperatively schedule lengthy homework assignments, project due dates, and major tests so students do not have three or more of these on the same day.

Too much homework / it's just busywork (9)

- *Teachers believe that they are the only ones to give us an hour or more of homework and that we have no personal life. 12th grade girl*
- Cheating on homework is less offensive to me because I place less value on busywork. 12th grade girl
- *I look at work as a waste of time because on tests I usually score 90% or higher. If you don't need the practice then why do it? 12th grade boy*

Friends help me / expect me to share homework (5)

- *My friend let me copy her homework and we got caught. There weren't really any consequences. 8th grade girl*

Author's note: Student comments are unedited except for the use of [Teacher] to replace any teacher's name in a response and some spelling errors corrected automatically by our word processor.

Justice or Just Us? What to Do About Cheating

(abridged, see below for complete article online)

Jason M. Stephens

Adults always seem shocked and surprised to learn of student cheating, especially in high-achieving and high-socioeconomic schools. They shouldn't be so surprised. Research in high schools shows that two thirds of students cheat on tests, and 90 percent cheat on homework. The figures are almost as high among college students. Furthermore, it is clear that rates of cheating have gone up over the past three decades.

Why? Do students fail to understand that cheating is wrong? Well, yes and no. In a recent study of high school students that I conducted, many students acknowledged that cheating is wrong but admitted they do it anyway, seemingly without much remorse. They cheat for simple, pragmatic reasons—to get high grades and because they don't have time to do the work carefully. Especially for college-bound students, the pressure for grades is real. According to the Higher Education Research Institute's annual survey, 47 percent of incoming college freshmen in 2003 reported having earned an A average in high school.

But despite the pressure for consistently high grades, students don't generally cheat in all of their classes. And somewhat surprisingly, it is not the difficulty of the course that predicts in which classes they are more likely to cheat. Instead, I found that high school students cheat more when they see the teacher as less fair and caring and when their motivation in the course is more focused on grades and less on learning and understanding. At least in these classes, they can justify cheating. They don't claim it is morally acceptable, but they don't seem to feel that it really matters if they cheat under these circumstances.

In most studies of cheating, the researcher decides which behaviors constitute cheating, and students are only asked to report how often they engage in those behaviors. In my survey of high school students, I asked them to report both their level of engagement in a set of 11 "academic behaviors," as well as their beliefs concerning whether or not those behaviors were "cheating." Not surprisingly, the vast majority (85 percent or more) indicated that behaviors such as "copying from another student during a test" and "using banned crib notes or cheat sheets during a test" were cheating. However, only 18 percent believed that "working on an assignment with other students when the teacher asked for individual work" was cheating.

Subsequent interviews with a small sub-sample of these students revealed that students regarded this forbidden collaboration as furthering their knowledge and understanding, and therefore saw it as an act of learning rather than a form of cheating. These findings suggest that students make a distinction between behaviors that are overtly dishonest (such as copying the work of another, which effectively serves to misrepresent one's state of knowledge) and behaviors that are not inherently dishonest (such as working with others, which can serve to enrich one's interpersonal skills and academic learning). Educators, too, should be cognizant of this distinction and be judicious in prohibiting collaboration.

With this pervasiveness of acceptance by students, is it acceptable to us as a society to tacitly accept cheating as a fact of life and not be so shocked when it comes to light? I don't think so. Cutting corners and compromising principles are habit-forming. They don't stop at graduation, as we have seen in recent scandals in business and journalism. And cheating or cutting corners in one's professional or personal life can cause real damage—both to oneself and to others. We need to care about it.

And I believe we can do something about it. The best ways to reduce cheating are all about good teaching. In fact, if efforts to deal with cheating don't emerge from efforts to educate, they won't work—at least not when vigilance is reduced. These suggestions are easier said than done, but I believe they point in the right direction, both for academic integrity and for learning more generally.

- Help students understand the value of what they're being asked to learn by creating learning experiences that connect with their interests and have real-world relevance.
- Consider whether some of the rules that are frequently broken are arbitrary or unnecessarily constraining. For example, is individual effort on homework always so important? Given the evidence that collaboration in doing homework supports learning, it doesn't seem so.
- As much as possible, connect assessment integrally with learning. Create assessments that are fair and meaningful representations of what students should have learned. Make sure assessments provide informative feedback and thus contribute to improved performance. When possible, individualize evaluations of students' progress and offer them privately. Avoid practices that invite social comparisons of performance.
- Give students images of people who don't cut corners: scientists who discover things they don't expect because they approach their work with an impeccable respect for truth and a genuinely open mind; business people who exemplify integrity even when it seems like it might cost

them something. But don't preach. Take seriously the fact that, in some contexts, being consistently honest can be hard.

Finally, as educators, we must do our best to exemplify intellectual integrity ourselves—in everything from how we treat students and each other to how we approach the subject matter, to how we approach mandatory high-stakes testing, to how we think and talk about politics. We need to look for ways to make deep and searching honesty both palpable and attractive.

[Abridged and reprinted with permission of the author and The Carnegie Foundation for the Advancement of Teaching. The original article was published in the May 2004 issue of *Carnegie Perspectives,* online at www.carnegiefoundation.org/perspectives/perspectives 2004.May.htm.

Dr. Stephens is on the faculty of the Department of Educational Psychology at the University of Connecticut. This article was written during his tenure as a research assistant at The Carnegie Foundation for the Advancement of Teaching.]

CHAPTER THREE

Responding to the Students

There are two types of cheaters in high school today. Type one cheats to get into Harvard or Yale. Type two cheats because cheating is easier than learning and the teachers just don't care. 10th grade girl

I would never cheat in [Teacher's] class because I know that would really hurt her feelings. Plus, she really does want her students to do well, and gives us lots of opportunities to do extra credit so we will make good grades. 10th grade girl

Student comments in Chapter 2 make it clear they recognize those teachers who actively work to prevent cheating and plagiarism. They also recognize the teachers who don't seem to care about cheating, do little to prevent it, or ignore it when they do see it. These are the teachers who leave the room or work at their desks during testing while students check their cheat sheets, call friends on cell phones for help, and share answers with each other.

Honest students become frustrated and angry when rampant cheating forces a seemingly impossible choice on them: join the cheating despite their own strong moral convictions against it, or watch their honestly earned grades lose value as cheaters move ahead of them to the top of the class and into the best colleges.

We *must* put an end to cheating and plagiarism to protect our honest students. Our instructional and assessment strategies *must* be changed to give honest students the level playing field they deserve. Assessments *must* reflect students' true academic ability rather than their skill in cheating and plagiarizing. Last, but by no means least, we *must* focus time and attention on the ethical and moral development of our students. Each of us has an important role to play in working toward these goals.

The role of the Board of Education

The Board of Education sets district policy. The adoption of an Academic Integrity Policy as official district policy makes a strong statement that the district is committed to honesty and integrity. This crucial first step in establishing the importance of the policy also provides the support needed by teachers and administrators who are charged with enforcing the policy, often in the face of aggressive parental opposition.

> Clearly, academic integrity is central to every institution's mission [and] trustees sometimes may be tempted to intervene directly in individual academic integrity cases. While some governing boards have the authority to decide these cases, such exercise of authority can be problematic...they risk undermining their institution's academic integrity procedures, especially in the absence of any stated reasons justifying their decisions. In general, direct trustee involvement in adjudicating academic integrity cases seems fraught with the potential of doing more harm than good....The single most important thing trustees can do, therefore, is to raise the issue. (Cole and Kiss 27)

In its role as policy maker, the Board is responsible for determining that the Academic Integrity Policy is fair. The Board is *not* responsible for implementing the policy; that is the role of the superintendent and staff. Neither individual Board members, nor the Board in its official capacity, should ever interfere with disciplinary actions taken by school administrators and teachers.

The role of the superintendent and district/school administrators

The superintendent is charged with policy implementation and is responsible for developing an effective Academic Integrity Policy. Teachers, students, parents, and community representatives should be involved in all stages of policy development, including publicizing and building support for the policy in the schools and community.

An Academic Integrity Policy committee includes, at a minimum, teachers and administrators, usually under the direction of the superintendent or principal. Student participation adds significantly to the strength of the committee. Parents are effective as committee members or in an advisory role; their cooperation is crucial. The support that evolves from such community-wide ownership of the Academic Integrity Policy is a major step toward successful implementation.

One of the most important factors for success is an administrative commitment of full support for teachers who actively enforce the Academic Integrity Policy and a stated expectation that all teachers will do so.

> [The] administration needs to assure the faculty that they will not be put on trial or endure a bureaucratic nightmare for simply maintaining ethical stan-

dards in their classroom. This means that the administration must be willing to stand behind the faculty when the students seek to mitigate or overturn their punishment. When the administration and faculty work together, it sends a clear and unified message to all students that cheating and plagiarism will not be tolerated in any class. (Heberling, par. 18)

Unfortunately, many administrators and School Boards do not "stand behind the faculty" when teachers prove charges of cheating or plagiarism and assign an appropriate penalty. This sends a dreadful message: Teachers, don't try to control dishonesty in your classrooms because we won't support you. Students, cheat and plagiarize without fear of consequences. Parents, we won't make you angry or create the possibility of a lawsuit.

Creating a school culture of honesty and integrity requires the commitment of parents, School Board members, administrators, teachers, staff, parents, and students. Strong and courageous administrative leadership creates an environment that supports teachers working with students in their classrooms to put these changes into action.

The role of the teacher remains the crucial one

The teacher plans instruction and decides what to emphasize in the classroom. The single most effective change a teacher can make is to focus on ethics, honesty, and integrity in every class; students then understand without doubt that these are important principles.

The researchers recommend the following for success in decreasing the amount of cheating in the classroom. First, the entire staff of teachers would need to be in agreement as to the definition and understanding of what actually constitutes cheating. Second, an agreement would need to be put in place, preferably in the discipline code, which would outline the definition and the consequences for those who are caught cheating....Third, it is important to follow through with a character education program on the importance of honesty and integrity. This kind of effort should start as early as the primary grades and be repeated at the start of each new school year....Finally, the researchers found through this study and action plan that there was a wide latitude of cheating that has become accepted in the classroom. When the clear definition of cheating is taught, modeled and reinforced by teachers, practiced and understood by the students, and supported by the entire staff, the incidents of cheating will decrease. (Bopp 47–48)

Extra effort is required of teachers who fully support honesty in testing and integrity in written assignments, and who assign penalties for proven cheating and plagiarism. They will make tests and testing procedures as cheat-proof as possible.

They will reduce plagiarism by developing written assignments designed to make the *process* as important as the final paper, or *product*.

In return, these teachers must be able to depend on strong, unwavering support from administrators, from Board members, and especially from parents. They also will have the support of the many students who want and deserve honesty in their classes.

Five COPY ME pages at the end of this chapter may stimulate your own creative approaches in dealing with these issues. Results of the "3-Minute Survey" indicate a need for greater emphasis on honesty and integrity in communicating with students and parents; the survey form is in Appendix B with permission to use and adapt it. "Focus on Academic Honesty and Integrity" reminds students of the importance of doing their own work to the best of their ability and notifies parents that teachers care about the integrity of student work. While we concentrate on the required curriculum, we may need to rethink how we assign class work and homework, and how we design our tests. "Whose Work Is Being Graded?" and "Help Students to Value Homework and Complete It Honestly" can initiate useful debate on this issue. Finally, "Simple Suggestions to Reduce Cheating" is intended to begin a discussion that can raise faculty awareness.

The role of students

Many students do not connect the value of a grade with the value of learning the material and completing assignments. Instead, they view testing and assignments as an obstacle course to twist and turn through with the least possible work required for the best possible grade. "Cheating is easier than studying so why not cheat?"

Teachers and parents can help students to understand how the knowledge and skills they are learning are important in their lives and for their future, and to value honest mastery. This can help reduce the number of students who deliberately decide to cheat or plagiarize.

Honest students will welcome and support an Academic Integrity Policy when it is enforced fairly in all classes. They want a "level playing field" that lets them compete with integrity. Then, when a fellow student asks to copy homework or test answers, the reply can be a simple, "No, it's against our Academic Integrity Policy."

References

Bopp, Mary, Patricia Gleason, and Stacey Misicka. *Reducing Incidents of Cheating in Adolescence*. Master of Arts Action Research Project. Chicago: Saint Xavier U., 2001. (ED 456127)

Cole, Sally, and Elizabeth Kiss. "The Delicate Task of Combating Student Cheating." *Trusteeship* 9.1 (2001): 24–28.

Heberling, Michael. "Maintaining Academic Integrity in Online Education." *Online Journal of Distance Learning Administration* 5.1 (2002). 18 Aug. 2004 www.westga.edu/~distance/ojdla/spring51/heberling51.html

Resources

COPY ME pages:

Bill Taylor: "Academic Integrity: A Letter to My Students"
Karen Farley: "Skills for Life in the Davenport Community Schools"
High School Students' Responses to a "3-Minute Survey"
Focus on Academic Honesty and Integrity
Simple Suggestions to Help Reduce Cheating
Whose Work Is Being Graded?
Help Students to Value Homework and Complete It Honestly

See Appendix C for related information in *Student Cheating and Plagiarism in the Internet Era: A Wake-Up Call:* Chapter 7, Integrity, Ethics, and Character Education; Chapter 9, Defining Cheating and Plagiarism for Students; Chapter 11, Reducing Cheating on Tests and Assignments.

Academic Integrity: A Letter to My Students

Bill Taylor

Here, at the beginning of the semester, I want to say something to you about academic integrity. Integrity is an essential part of any true educational experience, integrity on my part as a teacher and integrity on your part as a student. What does that involve for each of us in this class? Academic integrity means that we must consider our honor as we complete the exams and written assignments required for this class.

With regard to exams, the principles of academic integrity require that I:

- do my best during class time to prepare you for the exam
- be available to work with you individually if you need help to prepare for the exam
- develop exam questions that will be a meaningful test not only of the course content, but also of your ability to express and defend intelligent judgments about that content
- carefully monitor the exam so that honest students will not be disadvantaged by other students who might choose to cheat if given the opportunity
- give due and careful consideration to your answers when evaluating them and assigning a grade

With regard to exams, the principles of academic integrity require you to:

- come to class having done your best to prepare for the exam, including seeking my help if you need it
- make full use of the time available to write the best answers you can
- accept your limitations and not try to get around them by using cheat sheets, copying, or seeking help from another student
- not give help to other students, or make it easy for them to copy from you

With regard to written assignments, the principles of academic integrity require that I:

- devise meaningful assignments that grow out of and further the work done in the classroom
- provide you with a clear description of that assignment so that you know what is expected of you and what I'll be looking for when I grade it
- give due and careful consideration to your paper when evaluating it and assigning a grade
- confront you if I suspect that you have plagiarized or in other ways not handed in work that is entirely your own

With regard to written assignments, the principles of academic integrity require you to:

- start your research and writing early enough to ensure that you have the time you need to do your best work
- hand in a paper that you yourself have done specifically for this class and not copied from someone else, recycled from another class, copied from books or other print sources, or downloaded from the Internet
- not be satisfied with a paper that is less than your own best work
- seek only appropriate help from others (such as proof-reading, or discussing your ideas with someone else to gain clarity in your thinking)
- give full and proper credit to your sources

A challenge

I will do my best to live up to my responsibilities. If you feel I've failed to do so, you have every right to call me on it. If you do, I have a responsibility to give you respectful consideration. If you feel that I do not do these things, you have the right (and I would say the responsibility) to bring this to the attention of a school administrator.

At the same time, I have a right to expect you to live up to your responsibilities. If I think you're not doing so, I consider it a matter of academic integrity to call you on it.

Indeed, in certain circumstances, such as cheating or plagiarism, I may be required to charge you with a violation of the school's Academic Integrity Policy. Our school is every bit as committed to academic integrity as I am.

Personal integrity is not a quality we're born to naturally. It's a quality of character we need to nurture, and this requires practice in both meanings of that word (as in practice on the piano and practice a profession). We can only be a person of integrity if we practice it every day.

That is why it is essential for all of us in this class to practice academic integrity, in both senses of the word practice. For practice today will lay a solid foundation for practice tomorrow, and the day after that, and the day after that, so that through daily practice integrity will come to be woven throughout the fabric of our lives, and thus through at least a part of the fabric of society.

It also is important that your parents support and encourage you in your resolve to practice academic integrity. Your responsibility is to read this letter with your parents and discuss it together. Be sure you understand the value your parents place on academic integrity. They trust you to do your best and will value the grades you earn through your own honest efforts.

[Bill Taylor is Emeritus Professor of Political Science at Oakton Community College in Des Plaines, IL. This letter grows out of, and is based upon, ideas contained in the first draft of "The Fundamental Values of Academic Integrity," a document that was developed by, and is available from, the Center for Academic Integrity at www.academicintegrity.org.]

Skills for Life in the Davenport Community Schools

Karen Farley

The *Skills for Life* program was developed with the input of administrators, teachers, parents, and area employers. Many of the employers saw our students as being only marginally prepared for job success; the problem was not just literacy or basic math skills, but a lack of disciplined work habits. This program was created for our students to help ensure a productive learning environment.

Starting at the elementary level

- Caring—to feel and show concern for others
- Common sense—to use good judgment
- Effort—to do one's best
- Initiative—to do something, not necessarily for reward, but because it needs to be done
- Perseverance—to keep at something until one succeeds
- Responsibility—to take action when needed and be accountable for one's actions
- Teamwork—to work together to achieve a goal for the benefit of all concerned

Added at the intermediate school level

- Curiosity—to demonstrate a desire to investigate and seek understanding of one's world
- Flexibility—to be willing to alter plans when necessary
- Friendship—to make and keep a friend through mutual trust and caring
- Integrity—to act according to a sense of what is right and wrong
- Organization—to plan, arrange, and implement in an orderly way so things are ready to use
- Patience—to wait calmly for someone or something
- Problem solving—to create solutions in difficult situations and everyday problems
- Sense of humor—to laugh and be playful without harming others

Added at the high school level

- Courage—to act according to one's beliefs despite fear of adverse consequences
- Pride—to gain satisfaction from doing one's personal best
- Resourcefulness—to respond to challenges and opportunities in innovative and creative ways

The teaching of these skills is woven throughout all school activities—educational and social. "Target talk" reinforces students' learning of the *Skills for Life*.

For instance, a teacher might say, "Jose, you used the skill of *caring* when you helped Margaret find her books." Skills are discussed as they appear in stories read by the students. Even the evening news demonstrates such skills—or lack of them—in action. The students take pride in discussing how *Skills for Life* affect events in their lives.

Initial promotion of the *Skills for Life* program included poster sets of the skills for classroom use, screen savers for teachers, billboards, and a newspaper tabloid (paid for with grant dollars). Teachers and other staff attended in-service meetings on the curriculum, and teaching materials were developed.

What is the reaction of parents to the *Skills for Life* program? Ken Krumwiede, principal at Truman Elementary, reports, "Some parents were skeptical at first. But as they see their children blossom and excel, they share our enthusiasm and become our strongest supporters. The momentum is growing."

Cindy Winckler, Curriculum and Instruction Facilitator, believes the program does work for students. "The educational and social challenges our high school students face have changed dramatically during the past generation. As the *Skills for Life* program expands into Davenport's high schools this year, the program will help provide an important focus for students progressing toward graduation. These are definitely skills for a lifetime."

District: Davenport Community Schools
City, State: Davenport, Iowa
Principal: Norbert Schuerman, Ph.D.
Number of schools: 31
Enrollment: 16,377
Web site: www.davenportschools.org

[Additional information about the *Skills for Life* program in the Davenport Community Schools is online at www.davenportschools.org/curriculum/skillsforlife.asp.]

COPY ME

High School Students' Responses to a "3-Minute Survey"

Students coming into the high school library during one day in May, 2004, were asked to complete this survey and drop it into a box on the circulation desk. These results are from the 176 surveys received that day. Survey response options are boldface and the number of students who selected each response is in parenthesis.

How many of YOUR teachers have discussed cheating on tests and assignments in one or more of your classes this year?
  1 (19) **2** (23) **3** (32) **4** (31) **5** (36) **6** (26) **none** (8)

How many of YOUR teachers have discussed plagiarism in one or more of your classes this year?
  1 (41) **2** (42) **3** (22) **4** (11) **5** (20) **6** (12) **none** (20)

Have your parents talked with you about why you shouldn't cheat at school?
  yes, often (9)   **yes, a few times** (49)   **not this school year** (117)

If you copied a paper or part of a paper from the Internet, did your parents know about it?
  yes, they knew and said it's OK (11)
  yes, they knew and said it's not OK (11)

  What would they say about it?
    it's OK (21)   **don't do it** (118)

Do you know what your Student Handbook says about cheating and plagiarism?
  yes, I've read it (84)   **no idea, never read it** (92)

Do your parents know what the handbook says?
  yes (26)   **no** (75)   **I don't know** (75)

[Survey forms are in Appendix B]

Focus on Academic Honesty and Integrity

Consistent use of these statements emphasizes the importance placed on academic integrity and honesty by the individual teacher, the school, and the district.

Put this statement at the top of the first page of every test:

All electronic devices, except any calculators we provide for your use, are banned from this classroom during testing. Any electronic device that is visible, whether being used or not, will be confiscated and the test will be scored as a zero. Your parent or guardian will have to meet with me to have the electronic device returned. Advice? Keep cell phones and all other electronic devices turned off and in your backpack, purse, or otherwise out of sight during testing.

Put this statement at the end of every test and ask students to sign it:

I have neither given nor received assistance on this test.

Put this statement on every homework assignment and ask students to sign it, and ask a parent or guardian to sign it when appropriate:

I have neither given nor received unpermitted assistance on this assignment.

Send a statement home at the beginning of each school year, and in the packet for each new student enrolled during the year, with a form for every student and parent to sign acknowledging that they have read the Academic Integrity Policy. The statement below is adapted from the Washington County Public Schools (Maryland) statement:

I have read and promise to uphold the (School/District) standards for Academic Integrity. I hold the qualities of honesty and integrity in the highest regard and will not violate them or support those who do.

Student _____ Parent _____ Date _____

COPY ME

Simple Suggestions to Help Reduce Cheating

Cheating in classes is a way to survive in school; sometimes you are forced to cheat out of pure pressure. But it is not really cheating any more because it now is a way to survive, its helping the little guy out which could be seen as a noble cause to some. As for me, I do what it takes to get by and to keep on top, because of the fact that most core class teachers believe that they are the only ones to give us an hour or more of homework and that we have no personal life so we have hours to finish it. This is just not true for almost all students and they are overloaded with homework so they turn to cheating as their only way out. 12th grade boy

Coordinate assessments to reduce pressures that may lead to cheating

The faculty should coordinate assessments as carefully as sporting events and assemblies are scheduled. This would avoid the major stress created for a student who has one or two major tests and a major paper all due on the same day. Each academic department could designate one day of the week to give their major tests and one week each month when their major written assignments are due. Pressure is a major reason why students cheat. A reasonable schedule for tests and written assignment due dates reduces these pressures.

Keep these warnings in mind

If you rip up the test paper and assign a grade of zero, the paper won't be available as proof of cheating if the student or parent challenges you. It is better to file the paper with a written account of the incident.

Any parent or student can purchase a teacher's edition of the textbook with unit tests and answer keys for both homework and tests. These also may be available online. Always assume your students have access to the teacher's edition, workbook, and publisher's testing material.

Never give your computer password to a student. Even a trusted student aide can disappoint you. Or, if a hacker breaks into your gradebook program or tests, the student aide may be blamed unfairly.

Whose Work Is Being Graded?

The tests, reports, term papers, projects, homework, or other student work that we grade *must* be the students' own work, honestly completed under the conditions stated by the teacher. Our assessments then reflect students' true academic ability rather than their skill in cheating and plagiarizing. It is important that we

- design and administer tests that make cheating more difficult
- monitor and grade the research *process* as well as the research *product* to make plagiarism more difficult
- structure science fair projects and other "do-it-at-home" projects to reflect the student's independent work
- design science experiments to make it more difficult to create fake data or to copy data and procedures from another student
- avoid "busywork" homework assignments that encourage copying

Students are less likely to copy or cheat if they perceive assessment as relevant.

Making cheating more difficult

- Base grades on essay tests, research papers, individual class presentations, and the like.
- Emphasize critical thinking skills rather than rote memory of a great many facts.
- Give many small tests rather than one major test at the end of the unit.
- Give open-note tests with only one note card, the test, and a pencil or pen allowed on students' desks during the test. Stress that preparing a good note card is an excellent way to learn the material. Collect note cards with the test papers.
- Distribute five to ten short essay questions a few days before a test. On test day, one student draws a number to determine the one question to be answered; it may be different for each period.
- For short-answer, multiple-choice tests, hand out 5, 10, 20 or more questions the day before the test. Tell students which ones to answer on the day of the test. Change questions each period, sometimes repeating a question and sometimes not.
- Add one or more short essay questions to a multiple-choice test and check accuracy of facts in essay answers against answers on the rest of the test.
- Avoid take-home tests. Honest students will complete the test as instructed, while classmates who cheat by asking for help from parents, siblings, tutors, or friends will unfairly receive a better grade.

Help Students to Value Homework and Complete It Honestly

Well-designed homework assignments help students to prepare for the next day's class work, verify that they understand new concepts or skills presented, and provide practice with these concepts. Students should see the connection between homework and class work. Provide clear and specific answers to these questions:

- What is the teacher's goal in assigning homework?
- What amount and kind of help from parents is acceptable?
- Is collaboration with other students allowed or forbidden?
- Will homework be graded and returned or is it kept in the teacher's file?
- Is there time in class to explain the problems or issues?
- Is the teacher available before or after school to help the student?
- What should the parent do if a student complains the teacher never checks and never returns homework?

A school-sponsored homework Web site lets parents and students check to see what homework has been assigned. Teachers can post expectations for how students should complete the homework: alone, with some specified degree of parent help, with a friend, in collaboration with peers, and so on.

Review each day's homework in class to capture "teachable moments." Many students benefit from a review that checks quickly for problems and misunderstandings.

Permit collaboration on homework and other assignments

Two reasons support allowing students to do homework collaboratively: (1) students who work with an entire group solving each problem are helping to teach each other, and (2) being told to "do it alone" punishes the honest student who works hard to complete the assignment, only to receive the same credit as students who divided the work and copied each other's answers. A better approach is to permit collaboration that probably cannot be stopped and that may have some positive benefits. Then test for mastery to identify students who copied the homework without learning from it.

Check for honesty with a minimum of grading time

Each time homework is handed in, give a one-question test or have some other in-class activity that would be difficult to do well unless the student had completed the homework. Let students use their homework paper to answer the question but all books remain closed. Collect the test paper with the homework. The test or activity should be varied for each class period.

CHAPTER FOUR

Parents' Role in Developing Student Honesty and Integrity

We need parents with good moral values who will consider a teacher's point of view before automatically believing their kid is right—teachers have a reason for disciplining a kid, but parents believe the teacher is unfair. They should support the teachers. 10th grade boy

A special word to parents. If you're a parent, don't wait for the educational system to adopt character-education programs or serious honor codes. Make a commitment to integrity in your own home. Talk to your kids about why they should play by the rules—and honestly challenge rules they think are wrong. Teach them how to work through the tough ethical dilemmas in life. Create an environment where money and status do not loom in the children's lives as the greatest good. (Callahan 295)

This chapter is written for *you,* a concerned parent who wants to keep ethical issues, including academic cheating and plagiarism, "front and center" in your child's life. You are the primary role model for your child's values.

Yet only 23 of the 906 student comments from the surveys in Chapter 2 refer to parents. There were 13 students who listed parental concerns as a reason "why I don't cheat" and 10 students who listed parental demands for good grades as a reason "why I cheat." Students of parents who say "don't cheat" think their parents would be disappointed or might punish them for cheating. When less than three percent of students in grades 7–12 across five states make any mention of parental influence, it is time to look at the role of parents in developing student honesty and integrity.

Developing strong concepts of right and wrong

You are teaching right from wrong as you help your child process the often mixed messages received from television and radio, advertisers, teen magazines, newspapers, and—perhaps most important—from friends and peers. You do this in many ways.

- Clarify your expectations for your child's moral behavior.
- Help your child to develop a personal code of ethics.
- Discuss moral issues at dinner, in the car, as part of the family dialog.
- Discuss the day's news as related to moral behavior—why did the person act the way he/she did? What impact did those actions have on the person, on people who loved them, or on society? What could the person have done better?
- Keep lines of communication open with your child, teachers, and the school staff.
- Be sure your child understands the rules at school and the penalties for breaking them.
- Read and discuss the school's Academic Integrity Policy together.
- If your school does not have an Academic Integrity Policy, form a committee to develop one.
- Be realistic about your expectations for your child based on her or his abilities and watch for signs of stress.
- Stress that honesty is more important than getting an "A" by cheating.
- Encourage your child to "come clean" and take the consequences rather than lie.

By helping to clarify moral and ethical issues for your child you are laying the foundation for a lifetime code of honesty and integrity.

Helping with time management skills

Help your child learn to manage the time needed to complete assignments with integrity and to the best of her ability. This means limiting the time spent on television, video games, surfing online, or other more pleasurable activities while schoolwork is ignored.

It is the student's job to get an education. Part-time jobs during the school year can often interfere with schoolwork. Working students say they cheat and plagiarize because they don't have the time, or are just too tired, to study for a test or to complete assignments well. Limiting the number of hours your child works each week is your responsibility.

Dealing with plagiarism

Your child has easy access to the Internet's seemingly endless variety of online Web sites with thousands of term papers and reports on every subject. This access is an open invitation to plagiarism. Students during the 70s and 80s had to rely on books, encyclopedias, newspapers, magazines, and pamphlets to gather research material. Those who didn't want to write the paper had to find a friend to write it, or perhaps a parent or older sibling.

Today, a child who spends hours "writing" a book report or term paper may be plagiarizing from the Internet. Some cut and paste "research information" from a magazine article found in a library online database. Others rework a paper from a paper mill into a more age-appropriate version to fool the teacher. More sophisticated, or desperate, students send the parameters for the paper to a paper mill, provide a credit card, and receive a completed paper ready to be downloaded, printed, and turned in.

Your responsibility is to make sure your child completes the research and writes the paper independently. The best way to do this is to keep informed about written assignments and their due dates, then follow the process from initial planning and research to the finished paper. You may want to explore some of the Web sites listed in the COPY ME pages or ask your school to organize a back-to-school workshop about the Internet and today's research techniques (see "A 'Research Night Out' for Parents" COPY ME page in Chapter 9).

Being honest in the amount of help you give

You are cheating when you "help" by doing too much of your child's work for a class project or written assignment. This gives a teacher an inaccurate basis for assessment and teaches your child that cheating and plagiarism are acceptable. Kate Stone Lombardi recalls a display of students' reports in her son's fourth-grade classroom:

> My son is not much of an artist, but there next to his report on the Rev. Dr. Martin Luther King Jr. was a game attempt at depicting the civil rights hero. It was accompanied by a straightforward, chronological roundup of Dr. King's life. It wouldn't knock your socks off, but for a 9-year-old, it was O.K. His project was hanging next to one on Amelia Earhart, executed by an evident artistic prodigy who also had incredible literary talent.... The paper—also available as a PowerPoint presentation—speculated on Earhart's early impact on the feminist movement and her possible psychological motivations for flying. O.K., fine. Who cares if someone got a little too much help in elementary school? [But] even in middle and high school, many parents haven't stopped....One mother told me she was glad to do research and other "clerical work" for her child, because her daughter was far too busy with other enriching activities to do it herself. (Lombardi, par. 6–9)

Ask that the original instructions sent home with any project state clearly the degree and kind of help from parents or fellow students that is permissible. It is your responsibility to honor these instructions.

Suggest that your teacher or school create a pledge or statement for you and your child to sign verifying that the project has been completed by your child, not by you. Some teachers may require that each student write a reflection piece on "how I did this project" in addition to returning the signed pledge.

COPY ME pages as discussion starters

Some of the articles that follow speak directly to students, others to parents. All are formatted as COPY ME pages.

You may find the articles helpful in discussing these issues with your own children. Cheating and plagiarism are serious problems in our schools. You address these problems in positive ways when you model good values for your child.

References

Callahan, David. *The Cheating Culture: Why More Americans Are Doing Wrong to Get Ahead.* New York: Harcourt, 2004.

Lombardi, Kate Stone. "Haunted by Ghost-Written Homework." *The New York Times,* 2 Feb. 2003. ProQuest. Los Alamitos High School Lib., Los Alamitos, CA. 5 Nov. 2004 proquest.umi.com.

Resources

COPY ME pages:

Elaine K. McEwan: "'I Didn't Do It'—Dealing with Dishonesty"
Father Val J. Peter: "Nobody Likes a Cheat"
Michael Josephson: "Helping Our Children Learn to Make Good Choices"
Carolyn Jabs: "Preventing Plagiarism"
Elaine K. McEwan: "'The Dog Ate It'—Conquering Homework Hassles"

See Appendix C for related information in *Student Cheating and Plagiarism in the Internet Era: A Wake-Up Call:* Chapter 7, Parents: Vigilant, Informed, Involved.

"I Didn't Do It"—Dealing with Dishonesty

Elaine K. McEwan

What should I do if my child is cheating?

If you have discovered that your child is cheating, first think about possible reasons. Reasons are not excuses—to excuse the behavior would be a mistake. But you do need to determine why the cheating happened so you can take steps to make sure it doesn't happen again. Ask yourself the following questions:

- Am I unrealistic in my expectations or demands of my child? Do I continually emphasize the importance of winning or having top grades?
- Are my expectations far greater than my child could be expected to achieve, for example, expecting someone who isn't physically coordinated to earn a place in the starting lineup or expecting someone with average ability to win a scholarship to Harvard?
- Is my discipline so harsh and punitive that it engenders extreme fear in my children so that they cheat rather than face the consequences of failure?

Why did my child cheat?

Here are some of the main reasons children cheat and what you can do about them.

Competition and pressure. We want our kids to be number one—in academics, in sports, and in life. This intense pressure to be at the top of the heap engenders a "win at any cost" mentality that is very dangerous...unreasonably high expectations can push children to be dishonest in the achievement of their goals. If, after talking with your child's teacher, you determine that competition and pressure might be the reasons for cheating, lighten up. Major on praise and encouragement, rather than pressure. Avoid making comparisons between your child and siblings or friends with regard to report cards, sports achievements, or other accomplishments.

Feelings of inadequacy and unpreparedness. I've empathized with many a student whose parents expected As when they were only capable of delivering Cs. Their own feelings of inadequacy and need for parental affirmation pushed them over the line.... Solicit help from your child's teacher if she needs extra help in the classroom.

To be numero uno. This is the child who is naturally aggressive and needs to be first at everything (especially games and sports). He has an inordinate need to win, and if it takes cheating, he may even do that.... The impulsive, challenging child may need special help in this area.

Copy cat. Sometimes a younger child may see an older or more manipulative child cheat and win. She mistakenly assumes that this is the way "the game is played," and she lacks the maturity to realize the ultimate problems that cheating involves. Teach this child that cheating is wrong, and help her to understand that just because someone else does it, that doesn't make it right.

Laissez faire. Some parents are loath to come down too hard on their children, so they forgive a little "harmless fudging." They may even encourage it by doing homework for a child. Children are quick learners and will get the impression that a parent doesn't really care if they cheat. Before you know it, habits will be formed. Cheating is not a problem that will disappear with age. It will only grow worse. Don't ever let a child get away with cheating. If you do, he will come to believe that nobody cares.

Egocentricity. This is a younger version of "numero uno." The young child firmly believes that he is the center o the universe and demands to be first and best, and to win at everything. In a mistaken attempt to make a child feel good, parents often unwittingly create a monster—a child who believes he can have what he wants, no matter what the cost. Deal with this problem as you would deal with the "copy cat" by teaching firmly and clearly that cheating is not allowed.

These are the reasons that kids cheat. If you can step back from the emotionally charged reaction you had when you first discovered that your little angel's halo was a mite tarnished, you'll probably be able to make some adjustments, fine-tune your parenting, and move into a proactive program to deal with the problem.

[Reprinted with permission from "*I Didn't Do It*"—*Dealing with Dishonesty,* by Elaine K. McEwan (Shaw, 1996). Elaine McEwan is an educational consultant and a well-known author, lecturer, and workshop leader for parents, teachers, and administrators. For more information, visit her Web site at www.elainemcewan.com.]

COPY ME

Nobody Likes a Cheat

Father Val J. Peter

In movie Westerns, a cowboy who cheats at cards is usually shot right then and there. The sheriff doesn't intervene. That's frontier justice.

Nobody likes a cheat. Yet we live in a society known for getting around the rules. We all know what cheating is:

- not following the rules
- using other people's homework in school
- copying answers during tests
- cheating at cards
- cheating at games
- cheating at sports events
- just plain dishonesty

How do we teach our children not to cheat? How do we teach them honesty?

Teaching honesty

Don't let your children learn cheating from you.

It is pretty obvious that if you cheat (on your expense account, your golf score, your spouse), your children will grow up to be cheats. The contrary is also true. If you don't cheat and make every effort to teach your children that cheating is wrong, your children will grow up to be honest people.

I had a friend who cheated at everything. My parents' heated and repeated expressions of disapproval heightened within me my awareness of the importance of being honest. You can watch out for parenting strategies that make cheating attractive to your children.

Avoid unreasonable expectations about your children's grades in school. Why? Because unreasonable expectations can create conditions that make cheating an acceptable behavior to your child. Your child might think, "I'd rather get a good grade by cheating than be honest, get a poor grade, and have to face the wrath of my parents." Think of the pressure you put on your children via this parenting strategy:

- "Everyone in this family goes to Harvard."
- "I won't accept a stupid child."

Of course, you don't want your children to be lazy. The remedy for laziness is a series of positive and negative motivations served up with warmth and affection and stick-to-itiveness. If your child is lazy in school, get involved in his schoolwork. Meet with teachers who can help give you a realistic assessment of your child's potential. Use sports as an example. Most parents who attend their children's sporting events realize their children are not future NBA or NFL players. These are realistic expectations. They need to prevail in academics as well.

When your child cheats

What to do when your child is caught cheating on a test:

- The first thing that you need to do is to get the facts: "Is this the first event?" "Has it been going on for some time?" "Was it a prank?" "Was it serious?" "Was it peer pressure?"
- In addition to getting the facts, it is important to control your own emotions. There is a sizable difference between a disappointment and a disaster. Parents need to recognize that and communicate it to their children. It is a disappointment that your child was cheating on a test, but it is not the end of the world.
- Third, in addition to getting the facts and controlling your own emotions, it is important to find out what the pressures are on your child to cheat.
- Then help reduce those pressures.

Using these four simple steps usually produces an abundance of insights as to how to handle the situation. Usually your child will feel very embarrassed and ashamed. That is a great time to show a parent's love, especially if your child has "come to his senses." This presents you with an opportunity to give your child a big hug and not hold a grudge. "To err is human. To forgive is divine."

[Adapted with permission from *Dealing With Your Kids' 7 Biggest Troubles,* by Father Val J. Peter. Father Val J. Peter, Executive Director, Girls & Boys Town. Boys Town, NE: Boys Town Press, 2000.]

Helping Our Children Learn to Make Good Choices

Michael Josephson

In Florida two young men, eager to win the admiration of fraternity brothers, removed a stop sign and brought it back as a trophy. In Tennessee, a couple of teenagers were at a party in a high-rise apartment and one dared the other to slide down the trash shoot in the hall. In Colorado, an Air Force Academy cadet with a promising future played strip poker with a female classmate and, ignoring her protests, forced her to have sex.

The Florida boys were convicted of manslaughter after a fatal accident occurred at the intersection without the stop sign. The Tennessee boy who slid down the trash shoot was killed by an automatic trash compactor, and his friend is left with guilt and grief. The cadet's military career was destroyed and he may face criminal charges.

What makes these stories all the more tragic is that we're not talking about bad kids; we're talking about fundamentally decent kids who made really bad choices. That's the recurring nightmare of caring parents. Children seriously damaging themselves physically or emotionally by unwise decisions—engaging in reckless conduct to impress friends, endangering themselves through drugs, alcohol or imprudent sex, or getting involved with irresponsible, manipulative, cruel or selfish people.

Sure we want our kids to be successful, good-looking, and clever, but it's much more important that they make good choices. This requires more than cultivated instinct. It requires an ability and willingness to act rationally rather than impulsively and to evaluate situations and anticipate potential consequences.

Every good decision starts with a "stop"

Many of the choices we make can have a serious and lasting impact on our lives. What's more, most of our really bad decisions—the ones that mess up our lives—were made impulsively or without sufficient reflection.

Thus, the wisdom of the oldest advice in the world: "Think ahead." The maxim telling us to count to three when we're angry and to ten when we're very angry is designed to prevent foolish and impulsive behavior. But anger is just one obstacle to good choices. Others are fatigue, frustration, impatience and ignorance.

We can improve our lives immeasurably if we can get in the habit of self-consciously stopping the momentum of thoughtless behavior. We must force ourselves to reflect on what we are about to do. Just as we teach our children to look both ways before they cross the street, we can and should instill the habit of looking ahead in making decisions.

So each good decision starts with a stop. We must stop to sort out facts from rumors, to evaluate the evidence and devise alternatives so we can choose the most effective and ethical course of action. Stopping to think before we act also allows us to muster our moral willpower to overcome temptations.

The "Stop" is a break in the action that allows us to ask ourselves a few crucial questions that could set us on a better road: "Wait, what do I really want to accomplish here?" "How will my decision affect others?" "What are my alternatives?" "What could go wrong?"

Knowing when a decision is important

Abby doesn't know what she wants to wear today but she has to choose quickly or she'll be late for school. Ben is afraid of losing his athletic eligibility and is thinking of cheating on an exam. Cassie is urged by a friend to try the drug "ecstasy." Dirk's teammates want him to join in the taunting of a nerd. Ellie is thinking about lying to her mom so she can go to a party. Federico is dared by his buddies to take advantage of a drunken girl. Gwen is thinking about having sex so she won't lose her boyfriend.

Life is full of choices. Many don't require serious forethought because they're not important—like Abby's choice about her clothes. In such cases, there may be no bad decision and, in any event, the cost of error is minor. Thus, it's okay to rely on impulses and preferences.

But many everyday decisions have potentially momentous consequences, including choices about whether to cheat, experiment with drugs, lie to a parent or engage in sexual conduct. Even choices about whether to study for a test, cut school, lie to avoid an unpleasant consequence, talk back to a teacher or quit a job must be treated as important because a wrong choice can have a serious and lasting impact.

Generally, the greater the potential consequences, the more need there is for careful decision making. When we respond to impulse without reflection we stand a good chance of making a bad decision. Therefore, a first step in wise decision making is to know when to be especially careful.

Decisions are important when: (1) serious physical or emotional injury may result, (2) an important relationship can be damaged, (3) one's reputation or credibility can be seriously undermined, and (4) where the decision could endanger important long-term goals. So what do you do when the stakes are high? Be careful. Don't gamble. Think long-term.

If we take control, we have control

It's often said that our choices reveal our character, but it's also true that our choices shape our character. Thus, the more aware we become of the choices we make every single day—choices about our attitudes, our words, our actions, and our reactions—the more power we have over our own destiny.

According to Senator Bob Bennett of Utah, a big supporter of **CHARACTER COUNTS!**, "Your life is the sum result of all the choices you make, both consciously and unconsciously. If you can control the process of choosing, you can take control of all aspects of your life. You can find the freedom that comes from being in charge of yourself."

It's true. When we accept moral responsibility for our choices we take charge of our lives. Yet sometimes the power to choose is not self-evident, especially to teenagers who are struggling to deal with hormone-intensified impulses accompanying powerful emotions like excitement, desire, frustration, and anger. These emotions can be so strong that they create moods and urges that seem beyond control and, as a result, no attempt is made to control them.

At the root of good decision making is self-control and knowledge that no matter how difficult or confusing the situation, we always have the power to choose what we think, say, and do, even when we're under tremendous pressure and even when we don't like our options. Like a ship without a captain to steer it, when we hide behind our self-serving illusion of helplessness—"you made me mad," "you left me no choice," "I couldn't help myself"—our lives move in aimless and random directions and sometimes run aground. If we take control, we have control.

Seven rules of good choices

1. Because our choices can set in motion events that affect people and alter the future for ourselves and for others in serious and lasting ways, we are morally responsible for the consequences of our choices.
2. Though it can be difficult to overcome impulses and resist temptations, we always have the power to choose what we say (our words), what we do (our actions), and what we think (our attitudes).
3. Even choices made below the level of consciousness are still choices; even when we don't like any of our alternatives, we have a choice.
4. Choosing not to choose is a choice; choosing not to act is a choice.
5. We should be especially careful to avoid making bad decisions when we are: (a) under time pressure, (b) fatigued, (c) frustrated, (d) we have insufficient knowledge of facts and risks, or (e) we're under the influence of strong emotions such as love, lust, anger, fear, frustration, depression, grief, anxiety, resentment, jealousy, guilt, or loneliness.
6. Our choices are especially important when they can result in serious physical or emotional harm, damage important relationships, injure reputations, damage credibility, or interfere with the achievement of important long-term goals.
7. Good choices are both ethical—they honor core moral values such as trustworthiness, respect, responsibility, fairness, caring, and good citizenship—AND they are effective—they accomplish or move toward the decision maker's most important goals.

[Based on Michael Josephson's radio addresses from the week of March 17–21, 2003. Reprinted with permission from the Josephson Institute of Ethics. An archive of radio addresses is online at www.charactercounts.org. Michael Josephson is founder and President/CEO of the Josephson Institute of Ethics, sponsor of **CHARACTER COUNTS!** online at www.josephsoninstitute.org.]

Reprinted with permission of the authors: Guiding Students from Cheating and Plagiarism to Honesty and Integrity: Strategies for Change, *by Ann Lathrop and Kathleen Foss (Libraries Unlimited, 2005). Permission is granted to make print copies for class instruction, discussion groups, workshops, conferences, or newsletters. This material must not be placed on a Web site or distributed in any digital format. This statement must appear in its entirety on each print copy.*

COPY ME

Preventing Plagiarism

Carolyn Jabs

When our kids go back to school, we must think about desk supplies, new shoes, bus schedules, and plagiarism. Plagiarism? Yes. The Internet has made it so easy for students to "borrow" the work of others that this particular form of cheating is showing up as early as elementary school.

Many school districts are initiating programs to help students understand plagiarism and policies to punish those who cheat. As parents, we also have an important role to play. First, take plagiarism seriously. We knew it was wrong to copy word for word from the encyclopedia when we were in school. Lifting words from an Internet site is just as lazy. We'd be appalled if a child hired another kid to write his papers. Buying a paper from a website like *researchpaper.com* is every bit as reprehensible. Keep in mind that kids who plagiarize put honest students at a disadvantage. More important, stealing the words of others makes it less likely that kids will learn to think and write for themselves.

The best way to steer our children away from plagiarism is to talk early and often about why education is valuable. It's important for our children to understand that the goal of going to school isn't simply to finish assignments as fast as possible but to understand the ideas and master the skills behind them. If kids learn early to take pride in doing their own best work, they're less likely to succumb to the temptation of plagiarism. Here are other steps we parents can take:

- Check for a plagiarism policy when you look at the school's handbook at the beginning of the year. If there isn't one, talk to school administrators. Students who struggle honestly to do their own work should be protected from students who cheat.
- Talk to your child about stealing. Even little children understand they can't simply take what they want from a store. As your kids get older, explain that taking words someone else has written is just as wrong.
- When your child is assigned a report, ask how she's expected to handle source materials. Even young children should create a short bibliography showing what books and Internet sites they consulted. Older children should have detailed information about using quotes and creating footnotes for Internet sites as well as books. If your child isn't clear about what she's supposed to do, ask the teacher for clarification.
- Help your child manage time especially when there's a big writing project. Often kids copy other people's work because they get behind and can't see any other way to get the assignment finished in time.
- Read what your child writes. If you're used to reading her work, you'll recognize her natural style and be able to identify vocabulary that sounds too advanced and passages that just don't sound like her. Ask your child

to share her research materials with you and encourage her to show you early drafts.

- After your child has done his research, encourage him to close all the books and Web sites and tell you, in his own words, what he has learned. Summarizing the important points from memory makes it more likely that he will use his own words when he starts writing.
- Acknowledge that writing is hard. When you go over your child's homework, be gentle about pointing out errors in logic or grammar. Praise your child for doing his or her own work. Many kids cheat because they feel that they can't possibly live up to the standards of the adults around them. Make it clear that you value the effort as well as the results.

In the age of the Internet, kids need, more than ever, to be able to do careful research and reflect on what they've learned. They must be able to generate new ideas and express them effectively. Plagiarism undermines all these skills. If we expect our kids to know the difference between right and wrong, we have to start early so they will value the Internet as a resource instead of using it as the latest way to cheat themselves out of a genuine education.

[Reprinted with permission of the author. Carolyn Jabs writes "Growing Up Online," a nationally syndicated column that helps parents guide children as they use the Internet. She is a former Contributing Editor for Family PC and is mother to three computer savvy kids. Visit her online at www.carolynjabs.com]

Reprinted with permission of the authors: Guiding Students from Cheating and Plagiarism to Honesty and Integrity: Strategies for Change, *by Ann Lathrop and Kathleen Foss (Libraries Unlimited, 2005). Permission is granted to make print copies for class instruction, discussion groups, workshops, conferences, or newsletters. This material must not be placed on a Web site or distributed in any digital format. This statement must appear in its entirety on each print copy.*

"The Dog Ate It"—Conquering Homework Hassles

Elaine K. McEwan

Establish homework routines and be available to help

Even if your child's kindergarten teacher does not assign homework, establish a routine of spending time each day on a learning activity, for example, reading aloud, playing a word game, or drawing a picture about the school day. When formal homework is assigned, place a priority on completing school assignments. They should come before any extracurricular activities.

Habits established early in your child's school career will last a lifetime. Your role in helping your child become independent and responsible with regard to homework is that of a consultant. You should not be doing the homework for your child.... But being available to answer questions, proofread a paper, quiz on spelling words or multiplication facts, listen to a child read aloud, and teaching him how to organize the material for a test are perfectly acceptable examples of how you can help.

If you rush to the rescue at the least provocation, you're setting your child up for dependency and learned helplessness. Don't rush to the rescue.... The operative words are mastery, achievement, and independence.... Here are some reasonable expectations for your homework involvement at each grade level:

Kindergarten through third grade
- Check each day to make sure your child has a homework assignment.
- Tell your child when Daily Homework Time begins.
- Check to see that your child has all the necessary materials.
- Ask your child to tell you what the homework assignment is.
- If needed, read the directions together with your child. Make sure your child understands what is expected.
- If needed, get your child started by working on the first problem or question together.
- Praise your child's efforts.

Grades four through six
- Check to see that your child is doing homework at the proper time.
- Suggest that your child call a friend to get help, if needed.
- Give your child help only after he has been really trying on his own.
- Utilize study skills to help your child work independently.
- Praise your child's efforts.

Grades seven through twelve

- Other than occasional exceptions, your child should be working independently.
- If he or she is having a great deal of trouble doing so, you must back up and follow the suggestions given for younger students.
- The key is to start off with considerable involvement, then to reduce it gradually.

Create a learning environment in your home

Words and ideas are important. People talk to each other about what they are doing. They constantly add new words to their vocabulary, fostering language development.

Everybody likes to read and does it often. People read books, newspapers, and magazines, and they talk to each other about what they are reading. People read both silently and aloud to one another. Reading is a highly valued skill and activity.

Educational toys and materials are available. I would include computers and CDs in this category, as well as educational games, models, puzzles, and problem-solving toys.

Mother and/or father are available. Adults have a critical role in encouraging and affirming the learning process of children and young people.

Academic aspirations and expectations are high. Children are praised for their accomplishments. Parents talk about the future and what it holds in terms of schooling. They also talk about their jobs and the kind of education and training it takes to be successful in that job.

Learning behavior is modeled by parents. Parents tackle a new skill or field of knowledge and let their children see that learning is fun. Family members work on projects that require reading and math for completion. Everyone is encouraged to look up answers to questions in books and encyclopedias.

[Reprinted with permission from *"The Dog Ate It"—Conquering Homework Hassles,* by Elaine K. McEwan (Shaw, 1996). Elaine McEwan is an educational consultant and a well-known author, lecturer, and workshop leader for parents, teachers, and administrators. For more information, visit her Web site at www.elainemcewan.com.]

Reprinted with permission of the authors: Guiding Students from Cheating and Plagiarism to Honesty and Integrity: Strategies for Change, *by Ann Lathrop and Kathleen Foss (Libraries Unlimited, 2005). Permission is granted to make print copies for class instruction, discussion groups, workshops, conferences, or newsletters. This material must not be placed on a Web site or distributed in any digital format. This statement must appear in its entirety on each print copy.*

Part II

LEADERSHIP IN ACTION

CHAPTER FIVE

Effective Leaders
Create Effective Policies

I've never heard of an Honor Code or an Academic Integrity Policy before. Schools should adopt a code like this so students know the limits. At our school, during the first week, students are required to sign forms agreeing to the school dress code, attendance policies, homework policies, and drug policies. If students break these codes they know they are subject to punishment. If cheating and plagiarism guidelines aren't presented to students in writing, they'll get around them. We all know how to work the system. If punishments aren't clear, students don't fear the consequences of their cheating. 11th grade girl

The stories in this chapter are told by students, teachers, and administrators who decided it was time for a change. They attended conferences and training sessions, and initiated and conducted meetings with other students and teachers. They involved parents, administrators, School Board members, and their communities. They built support for positive change and helped to develop the school and district policies required. We hope their stories will encourage similar programs at other schools where cheating and plagiarism have been ignored far too long. We also hope they will prompt educators to listen to their students and to include them in all phases of policy development and implementation.

Trusting students to participate in the establishment, promotion and enforcement of community values is a difficult challenge. Traditionally, schools have been hierarchical with students being at the bottom. But educators are realizing that when trusted and when given an opportunity to participate in the vision of the school, students have a great deal to contribute. Moreover, the participation had had other positive consequences. Namely, the adolescent desire to belong results in expressions of loyalty to the school, rather than the sub-group. The more of this type of loyalty which we can inspire, the less cheating behavior we will see. (Kennedy, par. 26)

Six students and one teacher from *Marple Newtown High School* in Newtown Square, Pennsylvania, attended an Ethics in Education Conference at the University of Pennsylvania and returned to campus as strong advocates for academic integrity at their school.

The Honor Code at *St. Andrew's Episcopal School* in Austin, Texas, was developed in a series of open meetings of concerned students and faculty. Students accused of violating the Honor Code appear before an Honor Council made up of ten students elected by the student body and four teachers selected by the faculty. The Council is chaired by the Dean.

Students at *Staples High School* in Westport, Connecticut, asked their principal to help stop widespread cheating. A student article in the school newspaper brought campus attention to the problem and led to the formation of an Academic Integrity Committee made up of students, teachers, parents, and administrators. This committee led the development and implementation of the school's new Academic Integrity Policy.

A high school student serves as a member of the School Board of the *Washington County Schools* in Maryland. The School Board and Superintendent have set high academic standards accompanied by high standards for civic and ethical behavior. The Academic Integrity Policy developed to support these standards was a joint effort of the entire community. Parents, students, staff, PTA members, public and college librarians, community leaders, elected officials, civic groups, and religious leaders provided ideas and feedback. The policy has been adopted by the School Board as an official policy for all 46 schools in Washington County.

Three teachers from the physical education department at *Lennox Middle School* in Lennox, California, decided to tackle discipline and behavior problems that took too much time away from instruction. Rather than focus on punishing students, they initiated positive change by bringing the national **CHARACTER COUNTS!** program to their school.

Educational leaders at these schools are making significant progress in their efforts to change school culture. They took time from busy schedules to answer our questions and to share their stories. They have our sincere admiration and appreciation.

References

Kennedy, Robert. "An Epidemic: An Interview with Gary Niels." In *About How Widespread Is Cheating?* About, Inc., 2004. 18 Oct. 2004.privateschool.about. com/cs/forteachers/a/cheating_p.htm.

Resources

COPY ME pages:

Michael Josephson: "**CHARACTER COUNTS!**" and "The Six Pillars of Character"

See Appendix C for related information in *Student Cheating and Plagiarism in the Internet Era: A Wake-Up Call:* Chapter 8, Academic Integrity Policies.

Marple Newtown's Student Committee for Academic Integrity

Joseph Borson '03 and Jennifer Gordon '02

In 2001, six students and one teacher from Marple Newtown High School attended an Ethics in Education Conference at the University of Pennsylvania to learn more about the concept of academic integrity. At this time, our school had no formal policy on cheating other than vaguely worded clauses in the rarely read student handbook and what each teacher told students on the first day of classes. At a time when so much rides on performance levels in the classroom and on standardized testing when it comes to college admissions, a student may feel immense pressure to outperform his peers and therefore resort to cheating. At Marple, we realized that something had to be done.

The first stage of our campaign to promote academic integrity was to form a club recognized by our student council. We named it the Committee for Academic Integrity, "CAI" for short, in order to legitimately go about effecting the change that we recognized as being necessary. Next, we developed a clear definition of what constituted cheating, and official policies and procedures to deal with cheating. These new policies were added to the student handbook as part of the student discipline code approved by the Board of Education.

Our next step was to survey students regarding their views on cheating and the tactics they used to cheat. The survey disclosed an incredible prevalence of cheating in our high school. To effectively change these cheating behaviors required the support of our teachers. We knew that we needed to start young, as cheating habits can be formed and crystallized long before a student enters high school. Therefore, our next endeavor was to formally present the new policies to the high school and middle school faculties.

This faculty meeting was generally considered to be successful. We believed our presentations of both the formal policies and the techniques of cheating and plagiarism (such as placing answers on the labels of water bottles and taking cell calls during exams) helped to educate the faculty about the pressing problems of cheating. While teachers were willing to hear about the subject, being lectured by their own students came across as somewhat patronizing. Our committee never claimed, nor did we desire, to dictate policy toward either students or teachers. We wanted to be able to make recommendations and provide advice; our presentations met this goal.

We were approached by English teachers from the middle school who had decided to give their sixth graders prompts about the nature of cheating and integrity. A few weeks later, when we heard the prompts, we were all touched by the frankness and honesty the students expressed. It was clear that children were concerned with what it meant to have integrity, at least in the abstract. Reality, however, was rarely so simple.

In the spring of 2002, we were invited back to the University of Pennsylvania to speak about what we had done about the pressing and real issue of cheating in schools. We described how students can take actions to, if not completely solve the problem, at least open the problem to public discussion. We left Penn with a belief that we had made a difference; we had received recognition from schools across the greater Philadelphia area. We ended the year far better off than when we began.

That fall we decided it was not enough just to educate the faculty; we needed to educate the students. While the policy on cheating and plagiarism was in a handbook issued to all students, it was clear that not every student had read every word. Many students could, somewhat legitimately, claim they did not even know it existed. We decided to send two members from our committee to speak to every English class in the school. We delivered a standardized script stressing the importance of integrity and the severity of punishment, both in high school and beyond. We read the entire cheating and plagiarism policy aloud to each class. This ensured that everyone had heard and read our policies, and that ignorance of the law could no longer be an excuse.

Overall, these presentations went well. While some presenters in some classes were met with bored or apathetic stares, a significant number of students asked questions. In some classes there were debates about what constitutes cheating and what could be done about it. We now were sure students knew about the issue, knew about the Committee for Academic Integrity, and knew the school was serious about the issue.

We started many small projects designed to reduce cheating. In our school, events and functions are advertised by flyers and posters taped to hall walls. We posted anti-cheating slogans around the school, especially at exam time. These posters, some serious and some less so, were the subject of conversation for about a week. There even were a few parodies of our posters, proving students were thinking about the issues involved.

An anonymous "tip box" was established so students could inform administrators (through us) about any incidents of cheating they saw. However, it soon became clear that students didn't choose to use this box to the degree that we had hoped. We also had some concerns about whether students should be directly involved in the academic affairs of other students (as compared to merely advising and educating about policy), and the box was decommissioned. While it proved to be less than a success, it was a valid effort and we are glad that we tried it.

As the year ended, we returned to Penn, this time leading a question-and-answer forum for students from other schools. They raised serious questions about what policies would be considered appropriate, who should be in charge of setting policy, and who should be in charge of dealing with complaints and problems. They questioned whether such a policy should be so explicitly stated or left to individual teachers on a case-by-case basis. We left Penn confident that what we had started would survive and flourish, both in our hallways and in the hallways of schools in the greater Philadelphia area.

The original members of the Committee for Academic Integrity have not been students at Marple for several years, and yet what we started is continuing. We do not know what it will evolve towards, but we are confident that because of the efforts of CAI and those organizations like it, cheating and plagiarism will no longer be a third rail in secondary education, but a topic of discussion, debate, and relevance.

Addendum by Sandra J. Schaal, Faculty Advisor

The student Committee for Academic Integrity was established in 2001:

> *Purpose:* It is the mission of the Committee for Academic Integrity to encourage the school community to achieve academic excellence in an honest and dignified manner.

> *Goals:* Increase awareness of what cheating encompasses; Establish an Honor Code; Serve as a deterrent against dishonest practices; Prepare teachers to recognize all forms of cheating.

The revised section of the discipline code dealing with the issues of cheating and plagiarism was written by the Committee for Academic Integrity. It is now part of the student discipline code, as approved by the Board of Education, and appears in the student handbook.

Cheating/Plagiarism

Plagiarism or cheating, which are defined as the taking and use of another person's ideas, writings, or inventions as one's own, will not be tolerated. This includes:

- Turning in someone else's work (including homework) as your own,
- Copying another's lab report or similar assignment,
- Copying something word for word without putting it within quotation marks or citing the author,
- Paraphrasing another work without giving credit to the original author,
- Extensive paraphrasing, even when credit is given,
- Failing to indicate where borrowing begins and ends,
- Cheating on any assessment by using another person's work or allowing another person to use your work.

In the event of cheating or plagiarism, parents will be notified by both telephone and letter, the student will receive a zero (0) on the assignment, and the offense will be recorded in the subject department office. If cheating or plagiarism occurs a second time, the student will be subject to disciplinary action including suspension and/or expulsion.

Implementation

Simply stated, a student-driven program has more impact with students, and with teachers and parents as well. We want our academic integrity program to be real and to focus on the issues as they exist for students now. Student perspective is essential.

This approach has worked well. The students are enthusiastic, and with each new class, new ideas emerge. They struggle with how to relate to their colleagues who do not share their concerns, but are willing to go out on a limb to promote their ideas. The Committee for Academic Integrity has made a conscious effort to avoid being the "cheat-police" for the school. Rather, they try to keep students and teachers focused on the issue through education, discussion, and reminders.

The students who started our Committee for Academic Integrity were those who attended the Penn Ethics in Education Conference in the spring of 2001. They named the organization, established the mission, and began to carry it out. Among the first actions they took was to sponsor an assembly for the National Honor Society that featured University of Pennsylvania Honor Council members as speakers. National Honor Society inductees now sign an agreement to practice academic integrity.

Since then, CAI students have made presentations to faculty at both the high school and the middle school to help teachers combat cheating and plagiarism. They have made presentations to all incoming ninth-grade students and have held discussions with sixth-grade classes who have written essays on cheating. During exams, CAI students produce posters and TV spots for the school news program to encourage students to avoid cheating on exams. More recently students have worked collaboratively with teachers to produce a pamphlet on ways to combat cheating that is shared with new teachers during their induction training. Marple Newtown students have continued to participate in the Penn Ethics in Education Conference and have made presentations to students from other schools at two of the conferences.

Publicity beyond the walls has taken the form of articles written by students for the student newspaper, parent newsletter, and a local newspaper, *The County Press*. Marple Newtown's Committee for Academic Integrity was also featured in a front-page article in *The Philadelphia Inquirer.*

Disciplinary action

Some of the disciplinary action has been handled by departments and some by administrators. Some departments have developed form letters that are sent to parents for initial infractions. Ongoing problems or multiple infractions are referred to the assistant principals for disciplinary action. Every year there are a number of cases of students receiving zeros for assignments ranging from homework to term papers and final exams. We have rarely, if ever, been forced to impose the stronger disciplinary actions provided for in our policy. One of our assistant principals adds these comments about the policy from his perspective:

> In my two years as an administrator at Marple Newtown High School I have not seen a repeat offender for cheating in any form. The most serious event related to a final exam for all Western Cultures classes. A student or students somehow obtained a copy of the exam. They subsequently made an answer key that they sold to students for $5. Details of this situation came to light when a student anonymously reported to her counselor what had happened. Consequently, some students were suspended and given a zero for the exam. In addition, all exam grades were thrown out. Students were given the option of taking their grade as it would stand without taking the final or taking another version of the final.

Words of advice

Do involve students. The ownership that comes from student participation is tremendously valuable. Do take advantage of local institutions of higher learning. High school students are very receptive to advice from college students who are already "there" and know the ropes. The same thing is true of middle and elementary school students who respond very well to the wisdom and experience of high school students. At this point we have tried to avoid putting students in the position of "preaching" to other students as opposed to providing information and encouragement. In student-teacher collaboration, it has also been important to guide students and encourage a "we're in this together" attitude.

School: Marple Newtown High School
District: Marple Newtown School District
City, State: Newtown Square, Pennsylvania
Principal: John Sanville
Grades: 9–12
Enrollment: 1,160
Faculty: 95
Web site: www.mnsd.net

[Joseph Borson '03 and Jennifer Gordon '02 are currently students at Brown University. They are two of the original founders of the Student Committee for Academic Integrity.

Sandra J. Schaal is Faculty Advisor to the Student Committee for Academic Integrity and a social science teacher at Marple Newtown High School.]

The Student Honor Council at St. Andrew's Upper School

Bill Hayes

The creation of an Honor Code had been something that the entire staff had wanted to implement since the beginning of St Andrew's Upper School in the fall of 1998. At that time, a conversation was initiated with the first students (all ninth-graders) about an Honor Code. However, the students did not have the maturity necessary to discuss the topic. They could not get over the idea that an Honor Code would mean they would have to turn in their fellow students. With all the other items that were being created for a new school, this idea was tabled until the fall of 2001, when the same students were now in their senior year and had an opportunity to attend a conference on Honor Codes.

Students returned to the campus excited about how an Honor Code could positively impact the school community. Meetings were held during the lunch period once a week, open to all students and faculty, where questions were posed: What is honor? What does honor look like? How do you act in an honorable way? Why was it necessary to create an Honor Code? Doesn't everyone basically act honorably most of the time anyway?

Two key points emerged: (1) an Honor Code was necessary to focus the actions of both students and staff, and (2) acting with honor was not easy for anyone. It was this second idea that allowed the faculty to really buy into the time and effort necessary to rework their curriculums to embed this lesson within their classes.

An examination of other schools' Honor Codes revealed two basic types, a "Ten Commandments or Thou shalt not" code and a more positive code that states what students will do. We adopted the philosophy of the second type for our Honor Code. Brainstorming sessions identified the qualities that St. Andrew's truly values: safety and respect, personal responsibility, and academic integrity. We then began to write our statement. After two months of meeting once a week the results of all the rewrites was:

As a member of the St. Andrew's Episcopal School Community, I accept personal responsibility for my actions and their impact on other members of our community. At all times, I will exhibit academic integrity, cultivate a safe and respectful environment, and encourage all others to do the same.

No discussion about creating an Honor Code is complete without addressing the "rat clause," or what students must do when they see another student cheating. One of our students came up with the phrase we use: "and encourage all others to do the same." We feel strongly about not forcing adolescents to take on the problems of other students, but we do want them to be empowered to address the situation in their own manner.

For example, when seeing another student cheating on an assignment or test, it might be best if students confront their peer individually. The value of peer pressure is generally a more effective means of changing behavior than is punishment from a faculty member. It also encourages students to take responsibility for their actions when they see something that shouldn't happen. Our goal is to encourage students to police themselves. This is not an easy thing and does not happen all the time. But when it does, it makes the school run more effectively and is extremely rewarding.

In May of 2002, the members of the open meetings presented the wording of the Honor Code to the student body during chapel and then to a meeting of the faculty. The wording was approved without change by both groups and became policy in 2002–2003.

In addition to the Honor Code, a daily reminder of our commitment to academic integrity is the Academic Pledge students are required to write on each major assignment (including but not limited to quizzes, tests, major papers, and lab reports). It states:

I have neither given nor received unauthorized help on this assignment.

Implementation

Our next priority was to make the Honor Code highly visible. Letters were sent to parents informing them of the new Honor Code. Posters were created and placed across campus in all classrooms, the gym and weight room, the library, all faculty offices, and the lunch line. The Honor Code is on our Web site at www.sasaustin. org/HTML/USHonorCode.html.

An important tradition of signing the Honor Code in chapel services at the beginning of each school year was initiated, with parents invited to attend. The homily, given by a senior member of the Honor Council, addresses the importance of the Honor Code within the community. Students and staff recite the Honor Code and then sign five Honor Code posters, one for each class and one for faculty and staff. These posters are displayed outside the main office and are the first thing seen by visitors to the campus.

Our focus on the Honor Code continues throughout the year. One thirty-minute advisory period each month is dedicated to some activity about the Honor Code. These include discussions of why students cheat, case studies of specific violations, pressures and stress that can lead to cheating, how the Honor Code affects choices students make off-campus, and how redemption for violation of the Honor Code is dealt with. Students and faculty on the Honor Council help to create these activities.

In each classroom, the Honor Code has caused teachers to adjust some of their assignments and to become more rigorous in defining the expectations for each assignment. Specific information in each class syllabus describes what is and is not allowed in terms of collaboration. Teachers discuss plagiarism and how the work of others is to be cited. Our librarian has become an expert on plagiarism and visits classrooms to help educate the students. "I didn't know," is no longer a valid excuse.

Violations and consequences

The implementation of an Honor Code does not mean there will be no mistakes made by students. Initially, there may be an increase in instances due to the new visible policy and focus on the topic by students and staff. Student will still make bad choices and, for some, there is real pressure from parents or other sources to "make the grade." It is important to stress it is the behavior of the student, not the student, that is being addressed. Making a bad decision does not make you a bad person. When a severe violation of the Honor Code occurs, students must appear before the Honor Council.

The Honor Council is chaired by the Dean of Students, who is a nonvoting member. Four teachers are chosen by the faculty. Students elect four seniors, three juniors, two sophomores, and two freshmen. Honor Council hearings are confidential so students and faculty can speak freely. Students know not to approach Honor Council members about a pending case.

Students who appear before the Honor Council may select a faculty advocate to be with them for support. The Dean of Students presents the facts of the incident as they are known and the student has an opportunity to respond. Members of the Honor Council question the student and any other students or staff who may have relevant information. The Honor Council then decides whether the Honor Code has been violated; if so, they recommend consequences for the student's action. Consequences have ranged from probation and community service, to restriction from representing the school in certain instances, to expulsion. The Head of the Upper School and the Head of School must then approve the recommendation. An appeals process is included in our handbook.

Decisions of the Honor Council are announced to the student body and staff in chapel. Care is taken not to mention students by name; only the violation and the consequences are stated. In my three years of working with the Honor Council, I never cease to be amazed how the students take their responsibility so seriously and how they always come up with appropriate consequences that are both compassionate for the individual and right for the school.

Results

In the short time we have had the Honor Code, we have seen great benefits for our students and community. We have a common language for the entire school. We can point to the Honor Code as a framework for decision making and accepted behaviors. An overall feeling of trust within the community between students and teachers pervades the campus. Not only do the faculty believe in the overall trustworthiness of the students, but the students are reassured that the faculty really believe in giving them opportunities to demonstrate they are worthy of this trust.

These positive results flow from the implementation of an Honor Code, but I am reminded on a daily basis that it is real work to have one. The expectations of everyone are raised and the consequences of violating the Honor Code are more severe than violation of a school rule. The rewards of community building, common language, and a framework for the life-lesson conversations with teenagers make it well worth all the effort needed, and still needed, in working with an Honor Code.

Comments from St. Andrews' students on a 2004 survey:

Describe one time when you could have cheated in school but you didn't. Why did you decide not to cheat?

Because I'm smart.

Cheating is just cheating. There are so many easy ways to cheat every day from a pop quiz to final exams. I do not cheat because it is part of my morals as well as the academic code.

I choose not to cheat because tests should show what you know, not what you can find out from someone else. Also it would be lying if I cheated because, if I signed the honor pledge and I really had cheated, it would not be honest.

I really have no desire to cheat because of my moral values, even if I am doing bad in a class. I would feel bad about it because I know it is wrong.

I could have cheated one time in math because I was taking a test and the teacher left the answers in the folder on her desk, and then left the room. I didn't because I knew my teacher trusted me and I didn't want to break that.

Why would you never cheat, even when other students are cheating?

It is against the Honor Code.

I hate the feeling of cheating. I would much rather earn a good grade on my own. I value the Honor Code as well.

Because by cheating, I will not learn the material that I need, and although I may get a perfect score on that exam, I would not learn and digest that material, so really, it does not benefit me much in the long run.

It's easy enough that I don't need to cheat, and if I did I would feel I wasn't living up to my full potential. I can appreciate a little challenge in math and science subjects.

I do not cheat because it is very dishonest. Honesty is a very important thing to me. I would always like to be honest and trusting and if I do something to betray someone's trust then that would hurt me very much and I would not be doing myself a favor and I would not be doing the people around me a favor.

Because I don't want my teacher to lose respect for me.

Because most students who cheat don't do it very secretly and they have a high chance of getting caught.

Because I realize that it only hurts me. By cheating, I may get a quick easy grade then, but in the long run it doesn't help. Besides, I don't believe in cheating. It is not a good way to go through life.

Cheating makes me feel guilt. It makes me feel like I am doing something very wrong. I also feel really paranoid about cheating, as if I would be caught the first second I tried. And it's probably something to do with when adults say it's cheating yourself.

School: St. Andrew's Episcopal School
City, State: Austin, Texas
Head of School: Lucy Nazro
Dean of Upper School (grades 9–12): Bill Hayes
Librarian/Technology Coordinator of Upper School: Barbara A. Jansen
Grades: 1–12
Enrollment: 742
Faculty: 128
Web site: www.sasaustin.org
Honor Code Web site: www.sasaustin.org/HTML/USHonorCode.html
Library Web site: www.sasaustin.org/library

[Bill Hayes is in his fourth year as Dean of Students and math teacher at St. Andrew's Upper School. He has a B.S. in Mathematics from the University of Massachusetts at Amherst and a Masters in Educational Leadership from Florida Atlantic University.]

Cheating—A National Issue Hits Home

John J. Brady

In the spring of 2003 Staples High School was confronted with the reality that cheating was a problem that could not be ignored. Students came forward and asked the principal for help in curtailing cheating. These students were tired of seeing peers cheat on tests and assignments only to get high grades and grade-point averages. Students pleaded, "Since many of us are competing for the same seats at brand-name colleges, seeing peers cheat and get ahead makes getting on the cheating bandwagon impossible to resist. Cheating is contagious. Please help us stop cheating."

When these hard-working, motivated, and committed students made this plea, our eyes were opened to a cultural phenomenon that is taking an ethical and educational toll on our young people. For the most part, our students want to do what is ethically right and our teachers need to know exactly what our students know and are able to do. Many have a strong drive to go to selective colleges and universities and to pursue successful, "high-powered" careers. They are exposed to messages from the school, community, and their families to act with integrity and to be responsible. They observe in their lives and through the media people who have gotten ahead by cheating. It is the squeeze of these conflicting pressures that compelled our students to reach out for help.

From an educational viewpoint, teachers have become aware of the fact that fabricated work, work plagiarized, homework copied, and exams cheated on created a web of academic deception that is very hard to pierce. They are eager to design new approaches to assessment and assigned work that discourage cheating.

Development of the Policy

Once students came forward to me, we had them meet with our Collaborative Team made up of teachers, students, administrators, and parents. We wanted to wake up the school to what I was convinced was a serious problem. As this meeting was being planned, one of our students wrote an article for the school newspaper stating that cheating was an important issue that should be addressed. This article helped to add urgency to the issue.

As a result of the meeting and our new sense of urgency, volunteers were easy to find for an Academic Integrity committee comprised of teachers, students, parents, and administrators. The charge to the committee was to come up with an Academic Integrity Policy to drastically curtail cheating and to consider and recommend preventative measures. The committee began meeting in September 2003 and presented its report to the Collaborative Team in March 2004.

The Academic Integrity Committee developed a new policy that covered cheating, plagiarism, and fabrication. This third category, fabrication, was included in the policy when committee members realized that one form of cheating is simply making up information or sources. We are now confident that our policy addresses all potential academic cheating violations.

The Academic Integrity Committee also looked at the issue of an Honor Code for our school. Some student members of the committee advocated strongly for such a code since they were aware of colleges that had instituted Honor Codes with reported success. After much discussion, the implementation of an Honor Code was not recommended. Committee members were unconvinced that signing a pledge would have the desired effect. The consensus was to implement the new Academic Integrity Policy during the 2004–2005 school year and consider an Honor Code once cheating has abated and a renewed commitment to high ethical behavior is in place The hope is to change behavior with the policy and a campaign to make the issue even more prominent in the school, and then consider asking students to pledge not to cheat via an Honor Code.

Implementation

We have begun to build faculty support by sharing the progress of the committee as they have done their work. We have the commitment of all department chairs to implement the policy in their respective areas.

Another issue we considered is how teachers can help prevent cheating in their classrooms. Departments have been discussing developing various versions of tests, assigning texts for analysis that have not been put on the Internet, not allowing students to remove tests from the classroom, providing classroom calculators for math exams, and simply being more vigilant in monitoring students during testing. We have had to adopt a more jaded view of students as potential cheaters instead of our once far more trusting attitude. This has been a very difficult challenge at our school since teachers and students, to a large degree, develop mutually respectful and trusting relations.

During the summer of 2004, we planned an implementation campaign for our new policy. We developed a brochure that details the new policy and mailed it to each student at home. We used the first faculty meeting in August to review the new policy in detail. We also used the first Lathrop and Foss (2000) book to provide practical tips teachers can use to identify cheating. We purchased enough copies for each department to have a copy and the department chairs have begun to use this material with their respective teachers. We reviewed the Academic Integrity Policy with our new teachers during our new teacher orientation program in August. Each teacher reviewed the policy with students during our opening day homeroom.

Each of these events focused on our understanding of what students told us when they brought the issue forward. They are feeling squeezed and they want the help of adults to align their beliefs with their actions. Our students know what is right and they want our help to do what is right. We also focused on the educational exigency of clear, accurate information about student performance. Our Collaborative Team has identified "academic integrity" as a key goal this year. They are investigating methods teachers have employed to design new "cheat-proof" assessments. Currently a parent fact sheet is being developed to help parents understand what is allowable assistance with school assignments and what crosses the line.

Our student government body is the Student Assembly. I meet with the executive board weekly. I reviewed the new policy with the executive board at our first fall meeting and asked them to discuss it in the Student Assembly. The current student body president was on the committee that designed the policy last year. Students have strengthened their plea for teachers to "make cheating as hard as possible." A student recently stated, "if students are given a chance, they will cheat."

All incoming freshmen received the policy in a mailing home from our grade 9 assistant principal. Throughout the school year, guidance counselors will review the policy with all incoming transfer students and their parents.

Looking toward the future

We are confident that our renewed focus on the issue of academic integrity will have the desired result and that cheating will decline dramatically. Our students asked the trusted adults in their school lives for help with this vital issue. It is our belief that, with the help and guidance expressed in the Academic Integrity Policy and its fair implementation, our students will be better prepared to act with integrity in all that they do here at high school and throughout their lives. A concomitant result will be that teachers will have more accurate data about student performance and can therefore design instruction that better matches student learning need.

Staples High School Academic Integrity Policy

Definition of Academic Integrity Violations

In accordance with our mission statement, we at Staples believe in the academic, social, and ethical well being of our students. As a result, the following policy was developed in effort to foster, teach, and encourage appropriate ethical behavior.

A. Cheating: An act or attempted act by which a student deceives, acts dishonestly, or misrepresents work that he/she has produced on an academic exercise or assists another to misrepresent his/her work.

1. Copying from others during an examination;
2. Collaborating on a test, quiz, homework assignment, or project with others without authorization;
3. Using unauthorized materials to complete an exam or assignment;
4. Programming of notes, formulas, or other aids into a programmable calculator or electronic dictionary without prior authorization;
5. Using a communication device such as a cell phone, pager, PDA, or electronic translator to obtain unauthorized information during an exam;
6. Using online resources such as Web sites or e-mail while completing an online exam without the permission of the teacher;
7. Copying computer files from another person and representing the work as your own;
8. Taking an exam for another student or permitting someone else to take a test for you;
9. Allowing others to do research or writing of an assignment; e.g.,
   a. Using the services of a commercial term paper company,
   b. Using the services of another person (family member, tutor, etc.) inappropriately, without acknowledgement;
10. Submitting substantial portions of the same academic work for credit in more than one course without consulting the second teacher

B. Fabrication: The use of invented information or the falsification of research or other findings. Fabrication *includes* but *is not limited to* the following examples:

1. Citation of information not taken from the source indicated. This may include incorrect documentation of secondary source materials; e.g., using the bibliographic information from a source instead of going to the original source yourself;
2. Listing sources in a bibliography not used in the academic exercise;
3. Submission in a paper or other academic exercise of false or fictitious data, or deliberate and knowing concealment or distortion of the true nature, origin, or function of such data;
4. Submitting as your own any academic exercises prepared totally or in part by another.

C. Plagiarism: The inclusion of another's words, ideas, or data as one's own work. This covers unpublished as well as published sources.

Complaint Resolution Process

When a teacher has reason to believe that cheating, fabrication, plagiarism, or other academic misconduct has occurred, the following steps will be taken:

A. Teacher/Department Chairperson Action

1. The teacher will investigate the matter with the student(s) involved.
2. The teacher will communicate the outcome of his/her investigation to the immediate supervisor/Department Chairperson.
3. The teacher, in consultation with the Department Chairperson, may decide to issue a consequence, and will communicate this decision in writing to the student and his/her parents as well as the guidance counselor. This letter will be placed in the student's file. If a parent/student wishes to appeal the teacher's consequence, the Standing Committee on Academic Integrity may be convened to review the matter.
4. The teacher in consultation with the department chairperson may refer the matter to the appropriate grade level Assistant Principal. The Assistant Principal may conduct an investigation and issue consequences where it is determined that the Staples Code of Conduct has been violated.

OR

The teacher, in consultation with the Department Chairperson, exercising their professional judgment, may refer the incident to the Academy Integrity Committee for the following reasons:

1. The student denies the charge.
2. Several students are involved in the infraction, and the teacher does not have the capacity to perform a comprehensive investigation.
3. Other criteria warrant a broader investigation of the charge.

The teacher will forward copies of all information and written work pertinent to the Academic Integrity Committee prior to the hearing. A written request for a hearing, specifying the scope of the investigation, will be submitted and forwarded to the head of the Academic Integrity Committee.

B. The student

In those cases where teachers, exercising their professional judgment, choose not to refer the incident to the Academic Integrity Committee, the student may request that the Academic Integrity Committee review the incident.

C. Academic Integrity Committee

1. Upon receiving a referral, the Academic Integrity Committee will hold a hearing and investigate the charges.
2. In order to assure a student's due process rights, the counselor and parents of the student/subject of the charge will be informed prior to the hearing.
3. The student will have an opportunity to appear and may be accompanied by a parent and/or counselor before the panel to shed light on the charges.
4. The panel may interview other staff or students related to the inquiry.

5. The disciplinary consequences and outcome of the hearing will be delineated in writing to the student, counselor, and parents by the Chairman of the Academic Integrity Committee.
6. In all cases where a student has been found to have violated the academic integrity policy, a formal letter will be placed in the student's file, describing the action and confirming the consequence(s) meted out by the school.
7. The due process rights of students will always be ensured.

The Academic Integrity Committee will make the final decision concerning academic consequences on any case brought forward. The Committee may affirm the teacher/department chairperson's consequence or institute consequences with lesser or greater severity.

Standing Committee on Academic Integrity

This committee shall be formed in the spring of every year to begin its service in the fall of the next school year. Members shall serve for one year. The committee shall consist of five members: the grade level assistant principal, one administrator, and three classroom teachers (each teacher to be from a different academic department). Decisions of the committee may be appealed to the Principal within three school days and may be made only on the basis of new evidence.

The complete Academic Integrity Policy for Staples High School is online at: www.stapleshigh.net/

School: Staples High School
District: Westport School District
City, State: Westport, Connecticut
Principal: John J. Brady, Ed.D.
Grades: 9–12
Enrollment: 1,475
Faculty: 170
Web site: shs.westport.k12.ct.us

[John J. Brady, Ed.D., served as principal of Staples High School from 2002–2004. He presently is Superintendent of Schools of the Amity Regional School District I Connecticut.]

"Democracy in Action" in the Washington County Public Schools

Shulamit Finkelstein

The 46 Washington County Public Schools are nestled among the rolling hills, cultivated valleys, and small woodland areas in western Maryland. Enrollment tops 20,000 students, one-third of whom come from poor families, yet are among the highest achievers in the state. The vision of the School Board and Superintendent is nothing less than to create a world-class school system by setting the highest academic standards. While high academic standards are necessary, they are not sufficient. They must be accompanied by high standards for civil and ethical behavior, including academic integrity. Over the past three years, the Board and staff have engaged our various stakeholders in shaping what those standards should be. By spring 2004, the Board had approved three new policies that codified our community's expectations for academic integrity, conduct, and dress.

As with all of our major initiatives, we used "democracy in action" to develop our Academic Integrity Policy. We called for volunteers to serve on an advisory committee; they represented staff, students, parents, the public library, and the community college. We examined numerous academic integrity codes from schools and colleges, public and private. We deliberated and drafted a policy. We then sent the draft to schools, student government leaders, and more than 200 elected officials, community leaders, PTA groups, civic groups, and religious leaders for review and feedback. We were heartened by their positive comments and suggestions. The feedback helped us develop a policy that reflected the highest values and aspirations of our community. We received comments such as, "I agree with this policy. I think it is great!" (from a student); "Good to see that the Board is taking a position and developing a policy on academic integrity. Thank you" (from an elected official); "Great to promote awareness of ethics and integrity" (from a citizen); "Thank you for allowing me the opportunity to make recommendations to the proposed policy" (from a parent).

After two formal readings and postings of the draft on our Web site, the Board adopted the Academic Integrity Policy for which all faculties, students, and parents are held accountable. The official policy is on our Web site, posters were sent to each school for display, and the policy is included in the student handbook. Cards with the policy, including a tear-off "promise" card to be signed by student and parent, were created for every student. Teachers received in-service training on the policy and developed a sample lesson, the Plagiarism Mock Trial (www. lincoln.edu.ar/hs_library/plagiarismtrial.html).

While it is essential for all in our community to be clear on what academic integrity is and the high value our community places on it, the best antidote to cheating is good teaching. When talented and creative teachers inspire and excite students about learning, motivate and intellectually stimulate them, and create learning communities in which students play an integral part, cheating becomes unthinkable. Our new Center for Peak Performance and Productivity provides continuous, high-level professional development to produce peak-performing teachers who inspire our students to be their best.

Excerpt from the Academic Integrity Policy

Students have an obligation to their school, teachers, peers, parents, and the community to act with integrity in scholarship and in general academic work. Expression of original, well-formulated ideas is a fundamental skill for academic and career success. Staff, parents, and the community must be able to trust that the work of students is the product of their own learning and academic effort. Grades and diplomas must represent honest work and accomplishments. In a competitive world, it is essential that all members of our school community uphold a standard that places the integrity of each student's honestly earned achievements above higher grades or easier work dishonestly attained.

Each student's work should be held to the highest standards of honesty. Academic dishonesty in any form demonstrates a lack of integrity, shows character that is inconsistent with the goals and values of the Washington County Public Schools, and violates an ethic of mutual regard. It impairs the school's educational role and defrauds all who comprise its community. It skews the learning process and interferes with the assessment and feedback process necessary to promote academic growth. It compromises the instructional process by giving teachers and parents a false view of a student's academic ability and effort. Academic dishonesty may prevent further needed instruction and delay a student's reaching his or her potential.

All students will sign a statement of promise to uphold academic integrity. Parents must also sign the statement to acknowledge that they are aware of the standards of integrity to which students will be held. Consideration will be given for the developmental appropriateness of instruction with respect to the policy. The statement of promise will be included in the County Handbook for Parents, Guardians, Students, and Staff, and will read as follows:

I promise to uphold the Washington County Public Schools standards for Academic Integrity. I hold the qualities of honesty and integrity in highest regard and will not violate them or support those who do.

Student_____**Parent**_____**Date**_____

The signed promise will be submitted to and retained by the appropriate teacher at each school.

Washington *County Public Schools Academic Integrity Process and Procedures* is online at: www.wcboe.k12.md.us/downloads/Policies/PolicyJ_integrity.pdf

Student Leadership in the Washington County Public Schools

Brian Williamson

Most educational policies impact students. Most students, however, do not have the opportunity to impact the policies. As student member on our local Board of Education, I was able to sit on the committee that developed the Academic Integrity Policy for our county schools. Being the only student on a committee with adults was a daunting task. Overall, I felt welcomed and respected in the group. I knew that to properly represent the students I needed to be logical and also to be willing to voice my ideas. After nine months of meetings, a policy was developed. The process was long, but complete.

Initially, the group had planned on developing a plagiarism policy. We quickly realized that the policy needed to be broader and expanded it to encompass plagiarizing, cheating, and facilitating in cheating. Throughout the process I believed that the policy was becoming more of an instrument to discipline students, rather than an aide in their learning. The spectrum ranged from zero tolerance, and failing the student, all the way to giving kids more than half credit on an assignment for infractions. My opinion fell somewhere in the middle of this spectrum. Students should not be able to get away with submitting someone else's work; making mistakes, however, even moral mistakes, is still part of the learning process.

My experience on the committee was a good one. While I did not always agree with group decisions, and was not always agreed with, the process still allowed me to voice students' views. I believe that I had a positive impact on the policy, as well as in the minds of my committee members. My hope is that Boards of Education around the country will recognize the student voice and utilize it in educational decisions.

District: Washington County Public Schools
City, State: Hagerstown, Maryland
Superintendent: Dr. Elizabeth M. Morgan
Number of schools: 46
Enrollment: 20,310
Web site: www.wcboe.k12.md.us

[Shulamit Finkelstein, Executive Assistant for Strategic Planning and Board and Community Relations, Washington County Public Schools Central Office.

Brian Williamson, Senior Class of 2005, North Hagerstown High School, Washington County Public Schools.]

CHARACTER COUNTS!
at Lennox Middle School

Carrie-Ann Ortiz

Four years ago, teachers in the physical education department at our school were unhappy with the attitudes and behaviors of our students. We had reason for our concern: 61 percent of our students believed it was okay to respond to an insult with physical force and 63 percent admitted to taking another student's property. We were spending too much time disciplining our students and not enough time teaching them the concepts and skills they needed to learn in order to meet the standards.

Rather than complain, we decided to do something about the situation. I was one of three teachers in our department who attended a three-day **CHARACTER COUNTS!** seminar to be trained as leaders. Today the 121 trained leaders in schools throughout our district include our deputy superintendent, coordinator of staff development, curriculum director, teachers, principals, counselors, staff developers, security personnel, parent coordinators, teacher's aides, and community members. If anyone had told me at my first seminar that in less than four years all of our schools would be embedding **CHARACTER COUNTS!** into their school culture, I would have said, "You're dreaming." Let me share with you what I think are the three most important factors for building success.

First and foremost, you need positive, motivated people who want to make a change. We started with three people. As our staff saw the positive changes taking place, they started asking questions. They realized that it couldn't be just "a P.E. thing." We *all* needed to work on improving the character of our students, as a team. By going slowly and modeling positive change, others bought in. They saw the changes with their own eyes and wanted to be a part. Don't get me wrong, a certain percentage will resist and respond negatively. Continue to focus on the positive people and highlight what they are doing. The negative group will slowly diminish and become less vocal.

Second, we chose **CHARACTER COUNTS!** because it is not one more thing to add on for teachers already overwhelmed with getting kids on grade level and making sure they are meeting the standards. **CHARACTER COUNTS!** doesn't take time away from an already packed schedule; it gives you more time to teach because less time is spent on classroom management. Instead of structured lessons, **CHARACTER COUNTS!** is a framework with common vocabulary that you can easily *infuse* into your current curriculum in a genuine and natural way. By teaching, enforcing, advocating, and modeling the Six Pillars of Character (Trustworthiness, Respect, Responsibility, Fairness, Caring, and Citizenship), everyone is speaking the same language. It is a matter of looking at everything you do through a different lens and integrating the Six Pillars into all facets of the school culture.

Finally, be sure to include all stakeholders in your journey: teachers, administrators, secretaries, aides, custodians, security and cafeteria workers, bus drivers, parents, and community members. Empower the students to take responsibility for their school and to be proactive in making positive changes. As the students hear the same language from all adults they come into contact with, they begin to internalize it. For example, if a student is disruptive in the classroom, the teacher has her reflect on her behavior and the choices she is making and complete a written reflection that connects the Pillars to her choices. If this same student then has a difficult time modeling respect on the playground during lunch, an aide will talk with her about her actions and the reasons why she is choosing to be disrespectful, again using the Six Pillars. It is extremely powerful and effective for students to hear the same language from *all adults* on campus. Also, it forces the students, through self-reflection, to be accountable for their own actions.

How do we know that we are making a difference and that it is working? I could share with you all of our statistics and data, but instead, I will paraphrase for you what a few eighth-grade students have told me about changes they have noticed since they were in sixth grade.

- Teachers are greeting students and being more caring by asking questions about their lives.
- Students are fighting less, and not tagging or damaging school property as before. Students are cleaning up trash and keeping the campus clean.
- Students care about their grades more and are doing their homework.
- Students are being more respectful to each other and to the teachers by saying, "Good morning, please, thank you, and excuse me."

I asked students in my eighth-grade physical education class, "What was the most important thing you learned in this class?" Of the 158 responses, 96 percent mentioned one or more character related traits, 61 percent mentioned **CHARACTER COUNTS!** by name, and 84 percent mentioned at least one of the Six Pillars. They told me what they learned:

I learned how to improve my character. I learned what I need to have to be
*   a great person with great characteristics.*
To be a person of good character. I learned to be nice to people, to work
*   as a group, cooperate as well as other things.*
How important it is to be a good person of character and how we can get
*   there.*

All the pillars and to follow them. They really helped.
I learned that by treating everybody equally it can change my life and my
personality also, it might change theirs.
Character Counts. This was important because I learn how to value things.
To communicate and work together, to achieve anything. Also, to be a
person of good character by following the pillars.
Being trustworthy really helped because everyone ended up trusting each
other.

And, from a student with a different focus, "*How to keep my heart rate up.*"

We are not where we want to be, but we are better than we were before. We will always be a work in progress and continue working towards improving the character of our students, staff, and community.

When it seems that you are at a standstill, remember that baby steps are still steps in the right direction, and focus on the positive changes that are taking place!

Time-Out Reflection Worksheet

Students placed in "time-out" often are asked to write a short essay about what they did and why they are in "time-out." At Lennox Middle School, students are asked five questions based on the Six Pillars.

1. Why are you in time-out?
2. Which character Pillar have you chosen not to model?
3. What could you have done differently so you wouldn't be in time-out right now?
4. Explain what your new plan is so that you will be more successful in class:
5. Are you ready to join the class again and put your new plan to work?

They sign their response and take it home to be signed by at least one parent.

Do YOU Need CHARACTER COUNTS! at Your School?

Brian Johnson

"How important is honesty and integrity in your school? What does **CHARACTER COUNTS!** have to do with you? Do you need it?

Actually you DON'T need it ... IF

*   your school already has a common language among staff, students, and community regarding important human values,

- students are honest, take responsibility for their behavior, respect other students and adults, can be trusted to do homework on their own, are good citizens in their community, and care about others, and
- administrators, teachers, other staff, and parents consistently model the Six Pillars of responsibility (with attendance, on time to work, and on time with paperwork), respect (for colleagues, administrators, parents, and students), fairness, trustworthiness, citizenship, and caring.

IF that does NOT describe your school, I recommend **CHARACTER COUNTS!**

I am principal of a 2,400-student middle school in a section of Los Angeles with very low socioeconomic status and with a high immigrant population where many parents struggle to make ends meet. If you visit our school you will be greeted politely by students, you will see students at passing periods moving towards classes politely and without touching others, you will see teachers waiting at their doors for students to greet them as they enter class, and you will attend in-service training, faculty meetings, and department meetings where character is an item on every agenda.

We have a common language about values, and we believe passionately that school is not just about the three R's; it is also about forming complete human beings. We believe we are moving toward that goal.

My Career Goal: Athlete

Samuel Uribe, Jr.

The career that I want to have is being an athlete. I want to be an athlete because I am good at soccer and because I like playing competitive games. I chose to be an athlete because I have been playing soccer since I was five. I also want to be an athlete because I like playing outside and playing with other competitive kids. I also want to be an athlete because they get a lot of money and they are famous.

The responsibilities that I will have are setting an example for littler kids that want to play soccer. I need to show them that soccer is not so that you can fight, it is to have fun and exercise. I also have to show them that when you lose you should not blame the other team and say that they cheated. When you win you should not call the other team names when you win. I will also tell them that you should not yell at the ref.

The skills that I already have are shooting from far away. Another one is passing the ball to my other teammates. What I need to improve on is passing harder. I also need to improve on kicking harder. I also need to improve on kicking the ball on the ground.

CHARACTER COUNTS! Is Good for My Children

Elizabeth Hernandez

I am a mother of five children. I have a thirteen-year-old daughter and a ten-year-old son who have been exposed to **CHARACTER COUNTS!** at school for the last two years. I have always taught my kids right from wrong but I had never used the Six Pillars to teach my kids. Since they have started seeing the Pillars at school I have seen a difference in their behavior.

Now instead of them tattling on each other all the time they talk to each other and question each other using the Pillars. My ten-year-old had the habit of telling little lies and thinking that it was not bad to do if nobody got hurt. Then my thirteen-year-old would simply ask him, "Are you being trustworthy doing that?" My son, being an older brother to a three-year-old, would do the big brother thing of smacking him on the head or shoulder as he walked past him, and my daughter again would question him with, "Was that very caring?"

I am very lucky that my two children are being exposed to **CHARACTER COUNTS!** at school because now they help me to actually use the Pillars with their younger brothers. When my three-year-old does not want to share, my ten-year-old will simply say, "Sharing is caring, we must be fair."

School: Lennox Middle School
District: Lennox School District
City, State: Lennox, California
Principal: Brian Johnson
CHARACTER COUNTS! Coordinator: Carrie-Ann Ortiz
Grades: 6th–8th
Enrollment: 2,400
Faculty: 120
Web site: lms.echalk.com

[Carrie-Ann Ortiz is Coordinator for **CHARACTER COUNTS!** at Lennox Middle School.

Brian Johnson is Principal of Lennox Middle School.

Samuel Uribe, Jr. is a fifth-grader at Buford Elementary School in the Lennox School District.

Elizabeth Hernandez is a teacher's aide at Lennox Middle School.]

CHARACTER COUNTS!

Michael Josephson

In my daily radio commentaries, I usually close with the phrase "character counts." You may not know that this is also the name of the nation's largest character development program. In fact, for the last 11 years the U.S. Senate has officially declared the third week in October as National **CHARACTER COUNTS!** week.

CHARACTER COUNTS! started more than a decade ago when 27 national organizations, including the YMCA, AYSO, Boys and Girls Clubs, 4-H, and major educational institutions formed a coalition. Today, the **CHARACTER COUNTS!** Coalition is more than 500 members strong and reaches *five million* young people. Its purpose is to promote a politically neutral character development strategy based on values shared by liberals and conservatives, as well as by those who come from both religious and secular orientations. These values—trustworthiness, respect, responsibility, fairness, caring, and good citizenship—are called the Six Pillars of Character.

By discussing these core values—in classrooms, living rooms, and locker rooms—young people get a consistent message about what truly matters. They also see other people getting it.

While the primary responsibility to develop good values in kids rests with parents, lessons taught at home do not always prevail if dishonesty, disrespect, and irresponsibility are permitted or subtly sanctioned in classrooms and playgrounds, as well as in popular music and television. And, by the way, lots of kids are not getting fundamental moral education at home.

How does it work? **CHARACTER COUNTS!** surrounds young people with reminders of good character and insights into it. **CHARACTER COUNTS!** is not a curriculum, but rather a *framework* for sustainable character education. It's not a set of lessons; it's the environment.

Teddy Roosevelt reportedly said, "To educate a person in the mind but not the morals is to educate a menace to society." Education's historic goals have been to help people become smart *and* to help them become good. Indeed, the American Founders recognized that for a democracy to work, the country needed "citizens of virtue."

Today, character education is widely accepted as a necessary and effective response to poor choices, irresponsibility, and attitudes of entitlement. **CHARACTER COUNTS!** is one of the most successful and by far the largest character education system in the country. Because **CHARACTER COUNTS!** is designed to permeate not only schools, but entire communities, it is not just a fad. It is sustainable.

CHARACTER COUNTS! has developed a wide variety of training workshops and materials, publicity and promotional kits, books, videos, and K-12 teacher support materials. Find out more about what's being done and what you can do by visiting the **CHARACTER COUNTS!** web site at www.character-counts.org.

[Michael Josephson is founder and President/CEO of the Josephson Institute of Ethics, sponsor of **CHARACTER COUNTS!** online at www.josephsoninstitute.org and www.charactercounts.org.]

COPY ME

The Six Pillars of Character

Michael Josephson

I've talked before about the importance of making moral judgments. The idea is not to encourage categorizing or labeling the character of others but to clarify personal moral obligations in terms of specific values and attributes that make us better people and produce a better society.

The most effective framework I know is built on six core ethical values called the Six Pillars of Character: trustworthiness, respect, responsibility, fairness, caring and citizenship. Thus, if you want to be a person of character:

First, be worthy of trust. Live with honor and integrity. Be honest, keep your promises and do what's right even when it costs more than you want to pay.

Second, treat others with respect. Live by the Golden Rule and avoid physical violence, verbal abuse, prejudice and all other acts that demean or offend human dignity.

Third, be responsible. Exercise self-discipline and self-restraint. Do your best, and be self-reliant and accountable for the consequences of your choices.

Fourth, strive to be fair. Don't cheat. Be open and consistent. Don't jump to conclusions and be careful in making judgments about others.

Fifth, be caring, kind, empathetic and charitable. Avoid selfishness. Do what you can to improve the lives of others.

Sixth, be a good citizen. Do your share to make your community better. Protect the environment and participate in democratic processes. Play by the rules and obey laws (unless you have a compelling conscientious objection).

This is Michael Josephson reminding you that **CHARACTER COUNTS!** [Apr. 3, 2002]

[Reprinted with permission from the Josephson Institute of Ethics. An archive of radio addresses is online at www.charactercounts.org. Michael Josephson is founder and President/CEO of the Josephson Institute of Ethics, sponsor of **CHARACTER COUNTS!** online at www.josephsoninstitute.org.]

CHAPTER SIX

Academic Integrity Policy or Honor Code? Dealing with the "Student Ratting" Issue

I can't tell on my friends, because you just don't do that. You'd rather hurt yourself than hurt the cheaters. If you tell on one of them, you have to tell on all of them, and then your friends will get caught. My friends know they're wrong and they'll get caught eventually—but you don't want to be the one to turn them in. I just thought, I'll just work harder to get better grades, and they'll eventually get caught cheating. So we both get better grades. 12th grade girl

A basic tenet of many traditional Honor Codes is a requirement that students report another student for cheating or plagiarizing. Students refer to this as "ratting" and many refuse to do so. An Academic Integrity Policy generally does not include this requirement.

Our current student culture regards "ratting" on another student as being worse than the cheating. Before demanding that students report on their peers we should consider the consequences the accusing student may face. No school should require or even encourage students to "rat" or "blow the whistle" without putting strong protections in place to protect them from possible retaliation.

An issue of choice

It is important to remember that a student who chooses to attend a private or parochial school with a strict Honor Code is exercising freedom of choice. Students attending a public school may have no alternative school open to them. What is their responsibility to obey a strict Honor Code, one requiring that they report a student who is cheating or plagiarizing, when they have a strong moral or personal belief that to report another student is wrong?

Legal ramifications of a whistleblower requirement as part of an Honor Code

- Check what the district policy and the state education code say about students' rights and teachers' rights, especially when one student is accused of cheating or plagiarism by another student.
- Review the Honor Code and any "whistleblower" requirement with the district lawyer.
- Require official action by the Board of Education to approve any policy that could put a student whistleblower in harm's way.

Implementation considerations

- Involve parents in developing the policy.
- Formally review the policy each year with faculty, students, and parents.
- Explain the policy clearly to incoming students and their parents.
- Display the policy throughout the school.
- Include the policy in the student handbook and on the district/school web page.
- Recommend that a student discuss the situation with parents before reporting another student for cheating.

Specific questions the policy should address

What rights and protections are available for the student making an accusation?

1. Will the student making the accusation be identified to the accused student and the student's family?
2. In what situations could a student report another student, teacher, or situation and remain anonymous?
3. Is there a written plan for faculty and teaching aides to follow to protect the accusing student from harassment, bullying, or being ostracized?
4. Does the school/district provide legal support for the student or teacher who accuses a student and is sued by that student's parents?

What rights and protections are available for the student who is being accused?

1. What protection is there against deliberate and malicious false accusations?
2. Are parents of the accused student informed as soon as an accusation is made, when the investigation is complete, or only when or if any disciplinary action has been taken?
3. Should the accused student have a parent (or lawyer) present when questioned by the teacher/counselor/principal?

4. Does the school policy protect the privacy of the accused?
5. How does anonymity for the accuser impact the rights of the accused student, teacher, or administrator?

One professor's view: It is not our students' responsibility to identify cheaters, it's ours

We should take the pressure off our students whenever we can. It is their job to excel; it is my job to assess and reward their hard work. It also is my job to maintain academic integrity in all my classes so the assessments are honest ones.

It *is not* the student's job to turn in cheaters (blow the whistle). It *is* my job to catch cheaters.

1. Student A may tell me that students B and C have cheated, then:

    *   I cannot rely on student A's word, because student A may have a grudge against B and C, and falsely report just to get them in trouble, so
    *   I will look for independent substantiating evidence.

2. If I find independent evidence, for example, test/row and seat number charts to reconstruct seating during the test, then I don't need student A.
3. If I do not find independent evidence, then student A's report is unsubstantiated hearsay and cannot be acted on.
4. Either way, student A is not involved.

I have no expectation that students should help to catch cheaters in my classes. Catching cheaters is my job, not theirs. It is my responsibility, not theirs, to create a level playing field for all students by maintaining high standards of academic integrity.

Finally, it the responsibility of the institution to provide legal protection for the teacher or administrator who accuses a student of academic dishonesty based on solid evidence. The institution also must support appropriate disciplinary action. Academic integrity demands this of us all.

[Statement made by a Professor and past Vice-Chair of Undergraduate Education at the University of California, Irvine.]

Concerns

The focus of this chapter is the "ratting issue," and it must be addressed clearly and specifically in school/district policy and in all discussions of the policy. Students and parents, especially, must agree to any policy requiring that students report other students for cheating.

It is not enough to develop and adopt such a policy. To effect change in student behavior and campus climate, positive action must continue throughout the school year. Parents and the larger community must be involved to the extent that they will provide support and encouragement to teachers and administrators charged with policy implementation.

The development and implementation of an Academic Integrity Policy is covered in detail in Chapter 8 of *Student Cheating and Plagiarism in the Internet Era: A Wake-Up Call,* and that information is not repeated here. The COPY ME pages at the end of this chapter can help focus attention on the effectiveness of an Academic Integrity Policy or Honor Code.

Resources

Article:

Gary Zingher: "Carrying Secrets"

COPY ME pages:

Roberta Ann Johnson: "What Could Make You Decide To Be a Whistleblower?"
Discussion Questions: Student Whistleblowers
Gary Zingher: "Snitching"
Robert Harris: "An Administrative Check List"
Keep the Academic Integrity Policy "Front and Center"
Diane Downey: "Students Respond to New Honor Code"
Academic Integrity Policies / Honor Codes Online

See Appendix C for related information in *Student Cheating and Plagiarism in the Internet Era: A Wake-Up Call:* Chapter 8, Academic Integrity Policies.

What Could Make You Decide To Be a Whistleblower?

Roberta Ann Johnson

Talk about actual whistleblower cases. Let students see how important the issues are and how serious the consequences can be for a whistleblower. Then ask students if they would do the same thing if they were in the same situation.

- How life-changing is it to blow the whistle on something or someone?
- If the wrong-doing were serious and the issue important enough, would you put your career on the line? Your reputation? Your colleagues or friends?
- What issue, what threat to the community, what act of unfairness or injustice is serious enough to blow the whistle over? (Note: public employees generally agree that they are more likely to blow the whistle in cases where public health and safety are at stake.)

Show selected segments of films that tell powerful stories in dramatic ways. Discuss the decisions made by the whistleblowers and the dire consequences to them as a result of their whistleblowing.

- *The Insider* (1999), directed by Michael Mann, with Al Pacino and Russell Crowe
- *Silkwood* (1984), directed by Mike Nichols, with Meryl Streep, Kurt Russell, and Cher
- *Serpico* (1973), directed by Sidney Lumet, with Al Pacino, Tony Roberts, and John Randolph

There are many whistleblower stories. Think about what prompted these whistleblowers to act.

What might prompt a student to become a whistleblower?
- The student believes the wrongdoing and its consequences are important enough to warrant the action. (In what ways is it important?)
- The student overcomes "bystander apathy" and any ambiguity in the situation. He/she must believe that the situation is really wrong. If the culture is cavalier about the action, and others don't seem to be concerned, the student may begin to wonder if he/she is wrong to think it is so important.
- Data based on hundreds of cases and years of study suggest that people who blow the whistle aren't trouble-makers. They aren't really different from others in the situation with them. They are real people who face real

choices and real consequences. They blew the whistle when their threshold of tolerance for the illegal, dangerous, immoral, wrong behavior was reached.

Caution: No school should have a program inviting students and teachers to report cheating without having strong protections in place.

[Roberta Ann Johnson is Professor of Politics and Director of the Public Service Program at the University of San Francisco. She is the author of *Whistleblowing: When It Works— And Why* (Lynne Rienner, 2003) and *The Struggle Against Corruption: A Comparative Study* (Palgrave/ Macmillan, 2004). She was the recipient of the College Service Award in 2003.]

Discussion Questions: Student Whistleblowers

The whistleblower says, "I did the right thing; society needs to know the truth."

- When and why can whistleblowing be valuable to society?
- What dangers does the whistleblower risk?
- Should we support whistleblowers?
- How would you react to a student who turns in another student for cheating?
- How do you think other students would treat this student whistleblower?
- How would you react to a student who turns in a student who has a gun at school?
- How do you think other students would react to this student whistleblower?
- What happens when the whistleblower is lying?

How should a teacher react when a student reports another student for cheating or plagiarizing?

- Discuss the school or district Honor Code with all students and be sure they understand any requirement that they report other students for cheating or plagiarizing.
- Let students know whether you encourage students to report cheating or plagiarizing, and if you will take any action based on such a report.
- Don't say, "I'll look into it" if you aren't going to do anything.
- Clarify whether you will accept anonymous accusations.

A student whistleblower policy should protect both the accused and the accuser.

- Take official action for the Board of Education to adopt the policy.
- Consider all relevant legal issues.
- Define the process, including how a hearing will be conducted and by whom.
- State the rights of the student whistleblower and the accused.
- Provide confidentiality for both the student whistleblower and the accused.
- Provide a process to inform the parents of the student whistleblower and the parents of the accused student.
- Warn the student whistleblower of possible repercussions.
- Protect the student whistleblower from retaliation as much as possible.

Warning to faculty, administration, and Board members:
These are very complex and serious issues. Consider carefully in advance how you will respond to any incident of student whistleblowing.

Carrying Secrets

Gary Zingher

Kids often carry secrets, things told to them in private, or troubling things they have observed. Having such knowledge can cause them to be anxious. If things go unresolved, secrets can gnaw at kids, making them feel awkward and edgy, sometimes interrupting their patterns of sleep. They may pull in and tune out as they search for channels of escape.

Secrets at home

When secrets are centered in their home world, kids can feel anxious about their family's financial struggles, housing problems, or health issues. They may be upset by an increasing level of tension between their parents and the possibility of a separation or divorce. Any of these factors can be overwhelming, often making kids feel powerless and resigned.

Kids who wish to seek help may not want others to know their secrets; they may feel ashamed. There also can be questions about family trust and betrayal, of kids making choices that may make them appear disloyal. Going outside the family circle for help may violate the family code.

School secrets

In their school world, kids also may harbor many types of secrets. Some are just the innocent kind regarding who likes whom, or who led the dancing conga line when the teacher was out of the room. Some secrets are much more serious because, if revealed, they can result in someone getting hurt. Other secrets, if not revealed, might result in serious injury or even death. Or telling a secret could actually cause a friend or classmate to received needed help. These serious secrets can be a heavy burden.

Knowing that others are cheating or plagiarizing is an example of a collective secret, a secret shared by many. Most kids are aware that these practices are widespread, but few may be willing to try to remedy the problem. They don't know who to turn to, and they haven't any guidelines.

Usually, in the end, a number of kids will succumb to peer pressure. Why put in the extra effort to ace a test or write an excellent paper? They are used to the hollowness of undeserved grades, and may even become cheaters themselves.

Besides, if any kids were to expose this secret, they are not sure what to expect. Will they be targeted? Will they be ostracized? Who will protect them? By making the right moral choice, they are likely to be punished by their peers while their difficult situation is ignored by adults.

Even the most conscientious students may choose to carry this secret, and to look the other way. They are not really consenting when they hold back. They simply understand the realties and consequences of whistleblowing. Why do the responsible thing and take a stand when they believe they will not be supported by their peers and by the adults at home and at school?

Our responsibility

Parents must take care that their children don't become over-burdened by whatever problems are occurring at home. This can be very difficult, but the alternative may be a child so filled with tension and distress that completing schoolwork either at home or at school is no longer possible. At the very least, keeping a teacher informed about secrets a child is coping with helps with understanding the child's performance and behavior at school. Teachers and educators can do very little to change a difficult home situation, other than to be patient and perhaps refer the child to a school counselor when one is available and the parents agree.

For school "secrets" about cheating or plagiarism, or even more serious issues like a gun on campus, it is our responsibility to have clear guidelines in place and to make our students aware of these guidelines. We must make it possible for students to take positive action without fear of being bullied or shunned. All students should know what is expected of them and be certain we will protect them when they do what we expect.

Student acceptance of, or apathy toward, widespread cheating and plagiarism should provoke dialogue and discussion in all the classes. We can involve students in exploring the ethical issues involved as they examine reasons why they or their classmates cheat and plagiarize. We can invite their involvement in developing and implementing an Academic Integrity Policy. The policy can provide clear definitions of cheating and plagiarism with guidelines for ethical behavior.

We, as teachers, also must explore ways to make tests and written assignments more creative and stimulating. We can help students to understand the relationship between the importance of what they are learning and the reasons why an accurate assessment of their learning is important.

Finally, the entire educational community must clarify for students what we expect of them in terms of becoming a student "whistleblower." Do they keep secrets, or do they tell them to a trusted adult? Do they only tell some of their secrets and, if so, which ones? Who do they tell, and when? These are important questions that must be answered before we involve our students in any whistleblower role, a role that often proves to be difficult and dangerous even for adults.

Discussion starters

A challenging debate can be built by asking, "What is a whistleblower?" One group can present the whistleblower as a "hero" who makes a valuable contribution to society while others see the same whistleblower as a "rat, tattletale, fink, stool pigeon, or informer."

Parents and teachers usually try to discourage habitual tattling by young children, yet teenagers may be told it is their absolute duty to turn in a classmate who brings a gun onto the campus and may be threatening to use it. Who is right, where do we draw the line, and who draws it?

In many cases, well-written stories with powerful themes can lead to meaningful discussions. The examples in the COPY ME page that follows are short excerpts from a much longer article in the January 2001 issue of *School Library Media Activities Monthly*.

[Excerpt reprinted here from the January 2001 issue of *School Library Media Activities Monthly* with permission of the author and the publisher. Gary Zingher is Library Media Specialist at Corlears School in New York City. He is the author of *At the Pirate Academy: Adventures with Language in the Library Media Center* (ALA 1990) and writes for *School Library Media Activities Monthly*.]

Snitching

Gary Zingher

Examples of snitches abound in books and film. Hetty, the little sister in *Caddie Woodlawn,* can always be counted on to point the finger or spill the beans. Tom Sawyer's half-brother Sid loves to monitor Tom's escapades and report them to Aunt Polly.

When the heroine in *Bootsie Barker Bites* complains to her mother that Bootsie is terrorizing and hurting her, mother doesn't listen at first or take her remarks seriously. The *Tulip Touch* chronicles the relationship between two girls who begin to grow apart when one begins to see her friend as devious, disturbed, and capable of enormous cruelty; she sets fires and abuses animals. Is there someone Natalie should tell about her friend?

Two girls who go through extraordinary inner struggles are Genevieve in *On Winter's Wind* and big-haired Tish in *Don't You Dare Read This, Mrs. Dunphey.* Both girls know the consequences of telling certain information could be severe. What is best for them? What is best for their families? They are tired of vacillating, weighing things, and feeling unresolved. They need, once again, to feel playful and unburdened.

Younger children can enjoy *Armadillo Tattletale* and then develop stories about other animal characters that are tattletales, perhaps dramatizing these as puppet plays. The tattletale hen, for example, could report the rooster for oversleeping.

These are only a few of the many books and videos that can be used to help students think through the serious issues involved when they decide whether or not to tell on a classmate or friend who is doing something they know is clearly wrong. It is our responsibility as teachers to bring "Secrets" and "Snitching" into the open.

Bottner, Barbara. *Bootsie Barker Bites*. Putnam's, 1992.

Brink, Carol. *Caddie Woodlawn*. Macmillan, 1935.

Fine, Anne. *The Tulip Touch*. Little, 1997.

Haddix, Margaret. *Don't You Dare Read This, Mrs. Dunphey*. Simon, 1996.

Hermes, Patricia. *On Winter's Wind*. Little, 1995.

Kettleman, Helen. *Armadillo Tattletale*. Scholastic, 2000.

Twain, Mark. *The Adventures of Tom Sawyer.* Various editions.

[Condensed with permission of the author and publisher from "Snitching" by Gary Zingher, *School Library Media Activities Monthly*, January 2001. Many additional books, films, and videos are introduced and discussed in the original article.]

COPY ME

An Administrative Check List

Robert Harris

When dealing with suspected cheating or plagiarism it is best to be prepared for the process ahead of time. We plan for fires, earthquakes, and strangers who may cause violence on our campus. Now, an increasing number of schools and districts are developing plans to deal with student cheating or plagiarism, a more likely day-to-day occurrence than are disasters

Preliminary considerations

Develop clear definitions of cheating and plagiarism.

- Define the levels of intentional and unintentional plagiarism.
- Identify specific cheating behaviors.
- Define the limits of permissible help from tutors, writing assistants, parents, peers, and so on.
- When collaborative work is allowed, be sure that guidelines defining individual responsibility are stated clearly. If cheating or plagiarism is found on collaborative projects, define how responsibility will be assigned.
- Identify responses that may rehabilitate rather than only punish the student, especially for a first offense.

Develop a clear process to be followed when cheating or plagiarism is suspected.

- What is the process for handling an accusation of cheating or plagiarism?
- Where are student rights delineated?
- In addition to the teacher, who should be involved?
- Who evaluates the evidence and decides if cheating or plagiarism has taken place?
- What are the penalties and are they appropriate to the offense?
- Are there rehabilitation alternatives available for the student?
- Can a teacher decide on the punishment or decide to stop the process?
- What are the channels for an appeal of the decision?
- Can a teacher's decision with respect to the student's grade on the test or paper, or for the semester, be overridden? By whom?
- When and how will parents be notified?
- What record, if any, will be placed in a student's permanent file?
- Is legal counsel available for a teacher who is threatened with a lawsuit?

Develop clear administrative guidelines.

- Are school, department, and district policies in alignment?
- How much teacher discretion is permitted in dealing with a case of cheating or plagiarism?
- Because plagiarism may not be discovered right away, is there a statute of limitations?

Institutional questions to consider

1. Is there an Academic Integrity Policy in place and has it been adopted officially by the governing board?
2. Is there a way to keep track of a student's repeated cheating or plagiarism in order to identify the habitual offender?
3. Would it be useful to implement a special transcript grade to identify cheating or plagiarism?

Conclusion

When a school or district makes the decision to develop an official Academic Integrity Policy, it is always wise to involve all members of the educational community. The faculty, administrators, parents, students, and community must understand and support the policy. It is even better if they have had input into its development. The faculty, especially, must agree with both the policy and the handling of offenses so there will be a consistent application of the rules. The governing board should adopt the policy officially. Parents and students must be as aware of this policy as they are of the attendance and dress code policies. The policy should be publicized throughout the community at regular periods during the school year, and training of all school personnel in its implementation is a must. Finally, the policy should be reviewed annually for any needed revisions; this also serves to bring it to the attention of the entire community at regular intervals.

[Adapted with permission of the author and publisher from *The Plagiarism Handbook* by Robert Harris (Pyrczak Publishing, 2001).]

Reprinted with permission of the authors: Guiding Students from Cheating and Plagiarism to Honesty and Integrity: Strategies for Change, *by Ann Lathrop and Kathleen Foss (Libraries Unlimited, 2005). Permission is granted to make print copies for class instruction, discussion groups, workshops, conferences, or newsletters. This material must not be placed on a Web site or distributed in any digital format. This statement must appear in its entirety on each print copy.*

Keep the Academic Integrity Policy "Front and Center"

To stay effective, the Academic Integrity Policy should be introduced to incoming students each fall. One effective approach is to make each year's seniors, or students in the highest grade at a middle or elementary school, responsible for a publicity campaign to review the policy and bring it to everyone's attention. Each fall, ask all faculty, students, and parents to sign a pledge to uphold the policy and abide by its requirements.

It is important to explain the Academic Integrity Policy to incoming students and their parents throughout the year. Include the policy in the New Student packet with a pledge agreeing to uphold the policy to be signed by student and parent. Newly elected Board members and new teachers must be briefed fully on the policy and their support assured.

Create a prominent link on district and school web pages

Emphasize the importance of the Academic Integrity Policy with a direct link from the school's home page. Too often, users to must search through several menu layers and finally guess that the Academic Integrity Policy is in the Student Handbook, or perhaps somewhere else. It often is much easier to find the attendance policy or dress code.

The school/district Web page also should have clear links to the following policies: acceptable use of the Internet and school computer labs; use of cell phones, calculators, and other electronic devices; and permissible collaboration or parent help on homework assignments. Explain any use of commercial plagiarism detection programs. Create an online template teachers can use to adapt policy information for their class syllabus.

Fitting the academic integrity policy into a crowded teaching day

The curriculum is filled with "must do" things that crowd the day; teachers may resist adding even one more thing. These suggestions can keep a focus on the Academic Integrity Policy without losing time needed for instruction.

- Put the policy at the beginning of every syllabus. Administrators will create a template on the school Web site that teachers can adapt for their syllabus.
- Print the policy in the student handbook.
- Print relevant sections of the policy in the student writing handbook.
- Hang a framed policy next to the clock or flag in every room.
- Print the policy on bookmarks given out free in the library.
- Print the policy on free book covers; add a few honesty and integrity quotations.
- Have a contest for original quotations about honesty or integrity and make bookmarks with the winning slogans.

- Create a pamphlet featuring the policy to be given to every student at the beginning of each school year and to incoming students throughout the year. Include a tear-off pledge for students and parents to sign.
- Publish articles in the student newspaper written by the staff and solicited from the student body and staff.
- Write articles for the local newspaper.
- Once a month, honor students who have "gone the extra mile" for honesty and integrity—publicize their names and deeds.
- Use stories in anthologies or textbooks to stress the important contributions of honesty or integrity to people's lives.
- Have the student newspaper sponsor "the most honest person I know" contest open to students, parents, and staff.
- Create original short lessons on integrity, cheating, plagiarism, and copyright to be used for an emergency substitute day or on shortened school days, a lesson that can be picked up and used by a teacher in a time jam.

COPY ME

Students Respond to New Honor Code

Diane Downey

These are a few of the comments written by students in my eleventh grade English classes at the International High School in Eugene, Oregon, two months after they had signed the Honor Code. I was touched by the responses, and I think they could help us to see the student point of view as we consider next steps for encouraging academic integrity.*

Honor Code

In light of North Eugene High School's commitment to "Highlander P.R.I.D.E," which honors **P**erseverance, **R**espect, **I**ntegrity, **D**iscipline and **E**xcellence...

1. I will not cheat during tests or during test correcting. In addition, I will not discuss test questions or answers with other students.
2. Though I may discuss homework with classmates, I will not share homework with classmates for the purpose of copying.
3. Plagiarism is presenting another person's ideas or writing—even a few words—as one's own. I will not plagiarize.

Date:
Signed:
Printed Name:
Witnessed by Parent:

The honor code is a good thing, and it has been a good thing for me. At the beginning of the year, I would try to find some excuse for not doing something or doing something. But the honor code has made me realize that excuses don't matter.... It has taught me to be much more responsible not only for good things but also for bad. Along with that comes the responsibility to do the work, which has become harder for me during this junior year. But I believe it has bettered me for college. Thank you.

I feel that the honor code forces people to take a look at themselves and ask if what they are doing is right. It makes them more conscious of it, and makes people want to change.

I feel good about the honor code. I felt very bad before, because I was having to read a bunch of pages from a book, while the afternoon kids could walk into class with the answers. This code makes me feel much better, and I know that we all have to do the same work. It restricts cheaters.

I think that it is a good idea because it makes you stop and think about making sure you do your own work. And if you ask someone else to copy their assignment and they tell you "no" because of the code, then it makes you just do your own work.

I want to get the grade I deserve. I wish that everybody would want that, but everybody doesn't. I do think it would help if we had a discussion with all our teachers, and signed honor codes for all our classes. I think that all freshmen that come into IHS should have to sign an honor code.

I am very glad you had a discussion with us and made us do it because it is important for students to know that the teachers know what's going on and that they care whether their students are honest.

It has made a difference; even my friends don't ask me to copy anymore. Thanks…it did help me to sign it. We all need a little reminder sometimes.

The honor code has been really effective. I think it is more than the honor code though—it's a teacher taking the time to talk about a subject like that. I think those are the teachers you respect and so you want to respect what you put your word to. Since the code was signed, overall I have seen a lot less cheating.

I think that the honor code has actually helped me not to cheat anymore. It gave me a challenge that I accepted and so far it's helped me with my studies. The honor code was like a motivation for me to get my act together and start getting down to business.

[*Excerpt from letter to the faculty, followed by the Honor Code and selected student comments. Diane Downey is English Department Chair at North Eugene High School in Eugene, OR.]

COPY ME

Academic Integrity Policies / Honor Codes Online

Avon Grove High School, West Grove, PA. www.avongrove.org/aghs/

Belmont High School, Belmont, NH. myschoolonline.com

Benjamin Banneker Academic High School, Washington, DC. www.benjamin-banneker.org/about_bbahs/handbook/honor_code.htm#honorcode

Blocker Middle School, Texas City, TX. www.texascity.isd.tenet.edu/

Bolles School, Jacksonville, FL. www.bolles.org/pages/?bollespage_id=668 — 37k

Brookwood High School, Snellville, GA. www.gwinnett.k12.ga.us/

Citizens' High School, Orange Park, FL. www.citizenschool.com

Cliffside Park School District, Cliffside Park NJ. www.cliffsidepark.edu/

Conard High School, West Hartford, CT. www.whps.org/school/conard/index.asp

Druid Hills High School, Atlanta, GA. www.dekalb.k12.ga.us/schools/high/druidhills/

El Toro High School, Lake Forest, CA. eths.svusd.org

Episcopal High School, Jacksonville, FL. www.episcopalhigh.org/

H.E. Huntington Middle School, San Marino, CA. henry.san-marino.k12.ca.us/~heh/index.html

Lakeview High School, Battle Creek, MI. remc12.k12.mi.us/lhslib/

Langley High School, McLean, VA. www.fcps.edu/LangleyHS/saxon/honor.html

Lexington High School, Lexington, MA. lhs.lexingtonma.org/

Lynbrook High School, San Jose, CA. www.lhs.fuhsd.org/

Morgantown High School, Morgantown, WV. boe.mono.k12.wv.us/

Mountain Lakes High School, Mountain Lakes, NJ. www.mtlakes.org/hs/honcode.pdf

North Hunterdon High School, Annandale, NJ. www.nhvweb.net/NHHS/

Notre Dame High School, St. Louis, MO. www.ndhs.net/

St. Andrew's Episcopal School, Austin, TX. www.sasaustin.org/

Staples High School, Westport, CT. www.stapleshigh.net

Stevenson High School, Lincolnshire, IL. www.district12.k12.il.us/

Thomas Jefferson High School for Science and Technology, Alexandria, VA. media.tjhsst.edu/pdf/honorcode.pdf

Timber Creek Regional High School, Erial, NJ. www.bhprsd.org/Timbercreekrhs/

Triton Regional High School, Runnemede, NJ. www.bhprsd.org/Tritonrhs/

Washington County Public Schools, Hagerstown, MD. www.wcboe.k12.md.us/downloads/Policies/PolicyJ_integrity.pdf

Webb School, Knoxville, TN (Honor Codes for lower, middle, and upper level schools).www.webbschool.org/

West Springfield High School, Springfield, VA. www.fcps.k12.va.us/west springfieldhs/

Woodrow Wilson Senior High School, Washington, DC. www. wilsonhs.org/

CHAPTER SEVEN

Librarians As a Force for Integrity

We in the School District of Springfield Township understand and value the concept of intellectual property. Therefore, we strive to teach students the ethic of responsibly documenting the ideas of others in all formats. To do so, we believe that we must not only teach the ethics and mechanics of documentation, but we must also hold students accountable for the ethical use of the ideas and words of others. Therefore, all teachers provide the instruction and scaffolding necessary for students to use research ethically, and all students are expected to exercise good faith in the submission of research-based work and to document accurately regardless of how the information is used (summary, paraphrase, and quotation) or regardless of the format used (written, oral, or visual). Plagiarism, in any form, is unethical and unacceptable. [Excerpt from Springfield Township High School Research Integrity Policy*]*

School librarians are an integral part of the educational team. They have access to teachers in all departments and grade levels, and knowledge of all curricular areas. This gives them a key role in creating an ethical school culture. They provide leadership in a variety of ways:

- Develop lessons and instructional materials in support of academic integrity.
- Publicize and promote the Academic Integrity Policy.
- Create a "virtual library" Web site as the hub of school instruction and a one-stop reference service area for students, teachers, staff, and parents.
- Establish appropriate links to sites for library research, classroom instruction, and student research at home.
- Establish links to sites that teach correct documentation of sources and to anti-plagiarism sites.

- Make teachers and administrators aware of problems associated with cheating and plagiarism in the school.
- Call attention to relevant articles, provide information about changes in copyright laws, and report on new trends in student plagiarism and cheating.
- Publicize library materials and procedures that support integrity in student writing.

Librarians can develop instructional materials to enhance the anti-plagiarism efforts of a single classroom teacher, then take that instruction across the curriculum to be shared and used by all. These instructional materials on bibliographies and citation formats, proper quoting, paraphrasing, and so on, can be shared in print and by posting on the library Web page.

These activities and many others are "all in a day's work" for the three librarians featured in this chapter. They have taken the initiative in creating workshops, pamphlets, library Web site materials, and virtual libraries in support of academic integrity on their campuses. Their library Web sites are effective examples of the "virtual library" concept. Students and parents have 24/7 access to a wide range of resources. There also are instructional materials to help students understand and avoid plagiarism.

Librarian Joyce Valenza and English teacher Carol Rohrbach led the faculty of Springfield Township High School in Erdenheim, Pennsylvania, in a coordinated effort to change student attitudes toward cheating and plagiarism. The resulting Research Integrity Policy is the foundation for all writing assignments across the curriculum. The "Clean Hands" workshop offers teachers a checklist to use in creating student assignments. The virtual library provides effective student and teacher tools to support the Research Integrity Policy.

Barbara Jansen, librarian at St Andrew's Episcopal School in Austin, Texas, maintains a multilevel Web site with specific resources appropriate for each level: lower, middle, and upper schools. Basic information on plagiarism and copyright includes intellectual property guidelines, student materials on citation rules, writing prompts, etc. She has developed a Web Site Evaluation Form to assist students in evaluating the information they find on the Internet.

Margaret Lincoln, librarian at Lakeview High School in Battle Creek, Michigan, is an effective leader in her faculty's efforts to reduce cheating and plagiarism. Her workshops and library Web page are packed with information and strategies to help both teachers and students reduce plagiarism. She generously grants other schools permission to copy or adapt the cheating pamphlet developed as part of this effort.

These three librarians represent hundreds more who work with students and teachers to promote academic integrity in their schools. They are all, individually and as part of their profession, a force for integrity.

Resources

Article:

Gretchen Pearson: "What's a Teacher or Librarian to Do?"

COPY ME pages:

Carol H. Rohrbach: "Take the 'Clean Hands' Test"
Joyce Kasman Valenza: "The Virtual Library at Springfield Township High School"
Barbara Jansen: "Support for Student Research and Writing at the St. Andrew's School Library Web Site"
Margaret Lincoln: "The Lakeview High School Library Web Site"

See Appendix C for related information in *Student Cheating and Plagiarism in the Internet Era: A Wake-Up Call:* Chapter 12, The Librarian-Teacher Team.

Changing School Culture at Springfield Township High School: A Research Integrity Policy That Works

Carol H. Rohrbach and Joyce Kasman Valenza

Three years ago, plagiarism was commonplace at Springfield. When we asked a group of academically gifted students to reflect on school culture, relating to cheating and copying, they giggled a bit, looked at each other and then responded almost in unison: "It's no big deal. Everyone does it and if you do it carefully, you'll never get caught."

It was clear we had a problem.

What was broke?

Concern about superficial cut-and-paste reports and epidemic plagiarism prompted our school-wide determination to make a systemic change in the way we approached research. Nearly weekly, a teacher would visit the library with a suspicious student project. Joyce, our librarian, would check it for proof that it was plagiarized. She very often was able to verify it as a plagiarized piece in just a few minutes. Video interviews with students revealed a less-than-ethical climate. Students almost cheerfully admitted that cheating was okay unless you got caught, and that intellectual property—films, images, music—were fair game, there for them to use.

As teachers, we were not only discouraged by students' blatant cheating. We were also concerned that many student products were little more than series of pasted quotes loosely woven together to resemble a paper or an essay. We couldn't hear the student writer's voice among those lengthy quotes. Most importantly, we didn't want our school to be identified by slacker attitudes and sloppy ethics.

Getting tough: thinking about policy and practice

The first step, our staff believed, was to get tough: establish a plagiarism policy and punish students who plagiarize. On the surface, it seemed reasonable that if we all held students accountable for their actions, if there were clear and consistent consequences to plagiarism, students would be more careful, and their products would improve. Yet, we had serious questions about a punitive approach to the problem.

- How do you prove plagiarism? We knew high-tech cheating was easier than ever, yet harder than ever to prove despite available online and software sources to combat it.
- Did students fully understand what we as teachers considered plagiarism?
- Were there ethical differences between intentional and unintentional plagiarism?
- Despite our district's articulated Language Arts standards-based scope and sequence, did all of our students know how to gather information, how to evaluate sources, how to synthesize information, or how to document accurately, in all their classes *across the curriculum?*
- Could we be certain that we had taught our students how to act like competent researchers, rather than regurgitators?
- Did we want to address the problem reactively or proactively? A whole school problem requires a whole school solution.

Working as a team: it's about culture

We knew that it would take a team effort and we knew that we could change school culture. As a team we had gone through Middle States assessment with an increased sense of collegiality. As a team we had planned the multimillion dollar renovation of the building. As a team we had developed a school mission and core values; one of these values is integrity.

As a team we developed a schoolwide plan for improving research. We saw academic integrity as directly connected to our efforts in improving research. If we were to change student culture, we had to change teacher culture. The problem was not a language arts problem—it ran across disciplines.

We hosted a full-day in-service on plagiarism to alert teachers to the problem, asking them to share their stories. We developed and shared an informational PowerPoint presentation, "What is plagiarism?" (mciu.org/~spjvweb/plagiarism. ppt). The first Lathrop and Foss book provided powerful activities including Leslie Farmer's assignment asking teams of teachers to plagiarize a paper on a group of assigned topics. Though we offered prizes for the best, it was difficult to select a winner; so many of the plagiarized papers were so good!

The Research Integrity Policy

We decided that well-articulated documentation and plagiarism policies, backed up by proactive changes in our instruction and assessment, offered the best approach. Our Language Arts coordinator drafted a Research Integrity Policy, our librarian reviewed and revised it, and the faculty gave practical "what if?" input. Over the next two years we identified areas of student confusion, and our team developed shareable tools for instructing and clarifying the stickier issues of plagiarism:

- how to paraphrase/summarize/quote
- how to weave quotes into text
- how to document traditional and emerging media formats
- the difference between Works Cited and Works Consulted
- how and when to document in-text or in-project

We developed organizers to help students restructure information, and we developed rubrics that value academic integrity and original thought and the research process itself. The organizers, rubrics, and several assessment tools are located on our Online Lessons and Activities page (mciu.org/~spjvweb/jvles.html).

Addressing attitudes and behaviors

In addition to explicit tools for instruction, we needed to address the behavioral and cultural side of the problem. In every classroom teachers discussed expectations for ethical behavior. Teachers themselves modeled respect for intellectual property in their own practice. Students realized that every teacher was on board. Teachers were checking sources, returning questionable work, and holding students accountable for the process. The message was clear: Springfield teachers valued academic honesty and active scholarship.

Yes, we wanted our students to know that integrity matters and that across grade levels and curricula all of us were serious about ethical research behavior. Yes, we wanted a policy that focused on consequences but, more importantly, we wanted one that focused on learning opportunities.

Including opportunities for learning

For a policy to be equitable, it must be both consistent *and* flexible. An oxymoron? We didn't think so. Our policy distinguishes between the blatant, intentional plagiarism of a dishonest student and the unintentional plagiarism of a student new to our school or one who clearly is struggling with some aspect of the research process. Our policy allows us the discretion to determine the best course for the individual student. For one student, it may be the consequence of a zero and its impact on a course grade; for another it may be retracing steps and resubmitting the product for reduced credit; for even another, it may simply be a conference with the teacher, or more involved, individual instruction to help in isolating the missing skill. All instances are noted in students' disciplinary files.

Our goal is to improve student products. Therefore, including learning opportunities in our policy sends this important message to our students. Some students would prefer to take the zero. Forcing them, with parental support, to "get it right" gives us one more chance at the learning we were after in the first place.

The role of the Academic Integrity Committee

Our Academic Integrity Committee consists of our principal, Language Arts coordinator, librarian, department coordinator, and the referring teacher. This committee works with teachers to help determine, within the policy, the appropriate response to each plagiarism incident. It provides support for the teacher and the student. The classroom teacher is *not* the lone voice of concern. The committee informs parents of the plagiarism incident and provides an opportunity for them to meet with the committee should they wish to do so. The outcome will not change, but parents should have the opportunity to see the evidence, to understand the decision, and to help their children learn.

One more policy

Finally, we added a Documentation Format Policy stating that any research-based product, regardless of format, must include a Works Consulted/Works Cited piece for visual, multimedia, audio, digital, and text documentation. Thus, we sent the message that documenting sources always matters—it matters even if the product is a poster, a speech, or a video. The issue is not the product; rather, the issue is appropriate documentation for all forms of media (mciu.org/~spjvweb/docguidelines.html).

Designing plagiarism-resistant (and engaging) projects: down with the report!

We wanted to be certain that our students developed the intellectual skills necessary for active rather than passive research. Before implementing our Research Integrity Policy, we had to deal with these nagging concerns:

- Had we done everything we could to make sure our students understood plagiarism?
- Did they have the tools, skills, and strategies to be effective researchers?

Adopting policies without changing our approach to research would not improve students' research-based products.

One of the main reasons that students cut and paste is because they can! Ask a student to do research for a planet report or a President report and what you get is encyclopedic information—no brainwork necessary. There is no evaluation of perspectives, no analysis of information, no judgments or application of knowledge.

Springfield's faculty eliminated the report assignment in favor of assignments that challenge our students to do something with the information they find—to solve problems, to make decisions. We changed the questions. We began to guide students explicitly through more thoughtful inquiry and thesis-driven projects that value the *research process* as highly as the *final product*.

Having "clean hands"

Having "clean hands" is a metaphor for ethical and responsible behaviors. We want our students' hands to be clean of unethical or sloppy research behaviors. We also use the metaphor as we discuss the tools, skills, and strategies we want to *put into students' hands.* The hand we want to see holds all five of the following: Ethics, Accuracy, Evidence, Thought, and Process.

We want our students to use ethically the ideas, words, and images that others have created; to document accurately; and to synthesize scholarly evidence for their assertions. We want them to use the research process to locate and evaluate sources. However, questions nagged at us about our assumption that we had equipped our students. Whose responsibility was it to "teach" research?

If we leave instruction only to the Language Arts teachers instead of teaching these skills across the curriculum, we deny our students the reinforcement, practice, and consistency of expectation that they need. In what ways were we unwittingly contributing to the problem of plagiarism? What roles did our current assignments, instruction, assessment, and attitudes play?

Could we say that we had done everything we could to make sure that we put the necessary research tools into our students' hands—*did we as teachers have "clean hands?"* This metaphor offered us the dual meaning we wanted: "putting into students' hands," and "having clean hands."

We adopted five responsible instructional behaviors across the curriculum: the challenging assignment, clear communication, focused instruction, curricular practice, and reflection. In-service workshops, department meetings, and faculty meetings devoted to professional development gave the staff the support to implement these instructional behaviors. We used the "Clean Hands" test to demonstrate teachers' responsibility. Only when our own hands are clean can we hold our students accountable and can we determine when an opportunity for learning would be more appropriate than a punishment.

What we learned

To make our efforts viable, we needed five elements to improve instruction and change school culture. We needed to: provide professional development, develop collegiality, include administrative leadership, seek consistency, and communicate.

We had administrative leadership in place. Our principal valued active learning, and our Planning Team (an advisory and decision-making representative group of teachers and department coordinators) provided the sounding board for how we would proceed. We learned along the way what professional development our staff needed and desired; we included teachers in planning and facilitating the necessary workshops. We created interdisciplinary teams for professional development, workshops, and for our tuning protocol sessions where together, in small groups, we shared and examined the student work resulting from our assignments.

We also provided one-on-one support for teachers as they designed assignments, implemented instruction and practice, and even modeled mini-lessons for classes. Finally, we provided tools for consistency such as "Five Tests for Thesis Statements" and graphic organizers as well as custom tools for individual projects. In short, we provided a full court press to deliver the message that we were raising the bar and leaving no one below.

We recognized that these changes involved the entire learning community. Communication with parents was necessary for student success. Using our Web site, faculty and student handbooks, letters to parents, and meetings with the PTA, we communicated what had changed, why the changes were important, and how parents could help. Back to School Night gave us the opportunity to talk to parents about how our approach to research affected each discipline, each grade level, each course.

Evidence of change

Following the first full year of our academic integrity thrust, we asked graduating seniors to comment about the ethical climate in our school. We videotaped the following responses:

> *As we've gone through the years things are hardening up. Our teachers can tell [when we've plagiarized]....As we've been developing our research skills, our teachers have been developing skills, too.*
> *Before, if I had paraphrased I'd think it wasn't plagiarism. But now I know if you simply take someone else's idea and paraphrase and change sentence structure around it is plagiarism. Not only is it unethical, it isn't learning, it doesn't further your argument. When you are doing research, you have to distance yourself from your sources.*
> *From what I hear about the policies, I wouldn't want to get caught plagiarizing. People are very discouraged [from plagiarizing] by it.*
> *It seems that the systems and guidelines that are set up are successful in deterring students from plagiarizing. It seems like people know it's a very big issue.*
> *It's not taken lightly. All the teachers enforce that it's unacceptable and it's not what we're here to do. We're not here to copy what someone already said.*

Final comments

In a culture of inquiry, in a culture of academic integrity, all of the stakeholders need to understand the process of research, why process assessment is important, how collegiality makes the difference, and why ethics matter. Making it hard for students to take the superficial or the unethical route demands a communal, sustained effort, but the results—a culture of integrity, honesty, and pride—are well worth the cost.

Springfield Township High School
Research Integrity Policy

Rationale

We in the School District of Springfield Township understand and value the concept of intellectual property. Therefore, we strive to teach students the ethic of responsibly documenting the ideas of others in all formats. To do so, we believe that we must not only teach the ethics and mechanics of documentation, but we must also hold students accountable for the ethical use of the ideas and words of others.

Therefore, all teachers provide the instruction and scaffolding necessary for students to use research ethically, and all students are expected to exercise good faith in the submission of research-based work and to document accurately regardless of how the information is used (summary, paraphrase, and quotation) or regardless of the format used (written, oral, or visual). Plagiarism, in any form, is unethical and unacceptable.

Specifically,

It is the teacher's responsibility to provide:

- an assignment sheet with explicit requirements and directions
- a specific rubric for assessment of the process and the product
- checkpoints to facilitate the research process, to assist students in time management, and to provide opportunities to help students during the process
- availability for students who are having difficulty with note-taking, documenting, or formatting procedures
- clear guidelines for acceptable help from human sources (peers, adults)

It is the student's responsibility to:

- meet checkpoint deadlines
- ask questions and to seek help from teachers and librarian
- follow the School District of Springfield Twp. Research Guide guidelines and MLA or APA format per teacher direction (available online at SHS Virtual Library)

- submit an Acknowledgments page to credit help given by others (help that has been approved by teacher giving the assignment)
- use in-text or in-project documentation accurately and appropriately
- use Works Cited and Works Consulted pages accurately and appropriately
- submit only his/her own work

Plagiarism includes:

- Direct copying of the work of another submitted as the student's own (from that of another student or other person, from an Internet source, from a print source)
- Lack of in-text or in-project documentation
- Documentation that does not check out or does not match Works Cited/Works Consulted.
- Work that suddenly appears on final due date without a clear provenance (does not include checkpoint process requirements)

Consequences and Opportunity for Learning

1. The Academic Standards Committee (includes principal, librarian, Language Arts department coordinator, department coordinator, and teacher involved in referring issue) will confer to confirm the teacher's suspicion of plagiarism and to determine the options for the student to learn from his/her error in judgment. Upon confirmation of plagiarism, the student earns a zero for the plagiarism, the teacher files a disciplinary referral, and a member of the committee writes a letter to the student and parents to explain the decision and its ramifications, etc. Options include but are not limited to:
   - No second opportunity (Ex. A senior who is not new to the high school or any student who has blatantly copied a paper from another source, i.e., Internet source or another student)
   - Redoing the project (Ex. A senior who is new to the high school)
   - Redoing the project from an earlier checkpoint that was satisfactorily met (Ex. An underclassman who, as determined by the committee, will benefit from the opportunity to complete the process correctly)
   - Adding the appropriate documentation that is missing (Ex. An underclassman who has used a variety of sources and will benefit from the opportunity to add the necessary documentation)

Notes:

   - The student may choose not to take advantage of the second opportunity. If so, the zero stands.
   - A student may have only one "second opportunity" offer in his/her high school career.
   - A second offense automatically earns a zero without redress.

2. The teacher will assess the "second opportunity" work. If satisfactory, the zero will be replaced by the lowest passing grade. If the work is unsatisfactory, the zero stands.

3. It is possible that a student will fail a course if s/he plagiarizes a project of sufficient weight. In this case, the student repeats the course or attends summer school. The student's summer school experience must include satisfactory completion of a similar research-based project in order to earn course credit; otherwise, the student must repeat the course.

This policy is online at mciu.org/~spjvweb/acadintegrity.html.

The Springfield Township High School Virtual Library is online at mciu. org/~spjvweb.

School: Springfield Township High School
District: Springfield Township School District
City, State: Erdenheim, Pennsylvania
Principal: Joseph Roy
Librarian: Joyce Kasman Valenza
English Department Chair: Carol H. Rohrbach
Grades: 8–12
Enrollment: 900
Faculty: 63
Library Web site: mciu.org/~spjvweb

[Carol H. Rohrbach is the English Department Chair at Springfield Township High School in Erdenheim, Pennsylvania. She was a finalist for the 2003 Pennsylvania Teacher of the Year. During her 25-year teaching career, she has been named an Outstanding High School Educator by colleges such as University of Chicago and University of Richmond and nominated frequently by students for *Who's Who Among America's Teachers*. She is a Fellow of the Pennsylvania Writing and Literature Project, West Chester University. She presents workshops on literacy and research and has developed integrity/documentation policies and related documents that are currently being adopted by schools nationally and internationally.

Joyce Kasman Valenza is Librarian at Springfield Township High School (PA). She is the techlife@school columnist for *The Philadelphia Inquirer* and author of *Power Research Tools* and *Power Tools Recharged* for ALA Editions. She is a Milken Educator and an American Memory Fellow. Her video series, *Internet Searching Skills,* was a YALSA Selected Video for Young Adults in 1999. The video series *Library Skills for Children* was released in 2003, and her six-volume video series *Research Skills for Students* was released in Fall 2004. Her newest book, *Super Searchers Go to School,* was published by Information Today. Her Virtual Library won the IASL School Library Web Page of the Year Award for 2001. She is active in ALA, AASL, YALSA, and ISTE, and contributes regularly to *Classroom Connect, VOYA, Learning and Leading with Technology,* and *School Library Journal.* Joyce speaks nationally about issues relating to libraries and thoughtful use of educational technology. She is currently working on a doctoral degree at the University of North Texas.]

Take the "Clean Hands" Test

Carol H. Rohrbach

Each participant needs a pen, pencil, or marker, a piece of plain paper, and five small sticky notes.

Facilitator Instructs:

Trace your hand on the paper. Label each sticky note with one of the five responsible instructional behaviors: Challenging Assignment, Clear Communication, Focused Instruction, Curricular Practice, Reflection. Place one note on each finger of your traced hand.

As you move through the test, if you can place a check mark next to each criterion of the responsible instructional behavior, you may remove the applicable sticky note. At the end, if you have no sticky notes on your fingers, you have a "clean hand!"

Do you create a Challenging Assignment? For help, go to "Planning a Research Assignment: Checklist" (mciu.org/~spjvweb/researchassigncheck.html) and "Best Practice For Research-Based Instruction: A Checklist for Teacher Reflection" (mciu.org/~spjvweb/bestpractice.html). Does your assignment:

____ start as inquiry?

____ make it hard to download a paper or portions of a paper, or to cut and paste?

____ contain elements that change the approach, format, perspective?

____ change frequently and reflect the here and now of each class?

____ ask students to incorporate specified primary and/or secondary sources?

Remove the "Challenging Assignment" sticky note if all items are checked.

Do you Communicate Clearly? Do you give students (and parents!):

____ a rationale for the value of the assignment to student learning?

____ an explicit assignment sheet?

____ a rubric that assesses both process and product, given in advance?

____ a checkpoint calendar and step-by-step assessments to manage and monitor progress?

____ clear parameters for collaboration?

____ a climate that explicitly values ethics?

Remove the "Clear Communication" sticky note if all items are checked.

Do you Focus Instruction and provide the tools? Do you teach and/or review as they relate to your course content:

____ how to paraphrase, summarize, and integrate quotations?

____ how to use graphic organizers?

_____ how to document in-text?

_____ how to use graphs, charts, and so on?

_____ mini-lessons for reading comprehension of these texts?

_____ how to organize and format a Works Cited/Works Consulted page?

_____ Do you actively help your students think through the issues and solve problems by giving them graphic organizers, structures, and resources as the need arises?

_____ Do you help students locate materials meaningful to them and appropriate to their developmental and reading levels?

_____ Do you use time management intervention (parent contact, workshop points, etc.)?

Remove the "Focused Instruction" sticky note if all items are checked.

Do you provide Curricular Practice?

_____ Do you teach how to evaluate text?

_____ Do you provide opportunities within your curriculum to practice the higher-level thinking skills of synthesis and evaluating bias?

_____ Do you regularly provide class and homework activities that ask students to defend, justify, weigh, compare, develop criteria, work with primary documents?

_____ Do you use research-based class activities regularly: debates, interviews, and so forth?

Remove the "Practice" sticky note if all items are checked.

Do you Reflect?

_____ Do you use your students' work to reflect on the efficacy of your efforts?

Remove the "Reflection" sticky note if this item is checked.

So, are your hands clean?

[Carol H. Rohrbach is the English Department Chair at Springfield Township High School in Erdenheim, Pennsylvania. She was a finalist for the 2003 Pennsylvania Teacher of the Year. During her 25-year teaching career, she has been named an Outstanding High School Educator by colleges such as University of Chicago and University of Richmond and nominated frequently by students for *Who's Who Among America's Teachers*. She is a Fellow of the Pennsylvania Writing and Literature Project, West Chester University. She presents workshops on literacy and research and has developed integrity/documentation policies and related documents that are currently being adopted by schools nationally and internationally.]

The Virtual Library at Springfield Township High School

Joyce Kasman Valenza

A quality library program can make a dramatic impact on learners. But its impact is not limited to library hours and library space. Virtual school libraries are a second front door. They significantly expand and reinterpret the concept of library service. They meet young users' needs while respecting their sense of self-efficacy. They are virtual spaces where teacher-librarians can translate learner-centered instructional programs to an online environment, and meet young people where they live and play and work—on the Web. It is likely the twenty-first century school library Web site will have as broad an influence as its physical counterpart. A truly relevant school library should achieve its mission for learners both physically and virtually.

Our Virtual Library won the IASL/Concord Website of the Year award for 2000/2001 and has been featured in several educational journals and books. Over the course of nine years, the site has grown and changed as I continue to adapt it to meet students' research and learning needs.

Tools for Students

Our *Research Integrity Policy* sets the ethical tone for research across the curriculum. mciu.org/~spjvweb/acadintegrity.html

Our comprehensive *Online Research Guide* takes students through each step of the research process. www.sdst.org/rguide/Image:642004_13430_0.bmp

Our *Research Checkbric* reminds students of the importance of the process— planning, gathering, organizing, documenting, and reflecting—as they work. mciu.org/~spjvweb/checbric.html

Our *Pathfinders!* page clears a 24/7 path through the information jungle for students. It allows us to scaffold and model selection, evaluation, strategies, and balance without over-intruding. mciu.org/~spjvweb/pathmenu.html

Our *Catalogs and Databases* page leads students to a rich collection of databases beyond the free Web. mciu.org/~spjvweb/catalogs.html

Our *Search Tools* page has links to search engines, subject directories, search strategies, and much more. mciu.org/~spjvweb/searchtim.html

Our *Guidelines for Documentation Formats: Rationale* policy states that any research-based product, regardless of format, must include a Works Consulted/Works Cited piece for visual, multimedia, audio, digital, and text documentation. mciu.org/~spjvweb/docguidelines.html

Our detailed *MLA Bibliographic Style* guide has documentation examples for all likely resource types. mciu.org/~spjvweb/mla.html

Tools for Teachers

Our *Online Lessons and Activities* page features collaborative, inquiry-driven activities, student handouts, scaffolds, and professional development activities. mciu.org/~spjvweb/jvles.html

Our *Best Practice for Research-Based Instruction* is a checklist for teacher reflection. mciu.org/~spjvweb/bestpractice.html

Our *Planning a Research Assignment: Checklist* outlines the important points in design and assessment. mciu.org/~spjvweb/researchassigncheck.html

Our *Rubric for a Research Project* provides a framework for grading the process and the product. mciu.org/~spjvweb/resrub.html

Our *What is plagiarism?* PowerPoint presentation can be used with students or faculty; please credit our school. mciu.org/~spjvweb/plagiarism.ppt

Video: "Avoiding Plagiarism" ("Research Skills for Students" Series)

"Using someone else's words, ideas or artistic creations without acknowledgement is plagiarism—and whether it's deliberate or unintentional, it can have serious consequences. Plagiarism can be avoided by understanding how to organize time and research notes; quote, paraphrase, and summarize information; and properly document and cite sources. By following these practices correctly, students not only steer clear of plagiarism but also achieve the academic integrity that comes with creating a successful project with their own thoughts and ideas. Designed for students in grades 7–12." (Video description from catalog, Schlessinger Media, 2004. www.libraryvideo.com/sm/sm_home.asp).

[Joyce Kasman Valenza is Librarian at Springfield Township High School (PA). She is the techlife@school columnist for *The Philadelphia Inquirer* and author of *Power Research Tools* and *Power Tools Recharged* for ALA Editions. She is a Milken Educator and an American Memory Fellow. Her video series, *Internet Searching Skills*, was a YALSA Selected Video for Young Adults in 1999. The video series *Library Skills for Children* was released in 2003, and her six-volume video series, *Research Skills for Students*, was released in Fall 2004. Her newest book, *Super Searchers Go to School,* was published by Information Today. Her Virtual Library won the IASL School Library Web Page of the Year Award for 2001. She is active in ALA, AASL, YALSA, and ISTE, and contributes regularly to *Classroom Connect*, *VOYA*, *Learning and Leading with Technology*, and *School Library Journal*. Joyce speaks nationally about issues relating to libraries and thoughtful use of educational technology. She is currently working on a doctoral degree at the University of North Texas.]

COPY ME

Support for Student Research and Writing at the St. Andrew's School Library Web Site

Barbara Jansen

The St. Andrew's Library Web site offers links to pages selected specifically for each of our three major divisions: lower, middle, and upper schools. Each division page links to databases targeted toward that age group, useful subject-area links, and reading lists. We created our own original presentation guidelines, assignment organizers, questioning strategies, and a research assistant for the upper school students.

The site search on the front page was developed specifically for our school. A site map traces the links from the main page throughout the site. There are links to teacher resources, the online catalog, and the school's acceptable use policy.

Because awareness of intellectual property issues is a major concern for today's students, we developed copyright guidelines and plagiarism pages that spell out specific dos and don'ts for both. We expect our students to critically evaluate the free Web sites they cite in assignments; they use the Web Site Evaluation form developed for this purpose. We also developed a "Quick Guide" for bibliographies.

The St. Andrew's library page includes a section on how to avoid plagiarism. Definitions and suggestions are blended with study habits, writing practices, and personal behavioral tips that can enhance a student's chances for success. Students are encouraged to discuss why they might avoid doing a specific assignment. Rather than just "cutting and pasting" a paper, we challenge them to add to knowledge with their own original thoughts.

St. Andrew's subscribes to many online databases, including ProQuest, EBSCO, NewsBank, SIRS, Opposing Viewpoints, Britannica Online, Oxford English Dictionary, AccessScience, and Gale. Using online sources gives the students access to many more periodicals, journals, primary sources, and encyclopedia articles than a traditional print collection. In addition, the online encyclopedias are kept current. These are easily accessible on the QuickStart page.

The databases, accessible via IP authentication from school and remotely by password, are one of the most valuable resources we provide for student, teachers, and families. In addition to the subscription databases, the library pages link to sites on the free Web that may be of interest or help in academic studies. These general reference sources include current events, quotations, grammar, maps, almanacs, search engines, and virtual libraries. They are identified as appropriate for the lower, middle, or upper school students.

St. Andrew's library Web site was honored as the March 2002 "School Library Web Page of the Month" by the International Association of School Librarianship. Current students rate it highly useful and it continues to be of use even to our graduates, as some have reported using it instead of their college's pages!

Author's note: see page 79 for school and library information box.

[Barbara Jansen is the Librarian and Technology Coordinator for St. Andrew's Episcopal School's Upper School in Austin, Texas. She consults for Big6 Associates and teaches part-time at the University of Texas at Austin School of Information.]

A Proactive Response to Plagiarism

Margaret Lincoln

Students at Lakeview High School in Battle Creek, Michigan, are like their counterparts in many a suburban setting. A fair number are hard-working, college-bound, and academically motivated. They are increasingly technologically savvy and not unfamiliar with the ins and outs of Internet plagiarism.

Teachers at Lakeview High School are determined to proactively address the problem of online cheating. A group of staff members met in the summer of 2001 to draft *Cheating: An Insider's Guide to Cheating at Lakeview High School*. This pamphlet is incorporated into our high school student handbook and is distributed regularly to students at the start of each school year.

The cheating pamphlet

As a faculty, we address the problem with students by discussing *Cheating: An Insider's Guide to Cheating at Lakeview High School* in all classes. This is a straight-forward four-page document created with Microsoft Publisher. The language is grammatically correct, written in student-speak rather than educational jargon. Students appreciate the fact that they are not subjected to lengthy lectures about academic integrity. We spell out the rules, give definitions, and set expectations. The complete title catches students' attention and sparks lively discussions. A summary statement, also in the student handbook, reminds students and parents of definitions and penalties.

Cheating includes the actual giving or receiving of any unauthorized aid or assistance resulting in an unfair advantage on any form of academic work.

Plagiarism includes the copying of the language, structure, idea, and/or thought of another and representing it as one's own original work.

MINIMUM DISCIPLINE: 1-DAY SUSPENSION
AND NO CREDIT FOR ASSIGNMENT

Students are required to bring into school a signed form pledging that they have read all sections of the student handbook, including the cheating pamphlet in the cheating and plagiarism sections, and that they understand the rules and penalties. Parents must co-sign the form. Students and parents also co-sign an agreement to abide by the technology use stipulations in the handbook. In general, favorable comments are heard from parents, especially during conference time, about Lakeview High School's efforts to reduce cheating and plagiarism.

Faculty workshops

As library media specialist and the unofficial expert on Internet research, I have given several short, practical workshops to teachers on the detection and prevention of plagiarism. I describe the outline and talking points for these staff presentations in the January 2002 issue of *MultiMedia Schools* (accessible online at www.infoto-day.com/MMSchools/jan02/lincoln.htm).

The workshop can be conducted in a 45-minute staff meeting. I begin with statistics that reveal the widespread extent of the problem; for example, some 80 percent of high school students admit to cheating. Teachers reflect on reasons why students plagiarize and on how to recognize signs that academic honesty is being compromised.

I use a general Web site to demonstrate strategies to aid in detecting plagiarism and the particular techniques helpful in finding misuse of online database articles. Then we consider the important question of prevention.

- How can we best talk to students about overarching issues ranging from bibliographic citation to copyright and intellectual property rights?
- How can teachers structure assessments so students cannot readily cheat?
- What alternative creative written assignments can be used so students are less inclined to plagiarize?

Teachers take the information and skills from the workshop back to their students and classrooms, better prepared to recognize and prevent plagiarism.

Our challenge

Since our first attempts to address the problem of cheating, several classes of Lakeview High School students have graduated and gone on to college. These students have, undoubtedly, faced similar pressures and temptations to cheat at the university level. As teachers, we must continue to educate ourselves on how to deal responsibly with plagiarism and other forms of cheating in the electronic age. By challenging our students to submit quality and original work, we can take a proactive stance and work to prevent any form of dishonesty in our schools.

Permission to copy the pamphlet

We continue to receive a few requests each month from teachers and librarians around the country asking permission to use and adapt the pamphlet. Unequivocally, we answer yes! The pamphlet is available online and can be downloaded from our website. academic.kellogg.cc.mi.us/k12lincolnm/cheating98.pdf

Image:642004_13430_0.bmp

School: Lakeview High School
District: Lakeview School District
City, State: Battle Creek, Michigan
Principal: Dr. Steven Skalka
Librarian: Margaret Lincoln, Library Media Specialist
Grades: 9–12
Enrollment: 1,143
Faculty: 62
Library Web site: remc12.k12.mi.us/lhslib
e-mail address: mlincoln@bc-lakeview.k12.mi.us

[Margaret Lincoln is the Library Media Specialist at Lakeview High School in Battle Creek, Michigan. *School Library Journal* honored the Lakeview High School Library with the Web Site of the Month award in April 2002. Margaret Lincoln received the 2004 AASL School Library Collaborative Award for her work in Holocaust education. She was named an American Memory Fellow with the Library of Congress in 2000 and a Mandel Fellow with the United States Holocaust Memorial Museum in 2002.]

COPY ME

The Lakeview High School Library Web Site
remc12.k12.mi.us/lhslib/

Margaret Lincoln

Students quickly become familiar with the format and design of the LHS Library Web site because it is the default home page on all computers in the high school building. They appreciate being able to connect to the library's electronic resources from school, home, and other locations 24/7. Many students even e-mail reference questions to the librarian. *School Library Journal* honored the Lakeview High School Library with the Web Site of the Month award in April 2002.

Electronic Resources provides direct access to a wide range of full-text databases available from AccessMichigan and links to many additional research sites.
remc12.k12.mi.us/lhslib/Electronic.htm

LHS Library Research Guide is based on the Big6 problem-solving model and gives step-by-step help to students who are working on written assignments.
remc12.k12.mi.us/lhslib/Big%20Six1.htm

Copyright Basics and the Internet reviews copyright law and gives guidelines for usage. remc12.k12.mi.us/lhslib/Copyright.htm

How to Prepare the Works Cited and Bibliography leads students through the general rules of correct bibliographic citation and then provides specific examples. remc12.k12.mi.us/lhslib/works%20cited1.htm

Internet Plagiarism: An Agenda for Staff Inservice and Student Awareness www.infotoday.com/MMSchools/jan02/lincoln.htm

Cheating: An Insider's Guide to Cheating at Lakeview High School [pamphlet]. academic.kellogg.cc.mi.us/k12lincolnm/cheating98.pdf Image:642004_13 430_0.bmp

Schools are granted permission to link to these sites from their own Web sites.

[Margaret Lincoln is the Library Media Specialist at Lakeview High School in Battle Creek, Michigan. She received the 2004 AASL School Library Collaborative Award for her work in Holocaust education. She was named an American Memory Fellow with the Library of Congress in 2000 and a Mandel Fellow with the United States Holocaust Memorial Museum in 2002.]

What's a Teacher or Librarian to Do?

Gretchen Pearson

Cyberplagiarism, cut and paste, cybercheating, high tech cheating, "patch writing," theft of intellectual property: all these terms describe ways students use others' words and ideas without attribution.

Students under pressure because of work in other classes, jobs, athletics, or other activities may not think it is worth their time to write an original paper, especially if they are not interested in the topic, or see it as busywork. They may know of peers who have plagiarized successfully, which in turn discourages them from doing their own work. Remember, those who don't get caught talk, while those who get caught don't talk, so the perception among students is that everyone who cheats gets away with it.

Our response as a teacher or librarian will depend on whether the student's plagiarism is intentional and deliberate or unintentional due to lack of skill or understanding. One calls for penalties and punishment, and the other for better instruction. In either instance, we will do well to encourage ongoing discussion of the importance of ethical behavior.

Focus on ethics

Class discussions can help to discourage intentional plagiarism by emphasizing the ethical issues involved. They can help to discourage unintentional plagiarism by motivating students to learn to complete written assignments in an ethical manner.

- Discuss plagiarism often, not just in the first five minutes of the first class. Talk about the role trust plays in students' own lives, and why they want to, and should be able to, trust their peers, friends, and families.

- Present plagiarism as an ethical and moral issue of fair use and intellectual property, an issue of trust between student and teacher, and among peers.
- Discuss ethical issues that affect their lives such as Napster, or receiving a low grade for plagiarism, or even failing a class or being expelled for cheating on a test.
- Develop an ethics segment for your class, or integrate discussions of ethical issues throughout the semester.
- Discuss your school's Academic Integrity Policy. If neither your school nor your department has a policy, work with your students and faculty to create interest in developing one. Help organize a committee of faculty, administrators, students, and parents. All of these groups must "own" the policy; a policy written without the support of everyone involved and affected will have little value.
- Develop a Research Integrity Policy. Discuss ideas related to integrity in research with your students, and with your faculty. Ask students to discuss the ideas with their friends, other teachers, and parents. Start with a policy for your own class; perhaps it will spread throughout your department, school, and district.
- Invite a college teacher to talk about the ramifications of cheating and plagiarism in college. Anecdotes about students not being admitted to college after plagiarizing in high school can be used as illustrations.
- Talk about past cases when other students at your school have been caught plagiarizing and discuss the penalties that were assigned.
- Talk about why and how scholars use citations and references, so that students don't think of it as busywork.

What's a librarian to do?

Collaborate with teachers across the curriculum in teaching students to locate, evaluate, and use information effectively in all subject areas.

- Teach the search strategies that will be most useful in online searching.
- Teach students to evaluate the information they find and to evaluate the credibility of the Web site they are using.

Become the school expert on plagiarism.

- Be familiar with the tools and sites students use for research and how they use them.
- Help teachers track down original sources in cases of suspected plagiarism.

Provide leadership in developing policies and handbooks.

- Help create interest and organization to develop an Academic Integrity Policy and a Research Integrity Policy if your school does not have one or both.
- Offer to help the English teachers develop a Writing Handbook or to revise an existing one to include guidelines that can help to prevent plagiarism.

Develop instructional materials and Web sites.

- Work with teachers across the curriculum to develop writing assignments that are interesting and challenging, ones with specific requirements for content or references that can help to make plagiarizing more difficult.
- Provide print and online guides for citing information correctly (MLA, APA, etc.).
- Refer students and teachers to online writing centers that focus on teaching the skills of quoting, paraphrasing, summarizing, synthesizing, and correct citation.
- On your school library Web site, provide links to online writing centers and to anti-plagiarism instruction sites.

Deterring unintentional plagiarism

Define and discuss the many aspects of plagiarism.

- Make sure students know what plagiarism is. One student said that it wasn't plagiarism because it was on the Internet; another said it wasn't plagiarism because there was no copyright symbol.
- Clarify the issues of copyright and intellectual property so students won't confuse fair use with not needing to cite sources.
- Discuss and clarify the concept of "common knowledge." One professor reportedly told students that it's not plagiarism if you take it out of an encyclopedia because "that's common knowledge."

Teach the skills students need to have confidence in their own research abilities.

- Collaborate with your librarian to teach effective search strategies for both print and online sources.
- Conduct several online searches as a class.
- As a class, critically evaluate the information available at a variety of online sites.

- Contrast scholarly or peer-reviewed sources with Web sites that lack credibility or have an obvious bias.
- Provide guided practice in ways to integrate information from their sources into their own paper (quote, paraphrase, summarize, etc.).
- Encourage them by letting them know you think they could do better.

Deterring intentional plagiarism

Point out the penalties for plagiarism and stress that penalties are likely to be even more severe in college.

- Make it clear that penalties for handing in a plagiarized paper are much more severe than penalties for using the wrong margins or forgetting an apostrophe.
- Emphasize the importance of learning to complete an honest written assignment in high school as good preparation for college.

Share your knowledge about the paper mill sites, and Web sites and software designed to help you catch plagiarism.

- Analyze a bad paper from a paper mill with your students. Use it to help them identify the criteria of a good paper.
- Most of these papers are not very good, so critiquing one in class will bring that home.
- Talk about the lack of any quality control when buying a paper without seeing it first.
- Discuss the possibility that another student in your class might buy and hand in the same paper.

Don't let the students write about "anything."

- Make the topic of the paper a response to a specific question, class topic, or reading.
- Assign specific topics and change the topics each semester.
- When possible, make the topic a current one.
- Require current references. Most of the sources used in the papers from paper mills are several years old.

Structure writing assignments to make plagiarism difficult or less necessary.

- Assign the paper and start the process early to avoid procrastination and last-minute panic that can encourage plagiarism.
- Reduce the stakes. Instead of one large grade at the end of the project, grade each part of the paper as it is developed.

- Require that drafts be handed in as they are written and provide feedback on each.
- Give them opportunities to learn and practice summarization and paraphrasing.

Conclusion

Collaboration is essential to preventing plagiarism. Tackling the problem requires the cooperation of teachers, administrators, librarians, parents, and students. Only by working together can we hope to reach young people, to teach them ethical ways, and to impress upon them the importance of trust: trust between teacher and student, student and parent, and student and student. It is not just one person's responsibility.

Remember that many students don't plagiarize, and those who do plagiarize hurt those who don't. It's our job to take actions that can help level the playing field to make it fair to all.

Many of these ideas are developed more fully on the author's **Electronic Plagiarism Seminar** Web page at www.lemoyne.edu/library/plagiarism/index.htm. The seminar offers additional information and references on detecting plagiarism, search strategies, definitions, instructional strategies, policies and procedures, and a selective bibliography.

[Gretchen Pearson is the Public Services Librarian at the Noreen Reale Falcone Library at Le Moyne College, Syracuse, NY. She is Copyright Officer for the College, and the campus administrator for Turnitin.com. She conducts plagiarism workshops for college and high school classes. She can be reached at pearson@lemoyne.edu.]

CHAPTER EIGHT

Pursuing Victory With Honor

I can get an advantage by knowing the pressure points (pinching a nerve) so I inflict pain, this isn't illegal. On the offense, I hurt him so he gives in. Coach teaches us how to inflict pain to get an advantage. You win any way you can. All the teams wrestle dirty. 10th grade boy

Do coaches teach illegal moves? Yes, virtually all of them at higher competitive levels. They say, "Be a good sport, but win." High school parent

Youth sports are a vitally important factor in the lives of many students and their parents. Young athletes are influenced by their coaches and teammates as they develop their own ideas of what it means to be a "good sport" and what "sportsmanship" involves. Too often, they are told to seek "victory with honor" but hear a hidden message that "win at any cost" is the true goal.

These issues are addressed in the articles that make up this chapter. Michael Josephson sets the tone with *Victory With Honor.* Robert Weinberg describes a recent baseball season when he took a strong stand in favor of doing the honorable thing even in the face of student and parent protests.

The Arizona Interscholastic Association established a statewide *Pursuing Victory With Honor* program in 1999. Chuck Schmidt describes the program and provides a COPY ME page for other associations that might be interested in developing a similar program. The *Pursuing Victory With Honor* program at Sabino High School in Tucson, Arizona, is described by Will Kreamer, and the program at North Canyon High School in Phoenix, Arizona, is described by Scott Brown. The chapter ends with words to his young gymnast daughter from Michael Josephson.

Support material and additional information about the national *Pursuing Victory With Honor* program is available from **CHARACTER COUNTS!** Sports.

There also is data on the results of the 2004 **CHARACTER COUNTS!** Sportsmanship Survey. These are online at www.charactercounts.org.

Resources

Articles:

Robert Weinberg: "*Pursuing Victory With Honor* at Sherman Oaks Center for Enriched Studies"
Will Kreamer: "CATS WIN at Sabino High School"
Scott Brown: "Where Attention Goes—Energy Flows"

COPY ME pages:

Michael Josephson: "Victory With Honor"
Chuck Schmidt: "*Pursuing Victory With Honor* in Arizona Schools"
Pursuing Victory With Honor—Arizona Interscholastic Association
Michael Josephson: "What I Want My Daughter to Get Out of Sports"

Victory With Honor

Michael Josephson

Not everyone likes sports. Many think it's a waste of time or, at best, the toy department of life. Yet, regardless of your personal views, it's unwise to underestimate the influence sports have on the quality and character of the American culture. The values of millions of participants and spectators, including their views on what is permissible and proper in the competitive pursuit of all sorts of personal goals, are shaped by the values conveyed in sports.

In February 2002, the Josephson Institute hosted a summit meeting of many of the most influential leaders in youth sports to develop standards and strategies to improve the quality of the sports experience for youngsters 12 and under. A lot of time was spent discussing bad sportsmanship, violent and abusive parent behavior, and other negative trends that demean and diminish the reputation and reality of kids' sports.

At the same time, many of us watched the Winter Olympics, a perfect backdrop to our conference because the growing gap between the ideals of the Olympics and some ugly realities of modern day competition parallels the mission drift seen in youth sports.

One common thread is the distortion of the gallant and uplifting goals of athletic competition into an unrestrained, obsessive, and unprincipled pursuit of personal glory and material gain.

Though the word competition is derived from the Latin word *competere,* which embodies the idea of "striving together," even in a youth context competitors are commonly viewed as enemies. Instead of striving for personal excellence and pursuing victory with honor, modern soldiers of sport want to win so badly that they shamelessly engage in aggressive, hostile, disrespectful, and dishonest behaviors.

The solution is so easy to articulate but so hard to achieve. All we have to do is take to heart the Olympic Creed: "The most important thing is not to win but to take part, just as the most important thing in life is not the triumph, but the struggle. The essential thing is not to have conquered, but to have fought well."

All youth sports programs can have a greater positive impact if they have the courage and integrity to pursue a child-centered mission: give kids a safe environment in which they have fun, build character, learn to practice sportsmanship and develop skills and traits that help them become responsible citizens and live happy, healthy lives.

Striving to win is an important aspect of competition but youth sports is not primarily about winning; it's about learning through effort and improvement. You see, kids like to win; but it's the adults who distort the experience because of their need to win. The fact is, with positive coaching, all the values of sport, including enjoyment and a sense of accomplishment, can be derived from the passionate pursuit of victory, regardless of the outcome.

This is Michael Josephson reminding you that **CHARACTER COUNTS!**

[Based on Michael Josephson's radio addresses on Feb. 11, 2002, and Dec. 9, 2002. Reprinted with permission from the Josephson Institute of Ethics. An archive of radio addresses is online at www.charactercounts.org. Michael Josephson is founder and President/CEO of the Josephson Institute of Ethics, sponsor of **CHARACTER COUNTS!** online at www.josephsoninstitute.org.]

Pursuing Victory With Honor at Sherman Oaks Center for Enriched Studies

Robert Weinberg

The Sherman Oaks Center for Enriched Studies is a grades 4–12 Magnet school in the Los Angeles Unified School District. We draw our 1,800 students from all over the enormous school district; 800 are in our high school. Our mandated ethnicity level of 60% minority and 40% Caucasian makes us diverse ethnically and socioeconomically, so we qualify as a Title I school.

We also are a very successful school academically, being ranked in the top 10 percent of schools in our district and state. We have a culture of high expectations and high success, both academically and in character development. Our school and local district have been **CHARACTER COUNTS!** and *Pursuing Victory With Honor* schools for more than four years.

Our interscholastic program offers most of the sports possible for boys and girls, except wrestling and football. Because of our size, and sharing students with other activities, the size of our teams is typically not large. This means that all students who go out for a sport really get quality playing time. We have been very successful in our league events, but usually struggle in playoffs against much larger teams.

Pursuing Victory With Honor is a natural progression of **CHARACTER COUNTS!** We meet with our athletes at the beginning of each season to discuss expectations and talk about the kinds of situations they will confront throughout the season. We ask them to think about their decisions and actions as they represent their school, their families, and themselves. We ask parents to sign a pledge that indicates their responsibilities as parents and spectators.

During the spring 2004 season, our baseball team had a strong record of 14–0 going into the last two games. Of the 12 players on the team, 4 were seniors. The next-to-last game happened to take place on the same day as our Senior Picnic.

The senior baseball players were told by several staff members that transportation back to school would be provided so they would be on time to start the game. The opposing team traveled 25 miles to find our school with only eight players; the seniors chose to stay at the picnic. We had to forfeit to a team we had defeated 35–5 earlier in the season.

The coach and assistant principal talked to the team after this, with a focus on sportsmanship and the importance of every game. The final game of our season came on the same day as the Senior Talent Show. History repeated itself when the seniors were too busy with jobs or getting ready for the talent show that night to show up for the game. Again, we had to forfeit a game.

Knowing we would be awarded a bid to the playoffs, the coach, assistant principal, and I discussed what had happened. We decided that, based on the poor character of the seniors on the team, we should decline the playoff bid. In all my years as a coach or administrator, working for victories and ultimately a shot in the playoffs had been the goal; now I knew there was a bigger issue at stake.

Declining a playoff bid had never been done in our district and even staff from the district's athletics office questioned our decision. When a front-page article appeared in the *Los Angeles Times,* three of the seniors' angry parents came to meet with me. After more than two hours of hearing their concerns, I informed them that if I had to make the decision again, I would decide the same way. We met with the team and, to my disgust, the four seniors said the two teams we had forfeited to didn't deserve another chance to play us. Fortunately, the rest of our school community supported our decision. E-mails and letters from all over the country overwhelmingly applauded a decision in favor of integrity and purpose over brashness and lack of commitment.

Schools implementing the *Pursuing Victory With Honor* program should realize that the administrators, coaches, and parents must support the program. They must talk to kids about the real-life issues and the decisions that will confront them. Otherwise, they may not get the results they want in the areas of integrity, fair play, and appreciation for the love of sport and competition.

At athletic competitions the administrators, teachers, and parents must step forward with action to stop taunting, poor sportsmanship, and badmouthing of the officials, opposing players, or coaches. Adults who don't outwardly and strongly oppose such behavior have just endorsed it by nonaction.

Each of you must model the behaviors you want, even if the costs are high and often unpopular or difficult. Only in this way are you and your teams truly *Pursuing Victory With Honor.*

School: Sherman Oaks Center for Enriched Studies
District: Los Angeles Unified School District
City, State: Tarzana, California
Principal: Robert S. Weinberg
Grades: 4–12
Enrollment: 1,786
Faculty: 70
Web site: soces.lausd.k12.ca.us

[Robert S. Weinberg has been Principal at Sherman Oaks CES for five years. He was inducted into the LAUSD Football Hall of Fame for his play at Monroe High School and San Fernando Valley State College (1968 Junior Rose Bowl). In education for over 34 years as a teacher, football and track coach, athletic director, assistant principal, and principal, he is very proud not only of his student-athletes who have gone on to become All Americans, All Pro, and Olympic Gold Medalists, but all of the other great students and athletes, especially those in his only losing season in 1983 at Taft High School, when the team went 0–10 and showed great courage, passion, and love of the game.]

COPY ME

Pursuing Victory With Honor in Arizona Schools

Chuck Schmidt

The Arizona Interscholastic Association (AIA) is a nonprofit volunteer organization of 239 member schools in Arizona. It serves as the statewide governing body for interscholastic athletics and activities.

The *Pursuing Victory With Honor* initiative is a voluntary effort established in 1999 on behalf of AIA schools in Arizona. AIA has conducted face-to-face trainings for administrators and coaches at the high school level, and for students involved in the interscholastic experience and their parents.

In planning to develop a *Pursuing Victory With Honor* program, it is important to focus on what will work in your school and community. Each local program will be different, but success for each depends on having "buy-in" and strong support from the School Board and the community.

Work with your coaches, teachers, administrators, parents, and students to identify the issues. Emphasize the role played by the coaches in the total educational process, not just in the sports arena. Then create an initiative that helps to teach young people to make healthy lifestyle choices.

The focus must be on *Pursuing,* more on the journey rather than just on the destination. The educational process that occurs within that experience will provide far-ranging results, victories that can be measured on and off the field.

[Chuck Schmidt is Assistant Executive Director of the Arizona Interscholastic Association, 7007 N. 18th Street, Phoenix, AZ 85020, www.aiaonline.org.]

Pursuing Victory With Honor

Arizona Interscholastic Association

Throughout its history, the Arizona Interscholastic Association and its member schools have used educational athletics as a vehicle to teach life lessons related to the promotion of healthy lifestyles and character development. Recognizing the many challenges facing modern-day interscholastic athletics, the AIA introduced its signature *Pursuing Victory With Honor* program in 1999 to assist all invested parties in maintaining and promoting the integrity and educational value of athletics.

Mission Statement

The AIA *Pursuing Victory With Honor* initiative will create an environment in Arizona where the student-athletes, coaches, officials, and spectators are committed to *Pursuing Victory With Honor* and teamwork through TRUSTWORTHINESS, RESPECT, RESPONSIBILITY, FAIRNESS, CARING, AND CITIZENSHIP.

Objectives

- To develop a comprehensive, pervasive and sustaining AIA *Pursuing Victory With Honor* initiative, through the framework of the Arizona Accord.
- To establish character development expectations for the AIA student-athletes, coaches, administrators, and spectators involved in AIA athletics and activities.
- To develop standards of accountability for all AIA member schools, student-athletes, coaches, administrators, and spectators.
- To implement a program of assessment and accountability of the AIA *Pursuing Victory With Honor* initiative for all participating AIA member schools.
- To incorporate community outreach as a part of a character development outreach for youth sports and activities.
- To establish a clearinghouse of information and research for member schools to affect character traits, educate people on character principals, and develop initiatives for character education.

Information on AIA programs is online at: www.aiaonline.org

CATS WIN at Sabino High School

Will Kreamer

Sabino High School is a 4a comprehensive high school with an enrollment of approximately 1,635. We graduated 96 percent of our students last year and 94 percent go on to a university, college, or junior college. Last year Sabino was one of only two high schools in the Tucson area designated "Excelling" by the Arizona Department of Education.

Pursuing Victory With Honor is being implemented primarily in our CATS WIN program. We are the Sabercats and CATS WIN was originally developed at Sabino to battle the drug, alcohol, and tobacco problems that most high schools in the United States face. Over the last two years we have participated in the *Pursuing Victory With Honor* program that emphasizes sportsmanship for our players, coaches, and parents.

One feature of the CATS WIN program at Sabino is CATS WIN Night. This is a mandatory evening meeting during the first week of school for all students in activities and sports. The meeting also is mandatory for all coaches, parents, and sponsors. We have a standing-room only crowd each year. The meeting usually lasts less than an hour. Our keynote speaker this year was Josh Pastner, assistant coach for the University of Arizona basketball team—he was terrific.

The rest of the evening is an introduction to the CATS WIN program and what it entails. We review **CHARACTER COUNTS!** and the Six Pillars of Character. We also added a parent component this year. In return for signing a pledge sheet agreeing to be a model of sportsmanship and good character, each parent received a *Pursuing Victory With Honor* t-shirt with our school name and logo on it. They loved it.

During the presentation, the CATS WIN student pledge sheet is introduced with a discussion of the consequences if the pledge is broken. This pledge sheet is the first page in their sports packet, which is filled out prior to the season and students are not eligible to participate until it has been completed. The main presentation is followed by break-out sessions when students and parents interested in each sport or activity meet with the coach or sponsor in predetermined class-rooms. The coaches discuss the CATS WIN message and how they will address it. For a student and parent who could not make CATS WIN Night, we offer two make-up sessions later in the year.

In addition to CATS WIN Night, we have a number of other activities in place. The Athletic Director and I meet with each team prior to competition to remind them of our emphasis on **CHARACTER COUNTS!** and *Pursuing Victory With Honor.*

Each season an athlete is voted Player of the Year for **CHARACTER COUNTS!** Our PTSA takes the winning athletes out for lunch. Our faculty infuses the Six Pillars of **CHARACTER COUNTS!** into their curriculum and it is part of their evaluation. They also choose a Student of the Month to be taken to lunch. This helps to develop the program with our entire student body.

We are developing a "Gold Day" when teams go in force and cheer for their classmates in other sports, ones they ordinarily might not attend. This increases solidarity and sportsmanship on campus, another goal of *Pursuing Victory With Honor.*

The CATS WIN program at Sabino High School is one that stresses *Pursuing Victory With Honor* in all of our sports activities. Our student athletes commit to the program and to its principles in their athletic endeavors and also in their daily lives.

School: Sabino High School
District: Tucson Unified School District
City, State: Tucson, Arizona
Principal: Valerie Payne
Assistant Principal for Activities: Will Kreamer
Grades: 9–12
Enrollment: 1,708
Faculty: 80
Web site: edweb.tusd.k12.az.us/Sabino

[Will Kreamer is Assistant Principal for Activities at Sabino High School, Tucson, AZ. A PowerPoint presentation about the CATS WIN *Pursuing Victory With Honor* program is online at www.sabinohighschool.com.]

Where Attention Goes— Energy Flows

Scott Brown

When I accepted the position of Athletic Director at North Canyon High School, my philosophy was "where attention goes—energy flows." By this I mean that if you give kids a sense of ownership and make them feel as though they are a part of the program, they will have pride in that program. By rewarding the positive behaviors, you encourage others to parrot those behaviors.

At North Canyon we have immense social, economic, and cultural diversity. This idea works to bridge all of those barriers. We have a group called Athletic Club whose members volunteer their time to work at games outside their own sport. This encourages different sports to support each other, something I feel is crucial.

When the Arizona Interscholastic Association adopted the *Pursuing Victory With Honor* concept, it helped to reinforce what was already in place here and gave us the opportunity to expand it in new directions. This same idea is now being applied to parents. We are implementing a policy that rewards the parents who show positive behavior and support at competitions, and encourages them to model that behavior for other parents who are caught up in negative actions. The bottom line is this, *Pursuing Victory With Honor* at North Canyon High School means that good choices have good rewards, and bad choices have bad consequences.

Our students agree:

"I feel like students come first at North Canyon. Being a part of sports and Athletic Club has given me a second home. It is so obvious how great the communication lines are when athletes come to the AD's office just to hang out."

"I'm glad I got a chance to help start the Athletic Club with Mr. Brown. Athletic Club is the only club on campus where the members work hard to make visiting schools and officials feel welcome. Too often students think they need to show they're better than an opposing school with negative behavior—Athletic Club shows that being positive and kind is a better way."

"I am involved in several clubs at North Canyon, but Athletic Club is the only one that makes me feel as though I'm helping make my school a better place. The coaches at North Canyon really care about each athlete, and Mr. Brown always has time to hear anything we might want to say."

School: North Canyon High School
District: Paradise Valley Unified School District
City, State: Phoenix, Arizona
Principal: Carol Pollack
Athletic Director: Scott Brown
Grades: 9–12
Enrollment: 2,451
Faculty: 120
Web site: northcanyon.pvusd.k12.az.us

[Scott Brown is Athletic Director at North Canyon High School, Phoenix, AZ.]

What I Want My Daughter to Get Out of Sports

Michael Josephson

My six-year-old daughter is about to enter her first gymnastics competition. I've never seen her more energized or focused and it both pleases and worries me. So here's a note I intend to read and explain to her:

My dearest Carissa, I hope you win but I want you to understand that the real purpose of sports is not to win but to experience satisfaction and joy in the competition itself.

I want you to love the sport so much that you can have fun, feel good about yourself and learn important life lessons no matter the outcome.

I want you to set goals and work hard at getting better but when things don't go well, I want you to be tough and tenacious, never giving up or giving in.

I want you to pursue self-improvement and victory with passion but I want you to do so for the pleasure and sense of accomplishment it gives you and not to please me or your mom or to get the approval of others.

I want you always to conduct yourself in a way that brings honor to your team, your coaches, your family and, above all, yourself.

I want you to be a model of good sportsmanship, treating teammates, opponents and officials with the utmost respect, resisting temptations to brag, argue, accuse or whine.

I want you to respect the sport and the letter and spirit of the rules that define it by avoiding cheap gamesmanship tactics and all forms of cheating.

And, most of all, I want you to know how proud of you I am.

This is Michael Josephson reminding you that **CHARACTER COUNTS!** [Jan. 9, 2003]

[Based on Michael Josephson's radio address on Jan. 9, 2003. Reprinted with permission from the Josephson Institute of Ethics. An archive of radio addresses is online at www.charactercounts.org. Michael Josephson is founder and President/CEO of the Josephson Institute of Ethics, sponsor of **CHARACTER COUNTS!** online at www.josephsoninstitute.org.]

Part III

INTEGRITY IN
THE WRITING PROCESS

CHAPTER NINE

Moving from Plagiarism to Integrity in the Writing Process

It's easy to use papers from the Internet. 7th grade girl

The only thing that I do is that I copy and paste off the internet, when I write a report. It's easier and even when I try to put a sentence I like into my own words it still sounds like the original which is still considered cheating. 12th grade girl

I have done it [plagiarize] because teachers never take the time to check our sources. 9th grade boy

Half the class copy some or all of their papers from the Internet and half write their own papers. It's harder to plagiarize now because you have to cite your sources, what books you used and what library you found them in, or what web sites you used. 12th grade girl

Students today write their papers on computers using automatic spelling and grammar checkers, citation format programs, and online access to the vast world of electronic information. Our responsibility is to help them locate and evaluate the information they need, and then use these new tools effectively in the writing process.

It is especially important that we offer thoughtful feedback on their papers. Students must believe their paper was valued, appreciated, and evaluated fairly. This validates the importance of a writing assignment that might otherwise be viewed as busywork.

The best anti-plagiarism strategy is good teaching with a focus on the writing process

Good teaching accomplishes two important goals: It helps honest students avoid unintentional plagiarism, and it makes pleading ignorance more difficult for a student who plagiarizes intentionally.

Grading the research *process* as well as the research *product,* or *paper*, is the most effective anti-plagiarism technique. This requires that each student produce all or at least most of these: a topic or question, outline, note cards, preliminary bibliography, one or more rough drafts, photocopies of book pages quoted or paraphrased, copies of pages downloaded from the Internet and the Web address of each, final draft, annotated bibliography that identifies where each resource was located, final paper, and a written reflection piece on the research *process*. Students can be required to turn in each of these parts at specified times throughout the research and writing process.

Although it might take a little longer during the semester to teach, monitor, and correct a research *process* with an assignment completed in parts, final grading will go more quickly because much of the paper was graded earlier. Instead of one large grade, students have many small grades to show they have done the work themselves. The research *paper* is still important but has become only one part of learning the entire research *process*.

You might invite students to make a one-paragraph response to your comments on their papers. Students can appreciate your comments, dispute your opinion of the paper, or even argue for a better grade. You then answer each student's response. In some cases, it may even be appropriate to change a grade in response to a student's well-reasoned and persuasive argument (Josephson 2004).

A strong emphasis on, and grading of, the research *process* may lead many students to decide that plagiarism is more trouble than actually writing the paper. Such grading makes it almost impossible to substitute a paper from an online paper mill. A few paper mills now offer to provide copies of cited articles for an added fee but they still do not provide all of the many "bits and pieces" required. The "Research Portfolio Cover Sheet" COPY ME page can document the research process for each assignment; copies kept in the writing portfolio can track a student's research over the years.

What is your goal in making research assignments?

Obviously our students are not going to reveal any startling new developments in world affairs. Nor are they are likely to offer new insights into scientific theories or other fields of learning. So why require reports or term papers or research assignments?

The answer is that students need to learn to read, analyze what they have read, and explain it clearly. A research assignment should help students learn to formulate a question or problem, identify and locate the information needed, evaluate and organize the relevant information, and then report their findings. Finally, they should reflect on the research process and what they have learned.

The teacher's role is to guide, inspire, and support students as they master the skills required. Students are to learn the process and perform each step correctly and with honesty. Students are more likely to complete writing assignments with integrity when they consider them to be important. Thus, it is important that the instructional goals and value of each assignment be clearly stated.

It is easy to forget how inexperienced and unprepared our students are when it comes to writing a formal paper based on their own "research." We make it easier for students to complete writing assignments without plagiarizing when we teach and re-teach the skills they need.

How can we develop absolutely Plagiarism-Proof assignments?

It can't be done. The determined student will pay a friend or paper mill to create an original assignment, talk a parent into writing it, use an old paper from a sibling, copy from some obscure print source, or find another way to avoid the actual writing.

What you *can* do is to emphasize and grade the research *process*. Hold students accountable for all the incremental "bits and pieces" that are due at specific dates across the semester. Check that they have mastered the variety of skills demanded for success and understand the importance of these skills. This approach yields educational benefits and can, in many cases, make plagiarism simply not worth the bother.

The authors of the articles that follow share their experiences and offer a wide range of perspectives on the prevention of plagiarism. All except the first two are formatted as COPY ME pages to use with students, faculty, or parents.

References

Michael Josephson, interview, August 26, 2004.

Resources

Articles:

Gary M. Galles: "Simple Strategies for Combating Plagiarism"
Greg Van Belle: "How Cheating Helps Drive Better Instruction"

COPY ME pages:

Tom Rocklin: "Plagiarism, Trust, and Fraud"
Rebecca Howard: "Plagiarism: What Should a Teacher Do?"
Alexandra Babione: "Plagiarism: How to Avoid It"
Robert Harris: "When There's a Questions of Plagiarism..."
How to Protect Yourself from an Accusation of Plagiarism
Research Portfolio Cover Sheet
Library Research Checklist

24/7 Online Library Services
A "Research Night Out" for Parents
School Library Web Sites That Support Integrity in Student Writing
Plagiarism Web Sites for Educators
Identifying a Plagiarized Paper—Not As Simple As It Sounds
Online Sites for Reports and Research Papers
Carol Simpson: "Copyright and Plagiarism Guidelines for Students" and "The Importance of a Copyright Policy"
Sources of Information on Copyright Policy
ISTE National Educational Technology Standards (NETS) Project

See Appendix C for related information in *Student Cheating and Plagiarism in the Internet Era: A Wake-Up Call:* Chapters 3, 13, 14, and 17.

Simple Strategies
for Combating Plagiarism

Gary M. Galles

Since writing is, in essence, formalized thinking, the educational purpose of writing assignments is for students to master the process of organizing and disciplining their thoughts about a topic. Therefore, the most productive approach to such assignments is with intense teacher involvement throughout a paper's development, with each stage subject to comments and suggested changes. That approach would also minimize plagiarism possibilities.

Unfortunately, class sizes and time constraints typically preclude the level of teacher involvement needed for such a "hands-on" approach, which opens the door for a vast range of Internet-fed plagiarism possibilities. However, there are some simple assignment strategies that can help reduce those possibilities, without hindering the learning we wish to take place or unduly burdening teachers.

Sources

Rather than the usual list of references, an annotated bibliography with a synopsis of each reference could be required. Similarly, references could be required to be photocopied or printed from the Web site, with the relevant sections highlighted and turned in with the paper. Preparing an abstract of every cited paper and Web site could be part of the assignment. Each would force students to do research for themselves and make plagiarism far more difficult.

Papers could require the inclusion of a few assigned sources, which is particularly effective if some are very recent, because that combination rules out most online papers. For some assignments, all references could be restricted to holdings in the school library, to the same end. First-person voice or applications could be required, since that would be unavailable from other sources. More in-class writing can also be used.

Assignments

Assignments could include a student description or journal of their research process, particularly how and where the utilized sources were found, making it extremely difficult to "defend" the use of other people's work. Further, each paper could require a personally conducted interview, survey, or experiment, which would preclude the use of already written papers.

Papers shorter than six pages (shorter than most available purchased papers) can be assigned. This trains students to be concise rather than to pad papers to reach longer length requirements and also reduces the time required for teachers to grade the papers. Topics that are idiosyncratic to a particular class or restricted to current events, and unlikely to be available on the Internet, can also be assigned. This is especially effective if direct references to in-class discussions are part of the assignment.

Presentations

Graded oral presentations of papers, with students required to answer questions and defend their arguments, would force students to learn their material better and give them valuable experience speaking in front of others. This also dramatically reduces the payoff to using someone else's work. Assigning papers on opposing views of a topic, with the writers debating the subject in front of the class, also requires that students know their material thoroughly.

Plagiarism is both unethical and subversive of the huge investment America makes in education. At a time when more than half of both high school and college students have admitted to cheating on surveys and plagiarism possibilities are always just a keystroke away, we need to take it seriously. These strategies, some of which can be utilized for writing assignments in any class, are steps in that direction that do not require bigger school budgets or onerous impositions on teachers.

[Gary M. Galles is Professor of Economics at Pepperdine University.]

How Cheating Helps Drive Better Instruction

Greg Van Belle

Cheating, and specifically the time-honored act of plagiarism, has been receiving a good deal of attention in education circles of late. The rise of the Internet as a virtual paper mill has tuned educators in to the fact that students, when given the chance, will often resort to dishonest measures in order to get high marks in a course. Many of my colleagues have reacted very strongly to the rise of Internet cheating. Some have strengthened their policies on the matter, others have added new paragraphs to their syllabi addressing the issue directly, and still others have been spending hours online trying to find any paper they believe to be pilfered from a source other than the student's brain.

I question this type of reaction. In fact, as an educator and a scholar interested in curriculum development and instructional methods, I welcome the new challenge of creating "cheat-proof" course materials. Because of my perspective on this issue, I am often the lone voice in opposition to tougher, "zero-tolerance" policies on academic dishonesty. Instead I would like to turn to the faculty and present this issue not as a problem deserving reactionary policies, but as an invitation to rethink our course content, how we present material to our students, and how we assess what we teach.

What follows are some simple measures we can all put into place to help slow the flood of plagiarized work.

Rotate the curriculum

Many of us teach the same class repeatedly throughout the academic year. It is a good idea to develop two essay assignments, each with a unique twist, and rotate them. This small measure is often enough to discourage cheating. Clearly, the more variety you have the better. This has the side benefit of keeping your preparation and instruction vitalized. Keeping the curriculum fresh helps keep students and teachers interested.

Build process-oriented assignments

Simply asking that your students provide concrete evidence of the process of their work is sufficient to stop "cut and paste" or paper mill cheaters. Create small, specific in-class exercises that provide evidence of the writing process. This can be as simple as asking the entire class to spend five minutes writing a summary of their argument. Don't wait until after the assignment is turned in.

Write original assignments

Take a moment to browse the paper mills and one thing becomes apparent: the variety of available work is not great. Write assignments that ask students to look at old materials in new ways, or write assignments that address new works. Asking students to write about the "hero syndrome" as it is portrayed in Hemingway's *The Sun Also Rises* will likely net you some stolen papers. Add a twist. Add an autobiographical element to the essay in which students have to relate the literature to their own lives.

Assign unique readings

Students have to read the classics, but in addition to the standards why not assign modern readings? Look outside of the anthologies and collections. Even in most standard texts there are ignored or forgotten pieces of literature. Look there for sources of original, thought-provoking essays.

Consider other assessments

I am not going to suggest that writing isn't important or that we should abandon composition as a demonstration of critical thinking ability, but by balancing this against project-based learning you can at least know that the student has to do some original thinking. Such an approach makes sense even if it clashes with our classical aesthetic. Students often resort to cheating because they can, not because they have to. It is very hard to cheat on a group project or an artistic response.

Working in peer groups also has a deterrent effect on cheaters. Conscientious students will often let you know if they think a classmate is not doing his or her own work.

Keep a file

I always assign an in-class, diagnostic essay in the first week of class, which I use for two purposes. One is purely diagnostic to help decide how much attention

I need to pay to grammar and mechanics. The other is to begin a file on each student. Before I return subsequent essays I photocopy the first page of every one and add it to the file. By the end of the term I have a running record of the students' growth and change. I don't do this to catch cheaters (that is merely a byproduct of my efforts). I use it as a piece of the assessment for the class. Once grades are posted I typically recycle these files unless I suspect there will be a problem later on.

Be proactive in policy and procedure

At the beginning of every term I walk my students to the computer lab where we search the Internet and school network for helpful sites related to the course material. In this demonstration I also show them the 10 most popular cheating sites. More than one student has commented that this let them know that I was "with it" and that cheating in my class wouldn't be the best gamble to make. Other instructors hand out a list of cheating sites with their syllabus.

Write a clear, concise statement on academic dishonesty. Be sure this policy is consistent with school policies and guidelines, and be sure you can enforce whatever you decide on. There is nothing wrong with telling students that you punish cheaters.

Conclusion

I have found that the perceived increase in student cheating has helped my teaching. Rather than resort to policing my classes for the dishonest, I have taken on the challenge of creating assignments that will challenge the honest, hard-working student and will ultimately deter the student with a tendency toward cheating. Even at large schools, students talk. They know which teachers won't put up with anything less than honesty.

Ultimately I have decided that I want to reward the honest student rather than spend my time punishing the dishonest student. I challenge you to use the threat of academic dishonesty as the fuel to revitalize your instruction, assignments, and assessments.

[Greg Van Belle, Department of English, Edmonds Community College, gvanbell@edcc.edu]

COPY ME

Plagiarism, Trust, and Fraud

Tom Rocklin

For me a dictionary definition of plagiarism obscures the key issue we confront when we discuss plagiarism in the context of academic integrity. The dictionary definition and common usage of the word *plagiarism* conflate two transgressions: theft and fraud. Certainly, I want my students to commit neither theft nor fraud in their academic work (or, for that matter, in other areas of their lives), but when a student turns in a plagiarized paper, it is the fraud that chiefly concerns me.

Whether a student has stolen a paper or obtained it "honestly" by purchasing it or receiving it as a gift, if the student didn't write the paper and purports to have written it, that student has engaged in academic misconduct. In fact, the fraud that the student has committed is a specific instance of the unifying element in all academic misconduct. I propose that academic misconduct occurs when a student misrepresents his or her engagement in one or more activities designed to promote learning.

Certainly, much of the plagiarism students commit is also theft. However, a lot of our students demonstrate that they don't consider ideas and/or the expression of those ideas to be private property when they reproduce music (and increasingly movies) for which they don't own the appropriate rights. Even students who do recognize a general theory of intellectual property might have a hard time seeing the use of a few paragraphs of another's words as theft. The value we assign to giving credit to the originator of an idea is not completely foreign to our students, but it certainly isn't particularly well articulated in their minds.

On the other hand, discussing plagiarism as fraud puts the issue of student learning at the center of the discussion. Such a discussion puts us in a good position to make the case that the steps we take to help them avoid plagiarism are steps taken to enhance student learning.

This way of thinking about plagiarism as fraud has changed the way I want to talk with students about plagiarism. In addition, I am beginning to think that I should go further and more consistently down a path I have sometimes taken with students. Instead of thinking in terms of "write a term paper" as the assignment with the paper itself being the product, I am considering thinking (and speaking with students) in terms of assigning various learning activities.

The final written product, "the paper," will be only one part of the grade for the entire process. For example, I might want students to read opposing viewpoints on a current topic of environmental policy and then identify strengths and weaknesses in the arguments of both side. Grading the process as well as the product allows me to evaluate the effects of the students' engagement in all of the associated learning activities.

Once I have described an assignment in terms of the activities in which I want my students to engage (and the kinds of learning I think will result from that engagement), it seems natural to consider the kind of support they will need to be successful in the activities. Maybe they need examples, or a demonstration, or a handout with suggested steps. Perhaps I can provide students with a checklist or other guidance so that they can evaluate their work before turning it in. When I conceptualize the assignment as "write a paper," it's hard to imagine what specific support I should provide. When I've thought through the more specific activities that the paper is meant to document, it gets easier.

Providing that sort of support is my side of the educational alliance. When students do their own work with diligence, they are upholding their side of the educational alliance. It is only in the context of this alliance that we can expect learning to flourish.

[Tom Rocklin, College of Education, University of Iowa. Adapted with permission from "Plagiarism, Trust and Fraud" online at www.uiowa.edu/~centeach/talk/volume6/plagiarism.html.]

COPY ME

Plagiarism: What Should a Teacher Do?

Rebecca Moore Howard

You're in your office, you're in front of the t.v., you're holed up in the library with that well-known stack of papers—and you get that sinking feeling that something is very wrong with the paper you're reading. What do you *do?*

The first thing you can do is try to shake off the word *plagiarism*. It is time to think like a teacher, not like a judge. The high likelihood is that the situation is a purely pedagogical one, best remedied by your contact with the student rather than your frantic, tiresome search through the library or the Internet. Yes, you may have a cynical, unethical, fraudulent student in your class. Start, though, by investigating the more probable hypothesis: you have an unfinished learner in your class.

Sit down with the student and talk to her frankly about the paper. Be honest. Tell her that you were concerned as you read the paper. Ask her how it was composed, under what conditions, with what sorts of assistance—whether from other writers or from texts.

If the student knows that you are trying to understand her writing process and not catch her in the act, you are likely to get a frank response. And you are likely to discover that the student may have known she was transgressing (or may not have), but that the "transgression" was caused by her lack of understanding and skill. You are likely to find her perfectly willing to work some more on the task, under your guidance. Finally, you are very likely to feel, once it's all done, that you have actually *taught* a student more about how to learn and how to interact with source texts and readers.

I do not mean to suggest that we should not call to account those who submit papers under their own names that were written by others. I only mean to suggest that we *are* all victims if we allow the false umbrella term *plagiarism* to confuse us about disparate textual activities and to stampede us out of the classroom when it is a student's level of learning and not his level of ethics that is at issue. Let's keep fraud in the judicial arena, plagiarism and citation in the pedagogical arena. And let's keep our heads on our shoulders.

[Adapted with permission of the author. © 2001 Rebecca Moore Howard, Syracuse University. Presented at the Conference on College Composition and Communication, Denver, Colorado, 17 March 2001. The entire paper is online at wrt-howard.syr.edu/Papers/Syracuse/AddressSU04.htm.]

Plagiarism: How to Avoid It

Alexandra Babione

Some student scenarios

"Oh, I like the way the author expresses his ideas," you think as you read an article. "I'll just make some notes for my paper." You begin to copy the text but you forget to include quotation marks or some vital information such as title of the article, author, title of the publication, or date of the publication. Perhaps you do include the author and title of the article. But when you begin writing your paper, you include the notes you took and forget that these are exact phrases and sentences copied from the article. *You have plagiarized.*

You have been citing several sources and have incorporated several phrases into your own sentences. You think you have paraphrased, but you learn that your paraphrase is too close to the original. *You have plagiarized.*

You don't have time or don't want to take the time to write a paper. Your roommate has written one on the topic for your assignment. You pass the "borrowed" paper off as your own. *You have plagiarized.*

You think the author of a report or an article or an essay has said everything you want to say, so you submit it as your own. *You have plagiarized.*

In the first two examples, the plagiarism was the result of carelessness and misinterpretation. In the latter two examples, the "borrowing" is considered stealing. In all four examples, you have plagiarized.

What to do

Regardless of your intent, in each scenario you may be accused of plagiarizing and subject to punishment. To avoid being accused of plagiarism and possibly of fraud, you should follow some simple guidelines when you write your paper. Give credit if you do any of the following:

- cite statistics, facts, dates, or any information that may not be known commonly or that you did not know before doing research
- incorporate another person's theory, opinions, or beliefs that are not yours
- quote someone exactly, word for word
- paraphrase another person's ideas, opinions, or information that may be new to you
- want to demonstrate that you have researched the information

Yes, some ideas of your own may have been voiced before you have had a chance to express yours. When you acknowledge that someone else has thought as you do, you provide support for your ideas and opinions.

Some tips

Here are a few tips to consider before writing your paper, while you engage in research.

- Make sure you understand your teacher's definition and rules regarding plagiarism. If you do not, *ask* for an explanation. Request examples.
- Learn to manage your materials and resources. As you collect them, make sure to include quotation marks when you copy text exactly. Always add the information you will need later for your bibliography as well as citations within your text.
- If you photocopy portions of information from printed material, be sure to copy the page with the title, author, and publication information. If this information is not found on one page, find it and write on the back or top of the photocopy.
- Keep note cards of each citation, if this works for you. Some people prefer to keep a running list of citations and provide summaries of each.
- If you use electronic databases and Web information, cut and paste each citation into a word processing or notepad document and save to disk or e-mail to yourself as an attachment. Print at least one page from each online source to have as proof that you located the document yourself.
- Save a Web page to your disk. Some pages, particularly news pages, change frequently. The page may not be available at a later date. When you save a Web page to your disk, the URL is not saved unless it appears somewhere within the document itself. Always copy the URL and paste it either at the beginning or end of the article. Also note the date that you accessed the page; you will need the date for your bibliography.

COPY ME

When There's a Question of Plagiarism...

Robert Harris

It is sometimes said that the best plagiarism detector is the student who handed in the paper, because he or she already knows whether or not the paper is genuine, or what part is fraudulent. Therefore, you can sometimes enlist the student's help by discussing the paper and asking important questions without making any accusations. You must be very careful about accusing a student of cheating unless you have clear proof; a false accusation can be both cruel and reason for litigation. A student is always innocent until all the facts have been examined and the student clearly is guilty.

One of the simplest approaches is to ask the student to come to your office after school to discuss the paper in private. Be sure to keep a copy of the paper when you return the original so you can refer to it during the interview. By asking the right questions in the right way, you will often be successful in determining the truth of the situation.

Before meeting with the student

- Review all district, school, and department policies on plagiarism.
- Review your class syllabus and any instructions you have given about plagiarism.
- Take an "innocent-until-proven guilty" position. A previously lackadaisical student could become inspired by a topic that intrigues him or her.
- Even if the student is guilty, showing your regret and sadness for the wrongdoing may have more effect than a righteous vindictive tone.
- Consider all the various levels of plagiarism; some are deliberate, some due to lazy work habits, and still others due to ignorance.
- Gather all your evidence and secure it. Consider mailing a copy of any electronic evidence to an off-campus location.
- Consider asking another teacher, a counselor, or an administrator to be present at the meeting.
- Recognize the possibility that you may face parental pressure, including the threat of a lawsuit, in response to any accusation you make.

Meeting with the student

- Ask the student to bring to the interview some of the books or magazines used, or photocopies from the originals, and printouts from Web sites used.
- Treat the student with respect.
- Begin with a question such as, "Is there anything you want to say about your term paper?" Then wait quietly for the student to respond.
- Ask questions rather than make accusations and be prepared for evasions when the student answers. A student may respond better to a question on "not citing," "using someone else's paper," or "copying" rather than to a charge of cheating, stealing, or lying.

- When it seems appropriate, read any applicable policies to the student.
- Be prepared for rationalizations and excuses. Keep your focus on the paper and how it was developed or produced. Ask questions based on the content of the paper and start a discussion of some minor point in the paper.

Questions you may want to ask

- Did you write this paper?
- Did you cite every reference you used? (This can help to distinguish between ignorance and intentionality).
- Don't these words need to have quotation marks around them?
- What search terms did you use? Which ones were most useful? Which didn't help?
- What questions couldn't you answer, or what information did you need that you weren't able to find?
- Where did you find most of these sources? In what library? On what Web site? Say something like this: "The article by Edwards sounds interesting. Can you bring a copy to me at our next meeting?"
- What was the most difficult part of the process for you? What was the easiest?
- Are you familiar with the rules of paraphrasing and do you understand that you must still cite a source even though you put the author's ideas into your own words? (This may seem to imply that you have some evidence to the contrary.)
- When did you begin to work on this paper?
- Did you have any help with editing and revising the paper?
- Where and when did you print the finished paper?
- I'm curious to know why your writing style is so good in some parts of the paper and so poor in others. Why have you not shown such great writing on the in-class essays?
- Ask questions about the content, questioning vocabulary choices or phraseology: What exactly do you mean here by "dynamic equivalence?"
- Have the student read one of the more difficult sections of the paper aloud; few students use words they cannot pronounce. Ask the student to explain the passage in his or her own words.

Penalty Phase

- Summarize the interview and ask the student for any comments he/she may wish to make.
- Consider the nature of the offense. Was this the student's first act of cheating as far as you know (it is helpful for a school to keep a master file of cheating and plagiarism incidents). Was the plagiarism intentional

and blatant, for example, handing in a paper copied in whole or in large part from the Internet? Or was it unintentional, perhaps due to poor understanding of the rules of proper citation?
- Don't decide on the penalty immediately. You can tell the student you want to think about the case and will reserve judgment a few days or a week.
- Follow school, district, and departmental policies, rules, and guidelines.
- Consider the range of penalties available to you as well as rehabilitation measures.

Put your final decision in writing and include your reasons for determining that the student has, in fact, committed plagiarism. Specify whether, in your opinion, the plagiarism was intentional or unintentional. Recommend an appropriate penalty for intentional plagiarism, and perhaps an opportunity to rewrite the paper in cases of unintentional plagiarism.

[Adapted with permission of the author and publisher from *The Plagiarism Handbook* by Robert Harris (Pyrczak Publishing, 2001) and from "Anti-Plagiarism Strategies for Research Papers" on the author's Web site at www.virtualsalt.com/antiplag.htm.]

Reprinted with permission of the authors: Guiding Students from Cheating and Plagiarism to Honesty and Integrity: Strategies for Change, *by Ann Lathrop and Kathleen Foss (Libraries Unlimited, 2005). Permission is granted to make print copies for class instruction, discussion groups, workshops, conferences, or newsletters. This material must not be placed on a Web site or distributed in any digital format. This statement must appear in its entirety on each print copy.*

COPY ME

How to Protect Yourself from an Accusation of Plagiarism

Protect your work. You have spent many hours working on your term/research paper. The hours you spent choosing a topic, narrowing or expanding it, hunting for sources, taking notes, and finally writing the paper represent time you took from watching TV, hanging out with your friends, playing video games, going to the beach, or some other pleasurable activity. Your time and your thoughts are a valuable commodity.

Don't give or sell your paper to anyone. Later on, in college, some of the ideas you used in the paper you gave away or sold could now apply to a class you are in. If you use these ideas and your original paper surfaces in an online paper mill, you could be accused of plagiarism. Selling a paper is morally wrong; you are assisting in intellectual fraud.

Report the loss of a stolen paper immediately. Talk to your teacher. Your research portfolio on file with the teacher will help to support your allegation of loss or theft.

Make copies of your sources. These copies show the original authors' words. Your notes for the paper reflect your interpretation of what you thought was important in each source, stated in your own words. It is especially important to keep downloads from the Internet Web sites; these Web sites often disappear and your copy may be the only proof you have that a Web site ever existed.

Talk over your paper with your teacher. Discuss your progress and ask the teacher to indicate problems on your rough drafts. If you discuss your paper with other teachers or community experts, make written comments in the margins or on your note cards. For example, a teacher who served in the Korean or Vietnam wars may be able to give you some insight into post-combat stress, or a native speaker of a language you are writing about may be able to offer suggestions.

Keep a research portfolio. Keep copies of everything related to your paper in your portfolio. Photocopy your print sources, notes, note cards, rough drafts, and even make a duplicate of your final copy. Keep copies of computer printouts from home and from the libraries that you used while doing your research. These can substantiate your claim that you did the research required for your paper and will show the steps you took to complete the paper.

[Based on an idea from *Using Sources Effectively*, 2nd ed., by Robert Harris (Pyrczak Publishing, 2005). Additional material on plagiarism is online at the author's Web site, www. virtualsalt.com.]

Research Portfolio Cover Sheet

Student Name: _____   Period: _____

Teacher: _____

Topic: _____   Date due: _____

This sheet and the following items are to be included with the final paper.
(Any missing items will affect your cumulative final grade.)

Prewrite due: _____
For 5–10 minutes you will be writing what you know about your topic already and explaining what you would like to show or prove. Tell how you plan to investigate it.

Presearch of available materials due: _____
Presearch includes a check of the library holdings, a few searches on the Internet, and perhaps a call to the local public library to check on the amount and type of information available there. Documentation would be a list of several likely sources, note cards with titles and call numbers, photocopies of some materials found with call numbers and library location, printouts from the Internet, or similar materials.

Note cards due: _____
See writing handbook for note card format and style.

First draft due: _____

Second draft due: _____
Rough drafts of the paper will be required throughout the process. Drafts are checked for style and format as well as content. Each new draft is expected to show significant progress in the work accomplished.

Draft of working bibliography due: _____
This is due prior to the actual due date of the paper in order to check for format and content. Several class visits to the library will be scheduled, but some work may have to be done using local public libraries and university libraries. A list of local libraries with phone numbers and hours is available in the library.

Defending your paper:
After your paper has been turned in you may be called on to discuss it in class. Be prepared to explain your topic, defend your conclusions, and describe where you found your sources and where in the paper the sources were used.

Reflections on the research process:
This can be in the form of a diary or log and should document your search strategies, successes and frustrations, and the "ah-ha" moments in your research process. Turn it in with your paper.

Parent signature: _____ Date: _____

(For any questions about the assignment, please call or e-mail me at: _____)

COPY ME

Library Research Checklist

We have to bring in notecards, an outline, a rough draft, and a final paper with a sources list in the format set by the teacher. We pick our topic from a list of 100. Writing the paper in class will make it harder to plagiarize. Make students get started, don't leave it till the last minute. 11th grade girl

When taking precious class time for library research, it is essential to make sure the students are using the time for research instead of doing homework, visiting with classmates, or using chat sites and instant messaging. If this is a day with a substitute, it easily can become a totally free period for most of the class.

It is important to have an "end-of-period" check on student work in the library. This could be a list of sources that have been retrieved or a short paragraph of what was learned. In any case, students must produce some tangible item(s) by the end of the period. This helps to keep them on task and assures that the time set aside for research actually is used for that purpose. Before the bell, ask to see one or more of these:

- preliminary outline of the topic
- rough draft of a thesis statement or introduction
- list of keywords or search terms related to the topic, including any not useful
- list of potential sources in the school library
- list of specific reference books they have located and plan to use
- printouts from a specified number of Web sites with URL and note if site may be useful
- several note cards with full bibliographic information (on the second visit you can expect to see notes on these cards)
- printouts from one or more local college libraries or public libraries whose online catalogs they have searched for sources they may use (and explain how to get cards to use these libraries)
- for a controversial topic, one article representing each side
- questions they have not been able to answer or topics for which they have found no information despite the hour they have just spent searching
- names of people they may want to interview or authors whose work may be important
- outline of a survey they may want to conduct
- a short paragraph about "discoveries you made this hour"

COPY ME

24/7 Online Library Services

Students today have a multitude of ways to get information without leaving their homes. They can access the Internet or use online databases such as ProQuest, NewsBank, SIRS, or EBSCO. Now they have a new alternative, access by e-mail or phone to their local library's Web page where they will find the *Ask a Librarian* or *24/7* button. They can ask for help or even get the exact answer they have not been able to find for a homework question.

Ask a Librarian, or some similar *24/7* online service, is a fairly new phenomenon in reference service now being offered by many public libraries and the Library of Congress. These programs piggy-back on the idea of the central reference desk where a person could find assistance in answering a question. In an ideal situation the reference librarian would find a source or several sources to answer the question and then either get the materials or send the patron to the stacks for them. *Ask a Librarian* is the electronic extension of that program and is now available online twenty-four hours a day and seven days a week.

The *24/7* e-mail and phone numbers are run by a consortium of libraries and librarians that strive to provide library/information services to the public on a round-the-clock basis. While this service is still being discovered by adults, many students are beginning to explore the library Web pages that use the service. The upside is that students are being helped by professional library staff. The downside for schools and teachers is that the mission of public libraries is different from that of school libraries.

Public librarians locate the materials and information that their patrons request; school librarians teach students how to find the materials and information themselves. Whenever students venture into a public library and ask for assistance, most librarians recognize that they are students and try to do some quick on-the-spot instruction as they help them to find the answers they seek. The online service librarians are dealing with an unseen patron and so provide the information requested or, in the case of online services, give the Web address of one or more sites that can best answer the question. If the patron has problems finding answers from the Web site, the librarian may even highlight the needed information on the screen. This is a great help to adults, but defeats the "hunt for information" aspect of the research process that students need to master.

To level the playing field for all students, since there is no way to prevent a student from using this service or to track the students who use the service, teachers should make sure all students are familiar with *24/7* and *Ask a Librarian* programs.

COPY ME

A "Research Night Out" for Parents

Our librarian is planning an interesting evening to introduce you to the world of online information. [Name of administrator, teacher, counselor, etc.] will also join us to answer questions. Please check the topics you would find most interesting:

1. Standard Internet terminology: browser, search engine, Web site, and so on.
2. Internet Web sites versus traditional book material: accuracy, hoaxes, and misinformation.
3. How to evaluate a site for accuracy, authority, currency, objectivity, and coverage.
4. How information is indexed by search engines and how to find it: Boolean logic.
5. Homework helpers on the Web and what they do that a tutor does.
6. The 24/7 librarian help sites available through the public libraries.
7. ProQuest, InfoTrac, NewsBank, and other commercial online databases available at public and school library Web sites. We can do a show and tell about these databases.
8. Web sites elementary students can use for learning and fun.
9. Web sites parents can access with questions about parenting problems.
10. University library Web pages open to use by high school students.
11. Plagiarism and what parents can do to help students avoid it.
12. The school's Academic Integrity Policy or Honor Code, especially the sections that define cheating and plagiarizing, including a discussion with teachers, an administrator, or a counselor.

Please return this to [any teacher by date]. We look forward to seeing you in the library.

COPY ME

School Library Web Sites That Support Integrity in Student Writing

dewey.chs.chico.k12.ca.us/
Chico High School, Chico, CA
Peter Milbury

www.whps.org/school/conard/library/
Conard High School, West Hartford, CT
Katy Klarnet and Tobey Mintz

www.greece.k12.ny.us/ath/library/about.htm
Greece Athena High School, Rochester, NY
Nancy Dillon-Lyboldt and Will Haines

remc12.k12.mi.us/lhslib/
Lakeview High School, Battle Creek, MI
Margaret Lincoln

www.ncusd203.org/central/html/where/lrc/
Naperville Central High School, Naperville, IL
Thomas Bohdan and Jane Sharka

www.gananda.k12.ny.us/library/mshslibrary/indexgcl.htm
Ruben A. Cirillo High School, Walworth, NY
Jacquie Henry

mciu.org/~spjvweb
Springfield Township High School, Erdenheim, PA
Joyce K. Valenza

www.sasaustin.org/library
St. Andrew's Episcopal School, Austin, TX
Barbara Jansen

Note to our readers: Please tell us about other school library Web sites that help students learn the skills they need in order to avoid plagiarism.

COPY ME

Plagiarism Web Sites for Educators

Bates, Peggy, and Margaret Fain. "Cheating 101: Easy Steps to Combating Plagiarism." Coastal Carolina U. www.coastal.edu/library/presentations/easystep.html

Bombak, Anna. "Guide to Plagiarism and Cyber-Plagiarism." www.library.ualberta.ca/guides/plagiarism/why/index.cfm

Community Learning Network. www.cln.org/themes/plagiarism.html

Conradson, Stacey, and Pedro Hernandez-Ramos. "Computers, the Internet, and Cheating Among Secondary School Students: Some Implications for Educators." pareonline.net/getvn.

Council of Writing Program Administrators. "Defining and Avoiding Plagiarism: The WPA Statement on Best Practices." www.ilstu.edu/˜ddhesse/wpa/positions/WPA plagiarism.pdf

Kemmerer, Kathleen. "Techniques for Encouraging Academic Integrity." Pennsylvania State U., Hazelton. www.hn.psu.edu/faculty/kkemmerer/acadintegrity/ac-integ.htm

NCHS "Plagiarism Stoppers." www.ncusd203.org/central/html/where/plagiarism_stoppers.html

Pearson, Gretchen. "Electronic Plagiarism Seminar." LeMoyne College, Syracuse, NY www.lemoyne.edu/library/plagiarism/index.htm

Plagiarized.com: The Definitive Guide to Internet Plagiarism. www.plagiarized.com/

Pyatt, Elizabeth J. "Cyberplagiarism: Detection and Prevention." Pennsylvania State U. tlt.its.psu.edu/suggestions/cyberplag/

Stoerger, Sharon. "Plagiarism." www.web-miner.com/plagiarism

TLT@SUNY (Teaching, Learning and Technology). "22 Ways to Handle Technology Enhanced Cheating." State U. of New York. tlt.suny.edu/cheating.htm

UMUC Center for Intellectual Property (U. of Maryland University College). "Plagiarism." www.umuc.edu/distance/odell/cip/links_plagiarism.html

UMUC VAIL—Virtual Academic Integrity Laboratory (U. of Maryland University College). "Student Resources, Faculty Resources, Detection Tools and Methods." www.umuc.edu/distance/odell/cip/vail/home.html

Weisbard, Phyllis Holman. "Cheating, Plagiarism (and Other Questionable Practices), the Internet, and Other Electronic Resources." U. of Wisconsin www.library.wisc.edu/libraries/WomensStudies/plag.htm

Writing@CSU "Plagiarism: Understanding and Addressing It." Colorado State U. writing.colostate.edu/references/teaching/plagiarism/index.cfm

Evaluation of Plagiarism Detection Services

University of Maryland University College. www.umuc.edu/distance/odell/cip/links_plagiarism.html#detection

University of Michigan. www.lib.umich.edu/acadintegrity/instructors/violations/detection.htm

---

COPY ME

Identifying a Plagiarized Paper—Not As Simple As It Sounds

Many articles in magazines and on Web sites make it appear that you can find a plagiarized paper online easily and quickly by searching for a distinctive word string. Not so. For suspected plagiarism, if you begin your search with Google, you must also search Alta Vista, Dogpile, and so on. Then you must search EBSCO, SIRS, NewsBank, ProQuest, and other commercial databases. There are a number of reasons why you still may not find it.

Students have become sophisticated about breaking up distinctive word strings in a paper copied from the Internet. It's very difficult to "catch" a paper that has been put through a language translator from another language into English, from English into another language and back, or through the autosummarize function of a word processor. Many students then camouflage the paper by adding a few misspellings or grammatical errors to make it look more like a student-written paper.

Turning for help to an online plagiarism detection service offers a false sense of security. A service locates a paper only after it has been entered into their database, is online in the public holdings of a paper mill, or is included in one of the online periodical/newspaper databases searched by the service. Original papers written "to order" and purchased from online paper mills or other sources will not show up.

And what about the kid who still copies from an encyclopedia or other print source not yet online? Or students may invent a false book or journal to cite, or describe an imaginary interview for a paper that requires one. Plagiarized papers "written" by students using these techniques often go undetected.

Should you help a teacher who wants to search online to prove a paper has been plagiarized? Yes, of course. Take the opportunity to talk about restructuring a writing assignment to make plagiarism more difficult. Offer handouts to reinforce the message. At some appropriate time, offer to work with this teacher to develop collaborative lessons that can help reduce students' willingness and opportunity to plagiarize. Emphasize the benefits of focusing on and grading the research *process* as well focusing on the research *product,* or *paper*.

An attempt to catch plagiarizers after papers have been turned in can be a huge waste of time. In reality you usually catch only the truly clueless and lazy. It is not fair to catch a few and let the more sophisticated plagiarists get credit for papers they did not write. All plagiarism cannot be stopped, but applying many of the prevention techniques suggested in print and online articles can sharply reduce it in your classroom.

COPY ME

Online Sites for Reports and Research Papers

These five sites are representative of the several hundred online paper mills being used by students today. They were selected for their interesting disclaimers. All were available at the URL listed as of July 2005.

We listed 50 online sites in our earlier book; many are no longer available. Most of those still in business have updated their prices and many have added new features. The screen designs and search engines are more sophisticated, and most of them have a great many more papers available.

Many sites now offer copies of the research materials that support the article for an additional charge per page. This means that students who purchase their papers as soon as the assignment is given can have copies of the articles and a bibliography ready to turn in regardless of when the paper is due. Teachers can foil this service by requiring a preliminary bibliography within a few days of making the assignment and asking to see the actual book, magazine article, Web site printout, or other reference source.

ACADEMIC TERMPAPERS

www.academictermpapers.com

Disclaimer: "All reports are copyrighted by Academic Termpapers and are sold for research and reference purposes only and may not be submitted either in whole or in part for academic credit."

Description: "30,000 reports, essays, and expert custom research papers [with] experienced professionals writing in virtually all subject areas and can produce original research on your topic of interest."

Pricing: $7.00 per page with no charge for bibliographies, footnotes, or partial pages. Custom papers are $17.00 and up per page, with a five-page minimum.

CHEATHOUSE.COM

www.cheathouse.com

Disclaimer: "And don't be an idiot! If you hand in one of these essays exactly as it is, you ARE running a risk. IF caught, you could be kicked out of your school. It happens. Teachers have been known to check essay sites, and students have been caught. Instead of copying an essay, just use it—get inspired, use the bibliography and cite the essay. Simple and no risk."

Description: "50,000+ essays and papers. You can view as many essays you like, as many times as you like. Note that you pay for access to the database—we do not guarantee the quality, completeness or accuracy of any of the essays. And we regularly delete the worst essays, to stay on top." Has an article on Web site, "Using Sources Without Plagiarizing."

Pricing: $14.95 per month for access to entire database, or free access to 10,000+ essays if student contributes a paper.

EXAMPLE ESSAYS.COM

www.exampleessays.com

Disclaimer: "The papers contained within our web site are for research purposes only! You may not turn in our papers as your own work! You must cite our website as your source! Turning in a paper from our web site as your own is plagiarism and is illegal!"

Description: "101,000+ papers, most with bibliographies. ExampleEssays.com has high quality student written term papers, essays, and book reports. Most papers are written with recent, relevant, information on many different topics." Custom papers are available.

Pricing: $24.95 per month and up to print any number of papers.

REALPAPERS.COM

www.realpapers.com

Disclaimer: "Our work is designed only to assist students in the preparation of their own work. Review our papers for ideas, sources, & research information! Cite us as an academic source in your own paper!"

Description: "The Internet's premier term paper assistance service with more than 50,000 example papers to download & study from today! Struggling to find some last minute research articles, studies, and ideas to cite in your own term paper? Find an example paper to help you on this site! Shop Through Our Tens Of Thousands Of Professionally Created Papers by subject or by keyword & select the one(s) closest to the topic with which you're struggling! Just click our easy order button & receive the paper *TODAY!!*"

Pricing: $9.95 per page with free bibliography.

SCHOOL PAPER.COM

www.schoolpaper.com

Disclaimer: "The intended purpose of our term papers is that they be used as models to assist you in the preparation of your own. Plagiarism is a CRIME! IF YOU QUOTE FROM OUR WORK, YOU MUST CITE OUR PAPER AS ONE OF YOUR SOURCES. This service is NOT available to anyone who does not have a valid, ethical reason for seeking our tutorial assistance."

Description: "A large collection of high quality pre-written example papers at a low price [and] a database of literature summaries. Our summaries are specially written to give you a comprehensive understanding of the literature, when you're in crunch and are out of time to read them."

Pricing: $20.00 per paper regardless of length. Membership fee required.

COPY ME

Copyright and Plagiarism Guidelines for Students

Carol Simpson

1. You may make a single photocopy of any material you need to do your schoolwork, or for your own personal research. You may keep the copies you make as long as you like, but you may not sell them, nor may you make copies of your copies.
2. You must respect the copyright of the materials you use. Only the creators, or the persons or companies who own the copyright may make copies of the material, except as noted above. You may not modify or change the material, nor may you perform or display the material except in conjunction with class work.
3. You may use copyrighted material to do your schoolwork, but if you use an author's ideas you must give the author credit, either in the text or in a footnote. If you use an author's words, you must put the words in quotation marks or other indication of direct quotation. Failure to give credit to the author is plagiarism. If you use an extensive amount of a single work, you must obtain permission.
4. Use of copyrighted materials outside of regular class work requires written permission of the copyright holder. This includes graphic material such as cartoon characters on posters or other spirit or decorative matter.
5. You may not copy computer software from the school computers.
6. Information received from the school computers may be used only for regular schoolwork or personal research.
7. The source of any information used in your schoolwork should be acknowledged in the format prescribed by the teacher. Use of another's intellectual work without attribution is plagiarism, as outlined in the Student Code of Conduct.

COPY ME

The Importance of a Copyright Policy

Carol Simpson

Why bother to have a copyright policy? The purpose of a copyright policy is to state the school's intention to abide by the law. AIME (Association for Information Media and Equipment), the copyright watchdog group, boasts of its successes in redressing copyright infringement. The majority of the settlements involve the establishment of an institutional policy regarding copyright as well as comprehensive training and plans for tracking and monitoring copyright compliance. At a minimum, the following points should be included in a school or district copyright policy:

1. The policy states the institution's intention to abide by the letter and spirit of the copyright law and the associated Congressional guidelines.
2. The policy covers all types of materials including print, nonprint, graphics, and computer software.
3. The liability for noncompliance with copyright rests with the individual using the work.
4. The district mandates training for all personnel who might need to make copies.
5. The person using the materials must be able to produce, on request, copyright justification for its use.
6. The district appoints a copyright officer who serves as a point of contact for copyright information both within and without the district. That person will likely track licenses, serve as the registered copyright agent for the school's Web site and will oversee training of all students and teachers in copyright compliance.

[Abridged with permission from Chapter 15 of *Copyright for Schools: A Practical Guide*, 4th ed., by Carol Simpson. Linworth Publishing, 2005.]

COPY ME

Sources for Information on Copyright Policy

10 Big Myths About Copyright Explained, by Brad Templeton. www.templetons.com/brad/copymyths.html

Copyright, by PBS. www.pbs.org/teachersource/copyright/copyright.shtm

Copyright and Intellectual Property, by the American Library Association. www.ala.org/ala/ourassociation/governingdocs/aheadto2010/copyright.htm

Copyright Basics, by the U.S. Copyright Office. www.copyright.gov/circs/circ1.html

Copyright Compliance Made Easy! by Copyright Clearance Center. www.copyright.com

Copyright for Schools: A Practical Guide, 4th ed., by Carol Simpson. Linworth Publishing, 2005.

Copyright Hotline 1–800–444–4203, available to schools, libraries, and other public institutions by Association for Information Media and Equipment

Copyright Law and Fair Use, by PBS. www.pbs.org/teachersource/copyright/copyright_fairuse.shtm

Copyright Law in the Electronic Environment, by Georgia Harper. www.utsystem.edu/OGC/IntellectualProperty/faculty.htm

Copyright Web site. www.benedict.com

"The Importance of a Copyright Policy," in *Copyright for Schools: A Practical Guide,* 4th ed., by Carol Simpson. Linworth Publishing, 2005.

Q & A, by Association of American Publishers, Inc. www.publishers.org

COPY ME

ISTE National Educational Technology Standards (NETS) Project

International Society for Technology in Education

The goal of the ISTE National Educational Technology Standards for Teachers (NETS) Project is to guide educational leaders in recognizing and addressing the essential conditions for effective use of technology to support PK–12 education. The NETS standards span all subject areas and grade levels. The standards below are an excerpt from the "Social, Ethical, Legal, and Human Issues" section of the *National Educational Technology Standards for Students: Connecting Curriculum and Technology* (ISTE, 2003).

Profile for Technology Literate Students, Grades 6–8

Standard 3. Exhibit legal and ethical behaviors when using information and technology, and discuss consequences of misuse.

Profile for Technology Literate Students, Grades 9–12

Standard 4. Demonstrate and advocate for legal and ethical behaviors among peers, family, and community regarding the use of technology and information.

Standard 7. Routinely and efficiently use online information resources to meet needs for collaboration, research, publications, communications, and productivity.

Other publications in the ISTE series:

National Education Technology Standards for Teachers: Resources for Assessment

---

CHAPTER TEN

Lessons to Support Integrity in the Writing Process

Do you think you understand what the term **plagiarism** *means?*

- *Yes it is when you copie someone's work word for word but they have to have copie written it to file charges on you or to get you in trouble. 7th grade boy*
- *Depends on the definition. Plagiarism changes depending on where you work. 10th grade girl*
- *Yeah, it means a lot of different methods not just the copy and paste method. 11th grade girl*
- *Yes, yet if the paper you take doesn't have a copyright or says it can be used then plagiarism does NOT apply. 10th grade girl*
- *Not completely—with photocopying and stuff—but I think students are protected from that. But from books and stuff, yes. 12th grade boy*
- *Of course, but sometimes you have to do the wrong thing in order to get the job done. (As long as no one knows). 11th grade boy*
- *Yes, if I changed it and revised it to my style, so that's not really plagiarism is it? 10th grade boy*
- *Never seen the term before. 9th grade boy*

Many lessons are available in print and online to help teach students to avoid plagiarism. We selected four that we liked and wrote four of our own; we hope you find them to be helpful idea-starters for your own instructional program. All eight lessons are formatted as COPY ME pages.

The first two lessons are designed to help young students develop the concept of research as (1) a search for answers to questions, and (2) a way to write down, cite, or document the book, magazine, or Web site where the answer was found. They are simple in design and can be varied in many ways.

Murray Suid's lesson is designed for elementary students and could be adapted for middle school. His goal is for students to use and to think about encyclopedias in ways that do not promote direct copying.

The multigenre research paper, or project, is an excellent way to develop a writing assignment that would be difficult to locate online. The choice of topics can be limited and the list of genre controlled. The first multigenre lesson includes a list of the books, articles, and Web sites we identified as most helpful. "Your Multigenre Web" has many good examples and walks students through every step of the process. "Mrs. Juster's Virtual Classroom" is rich in examples matched to specific genre. The article by Ellen Goldfinch includes a sample evaluation rubric. The most thorough discussion of actual student experiences in writing multigenre papers is the article by Margaret Moulton, with many examples of student work and an extensive bibliography. Tom Romano is credited as the originator of the multigenre report format.

A very good example of the multigenre assignment is the lesson by Perkins and Guy. Students are asked to identify their own theme and then select a poem or song to reflect the assigned literary works. They write an essay relating the literary works to their theme and the selected poem or song. The assigned literary works and the focus of the essay can be varied each semester.

The last three short lessons give students practice with the skills they need to avoid plagiarism. They can be adapted for any grade level from upper elementary through high school.

Resources

Lessons as COPY ME pages:

Marcia Jensen: "Research in the Primary Grades: Spiders"
Beverly Schottler: "Fourth Grade Researchers"
Murray Suid: "How to Take Copying Out of Report Writing"
Kathy Foss: "Assigning a Multigenre Research Project"
Christine Perkins and Laurie Guy: "Identifying a Unifying Theme as a Final Exam in Literature"
Cite It? Don't Have to Cite It?
Practice for Note Cards, Paraphrasing, Quoting, and Summarizing
Cut-and-Paste Research

COPY ME page:

Teaching About Plagiarism: Resources

See Appendix C for related information in *Student Cheating and Plagiarism in the Internet Era: A Wake-Up Call:* Chapter 15, Tools for Writing without Plagiarizing; Chapter 16, Alternatives to Traditional Writing Assignments.

COPY ME

Research in the Primary Grades: Spiders

Marcia Jensen

In this day of easy access to lots of information, much of it in an electronic format, teachers want to facilitate honesty and integrity in the way their students "do research." Only a small number of students will master the necessary thinking and research skills without direct instruction. To encourage integrity in research, we must design assignments that encourage the continued growth of higher-order thinking.

The first question to ask when designing an assignment is, "What do I want my students to know and be able to do when they finish?" Next is, "How will I know that they know it and can do it?" These questions focus the development of the assignment into a manageable project. Close collaboration between the teacher and librarian in planning the lessons and identifying appropriate materials is important for success.

A primary teacher whose students are doing a unit on spiders wants to focus attention on the concept that answers to questions can be found in books.

Day 1: Read a storybook with a spider as a main character. Ask students what they know about real spiders and what questions they have. Write their questions on a large chart, leaving space for answers. One question my students had was, "Do spiders wear glasses?" (The storybook spider did.) We developed this question into, "What kind of eyesight do spiders have?"

Day 2: Read an easy nonfiction book about spiders to the students after reviewing their questions. Tell them to raise their hand when they hear an answer. Record answers they learn from the book under the appropriate questions. Say, "We are taking notes so we can remember what we learned." Be sure to write on the chart the name (title) of the book that had the answers and the name of the person who wrote the book (author).

Day 3: Go over the questions and read the answers together from the chart with the notes. Review the way the students developed their questions, found answers from the book, and recorded their answers as notes (information). Then have students make a picture of one thing they learned from their research. They can share their pictures and explanations based on information they learned from the book(s).

[Marcia Jensen, Library Media Specialist, Davenport Community School District, Davenport, Iowa]

Fourth Grade Researchers

Beverly Schottler and Martha Biggs

You are going to become a *researcher.* A researcher is someone who goes to books, magazines, encyclopedias, newspapers, Internet Web sites, or other *sources* to find information. The place where the researcher finds the information is called a *source.*

Letting others know your sources (documenting your sources)

Someone reading your report will want to know your *sources,* or where you found your information. Telling your reader about your sources is called *documenting* your sources.

You must tell the reader all of the details about the book, magazine, encyclopedia, newspaper, Internet Web site, or other *source* that you used for information. You must tell who wrote it, the title, where it was published, who published it, and the date it was published. For an Internet Web site, also tell the date when you found the information.

This information lets the reader know your *source* was good. The reader can go to your *source* for more information.

Reporting your information (so you are not plagiarizing)

You must report your information *by writing it in your own words.* If you use someone else's words or ideas, you must *quote and document* their words and ideas.

Using someone else's exact words without quoting them is a kind of cheating called *plagiarism.* You must either *quote your source,* using quotation marks, or write what you learned in your own words. You are cheating, also called *plagiarism,* if you:

1. copy some else's words or ideas without quoting them in quotation marks, or
2. you do not document your source by telling your reader where you found the information.

Writing your information in your own words

An important skill when using ideas from *sources* is how to put the ideas in your own words. Did you ever tell a four-year-old the story of *Goldilocks and the Three Bears?* Did you use the exact words from a book? You probably told the story in your own words but without changing the ideas in the story.

To be a *researcher,* you must first read carefully and think about what you have read, then take a new piece of paper and write the information in your own words. When you quote any words from your *source,* you must put those words in quotation marks to show you are using someone else's words. This *documents your sources* and keeps your report free of *plagiarism.*

This paragraph is about an elephant's trunk. It is from *Explore the World of Amazing Animals,* by M. Carwardine. How would you tell it in your own words? Be sure to include all the information you need, but don't change the meaning.

An elephant's trunk has many different uses. The animal can use it to pick fruit from high up in a tree, smell and touch things, and throw dust over its back while it is having a dust bath. The trunk is also used for drinking, by sucking up water and squirting it into the elephant's mouth, or as a loud-speaker for amplifying its trumpeting calls. Perhaps the most unusual use, however, is as a snorkel. As an elephant walks underwater along the bottom or a river or lake, it holds its trunk in the air to breathe (p. 14).

Documenting your sources—where the information came from

Carwardine, M. (1991). *Explore the World of Amazing Animals*. New York: Western Publishing Company, Inc.

Using My Own Words #1

The trunk of an elephant can be used like a snorkel. An elephant can be under the water and still breathe by holding its trunk above the water.

___ did not copy words of author
_X_ did not change meaning
_X_ included information I needed

Using My Own Words #2

The elephant uses its trunk for many different uses. An elephant can *use it to pick fruit from high up in a tree, smell and touch things, and throw dust over its back while it is having a dust bath.* Drinking, trumpeting, and breathing are other uses.

___ did not copy words of author
_X_ did not change meaning
_X_ included information I needed

Using My Own Words #3

The elephant uses its trunk for many different uses. An elephant can pick food from a tree, drink water, and trumpet with its trunk. It uses its trunk to smell, touch, throw, and breathe.

_X_ did not copy words of author
_X_ did not change meaning
_X_ included information I needed

[Adapted with permission from *A Handbook for Dealing with Plagiarism in Public Schools*, © 2003 by Beverly A. Schottler, Ed.D. and Martha Biggs.]

Reprinted with permission of the authors: Guiding Students from Cheating and Plagiarism to Honesty and Integrity: Strategies for Change, *by Ann Lathrop and Kathleen Foss (Libraries Unlimited, 2005). Permission is granted to make print copies for class instruction, discussion groups, workshops, conferences, or newsletters. This material must not be placed on a Web site or distributed in any digital format. This statement must appear in its entirety on each print copy.*

COPY ME

How to Take Copying Out of Report Writing: Activities That Spark Creative Thinking and Original Writing

Murray Suid

Now comes that thrilling moment: You announce your students' first research assignment. They are to select a topic, visit the library, gather facts from print and online sources, and write a report. Off they go, and if they are like most kids, they head straight for that most incredible of all resources, the general encyclopedia in print, online, or on a disc.

Sure enough, whatever the topic, there is a wealth of facts about it in the pages of these wonderful books. What's more, in today's home or school, the information is available electronically so students don't even have to write it out! They just pick the paragraphs they want, then cut and paste them together for a report.

Intuitively knowing that copying is wrong, students may try to retell the encyclopedia article in their own words. They switch around a few sentences and do a little paraphrasing here and there. The text becomes murkier, but at least the report isn't a word-for-word steal.

The more inventive and industrious kids, meanwhile, take the *smoosh* (that's the technical term) route. They copy a little from one encyclopedia, more from a second one, and add some interesting information they found on a Web site. Then they *smoosh* the facts together to create a new, chaotic version.

Report writing doesn't have to be like this. The print or electronic encyclopedia can be used to spark creative thinking and original writing rather than plagiarism. It can be used to promote inquiry rather than inhibit it. Here are three assignments designed to meet these goals.

Use the style of an encyclopedia article to write about a subject not found in the encyclopedia

Begin by studying biographical articles in the encyclopedia, selecting people appropriate to their grade and interest levels. The assignment is to interview a living person, then write an encyclopedia-style article about the person. Perhaps the class will publish its own encyclopedia with articles about local people, places, and events.

Of course, you must first teach your novice encyclopedists how to write encyclopedia articles, a kind of expository essay. There are two elements to point out: the lead and the body. Most encyclopedia articles use a one-sentence or one-paragraph lead that sums up the subject, similar to a dictionary definition. The main part, or body, of the article provides details. The paragraphs usually are arranged in chronological order: place and date of birth, early years, education, career, and significant accomplishments.

Articles dealing with places and objects use a more analytical organization. An article about a city or country can be divided into sections about geography, history, commerce, people, and arts. Reading several articles aloud and discussing them can help students get a feel for the different ways information can be organized.

Simplify an encyclopedia article for students at a lower grade level

Paraphrasing an encyclopedia article is a powerful way to master content and style. It becomes more interesting and creative when the paraphrasing is done to make material understandable to younger students. This activity has a number of benefits.

First, writing for younger children gives older students a sense of having a real audience. It stimulates analytical thinking as they learn to break down complex ideas into their basic components. Developing paraphrased sentences that are short and simple make students more aware of sentence structure. Finally, vocabulary selection is fine-tuned as they search for easier, more familiar words to use.

The culminating activity of this assignment is for the older students to share their articles with younger students to see if they can read and comprehend them.

Create adaptations using encyclopedia articles

Adaptation is the art of transporting material (text, facts, plots) from one format to another. This is not plagiarism if credit is given to the original source, but it can encourage higher-level thinking skills. Students might convert an encyclopedia article into a nonfiction picture book, the diary of an inventor, a puppet show of an historical event, a speech made by a famous person, a travel brochure, a game-show quiz, or a short story of historical fiction. The adaptation process is the same regardless of the format of the original or the adaptation.

- Study the information in the article carefully to become familiar with it.
- Choose an appropriate new format. An account of the Civil War could become a diary kept by a typical Northern soldier. An article about Cleveland, Ohio could be the basis for a travel brochure. A fairy tale could become a play or puppet show.
- Study the elements of the new format. The best way to understand the new format is to read several examples of it and look for common elements. Diary entries, for example, almost always begin with the date and usually are written in the first person.
- Write the adaptation. This will require deleting some material, writing new material, rearranging, compressing, and expanding.

Students must learn to keep the sense of the original while transferring the content and ideas into the new format. Doing this successfully is what makes this activity an intellectual and artistic challenge.

A process commentary encourages students to reflect on their writing experience

For any written assignment, students can be encouraged to reflect on the activity in a "My Process" section. You might list a few items that everyone should include: why I chose this topic or project, the tasks I most enjoyed in writing the report, problems I encountered, what I would do differently next time, strengths and weaknesses of my report, advice I'd give to another student writing this paper or doing this project, the grade I'd give this project, and why I'd give it that mark.

Summary

Creating their own encyclopedia articles provides students with practice in sentence, paragraph, and report structure. The simplifying activity leads easily into more sophisticated paraphrasing skills. The adaptations will challenge students' creative abilities. In these ways, students develop a better understanding of the concept of seeking knowledge for specific purposes. They also learn to repackage and present their new knowledge in useful and interesting ways that don't involve copying or plagiarism.

[© 2005. Murray Suid taught composition for 10 years at San Jose State University. He is the author of many books including *Recipes for Writing, Moviemaking Illustrated,* and *How to Be President of the U.S.A.* He also writes screenplays and is the founder of Point Reyes Pictures.]

Assigning a Multigenre Research Report

Kathy Foss

This is not your typical written essay, three to five pages type of report. For this project you will create original material in the number of different genres assigned. You might write a newspaper editorial and a poem, add a photograph, and write a short essay linking them together. They must have a common theme or focus with smooth transitions among all of the pieces, much as if you were showing someone a scrapbook of a trip or an event.

First select your topic or theme, then consider what genres would be effective for communicating with your audience. Your topic or theme must be one that has enough information available for effective research, and it must lend itself to this type of project. You will decide what information is important and how you want to present it. The two examples and the list of possible genres listed below can help you to get started. Finally, complete a bibliography and write a short reflection piece on your creative process.

Book report: *Farewell to Manzanar*

Perhaps write an opening essay on why Japanese-Americans were moved to internment camps, beginning by finding a newspaper account of the attack on Pearl Harbor. Add a short essay on why the attack happened and why we were not prepared. Other items could be a magazine photo of people being transported to the camps, a poster telling them what they could take, and a diary entry of a person seeing Manzanar for the first time. Discuss newspaper editorials with pro and con arguments about sending American citizens to internment camps. Interview a person who was at a camp or read an interview about an internee. Your story about the book (the "report") is woven through these items.

Research report on Dia de los Muertes (Day of the Dead)

You could begin with a newspaper article describing a local celebration. Find or draw a picture of celebrants in a graveyard. Make a personal altar or skeletal character for the celebration. Write a song or poem in English or Spanish, then translate it into the other language. Your written report can explain the activities on Dia de los Muertes, why it came to be a holiday, and how it differs from Halloween. It also brings together all the original pieces you have created and relates them to your theme.

A few of the many types of genre you might create (ask permission to add to list):

Advice column	Autobiography	Advertisement
Announcement	Book jacket	Campaign speech or poster
Cartoon or comic strip	CD cover	Character sketch

Collage	Diary entry	Encyclopedia article
Eulogy	Informative essay	Narrative essay
Eyewitness account	Graph/chart	Greeting card
Illustration	Interview	Job application
Letter	Mandala	Map with legend
Menu	Movie review	Newspaper article
Obituary	One act play	Photo with description
Poem	Puppet show	Quiz
Radio broadcast	Recipe	Resume
Song/ballad/rap	Travel poster	Wanted poster

[Ideas for the structure of this lesson came primarily from Ellen Goldfinch's article, "A Match Made in Heaven: The Multigenre Project Marries Imagination and Research Skills," in the April/May 2003 issue of *Library Media Connection*. Permission is granted to adapt this lesson.]

Resources for the Multigenre Research Project

Print Resources

Allen, Camille Ann. *The Multigenre Research Paper: Voice, Passion, and Discovery in Grades 4–6*. Portsmouth, NH: Heinemann, 2001.

Cate, Timothy E. " 'This Is Cool!' Multigenre Research Reports." *Social Studies* 91:3 (2000): 137–40.

Davis, Robert, and Mark Shadle. "Building a Mystery: Alternative Research Writing and the Academic Act of Seeking." *CCC* 53:3 (2000): 417–46.

Goldfinch, Ellen. "A Match Made in Heaven: The Multigenre Project Marries Imagination and Research Skills." *Library Media Connection* 21:7 (2003): 26–28.

Moulton, Margaret R. "The Multigenre Paper: Increasing Interest, Motivation, and Functionality in Research." *Journal of Adolescent & Adult Literacy* 42:7 (1999): 528–39.

Romano, Tom. *Blending Genre, Altering Style: Writing Multigenre Papers*. Portsmouth, NH: Heinemann, 2000.

Romano, Tom. *Writing with Passion: Life Stories, Multiple Genres*. New York: Elsevier, Reed, 1995.

Online Resources

"American Authors Research Assignment." www.ahs.asd103.org/Library/am-authorsc2.htm

"CD 315: Instructions for Multigenre Research Project (MRP)." www.bayarea-writingproject.org/15/stories/storyReader$24?print-friendly = true

"English 121: Research Possibilities—The Multi-Genre and Multi-Media Research Project." www.emunix.emich.edu/~adlerk/multigenre_instructions. htm, www.emunix.emich.edu/~adlerk/multi_genre_research1.htm

"Mrs. Juster's Virtual Classroom: Multi-Genre Writing." www.mrsjustersvir-tualclassroom.com/Am%20Htg%20Writing%20MG.htm

"Your Multigenre Web: Everything you need to know to succeed." www.sheboyganfalls.k12.wi.us/cyberenglish9/multi_genre/multigenre.htm

COPY ME

Identifying a Unifying Theme as a Final Exam in Literature (Part 1)

Christine Perkins and Laurie Guy

As the end of the semester approached, we started looking at ways to demonstrate to the students that many works of literature share universal themes and ideas that are relevant to everyday life. The four works we had read and discussed in class were *Antigone* (Sophocles), *Julius Caesar* (Shakespeare), Arthurian legends, and *To Kill a Mockingbird* (Lee).

The idea behind the poster project was to allow the students to come up with a theme that tied together any three of the works we had read over the semester, and then reflect on the significance of that theme to their own lives. Each student selected three of the four works and, as an individual fourth work, chose song lyrics or a poem to fit the theme identified for the project.

The results were better than hoped for, as many students thoughtfully analyzed significant ideas and really understood the greater importance of the literature we read as a whole, and not as individual works. While some themes tended to appear consistently, it was wonderful to see several students come up with a unique perspective on the literature. The students were then able to share their insights with the class.

[Christine Perkins and Laurie Guy are Language Arts teachers at El Dorado High School in the Placentia-Yorba Linda Unified School District in Placentia, CA.]

Reprinted with permission of the authors: Guiding Students from Cheating and Plagiarism to Honesty and Integrity: Strategies for Change, *by Ann Lathrop and Kathleen Foss (Libraries Unlimited, 2005). Permission is granted to make print copies for class instruction, discussion groups, workshops, conferences, or newsletters. This material must not be placed on a Web site or distributed in any digital format. This statement must appear in its entirety on each print copy.*

COPY ME

Identifying a Unifying Theme as a Final Exam in Literature (Part 2)

Christine Perkins and Laurie Guy

Instructions to Student:

The literature studied this semester has revealed strong characters and ideas that continue to be relevant to this day. There are important lessons to be learned and passed on in these works of literature. Take a closer look at the ideas expressed in these various genres, select three of them, and determine a common theme. Your theme is a message that you felt was an important understanding about life or human nature. Once you have determined a theme, create a carefully worded theme statement that reflects your understanding of the ideas conveyed in these three works. Then, choose a poem or song that also contains the same message. Next, in your own words, explain how this theme applies to each work and the song/poem you have chosen. Support your ideas with examples from the text. In a final paper, reflect on the significance of this theme in literature and in life in general. Each of the five papers is to be no more than one page in length. Arrange your replies on a poster board as follows:

Theme Statement

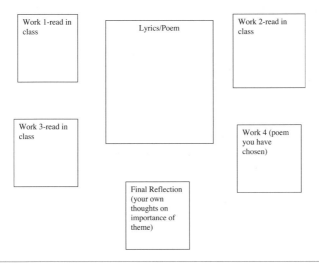

[Christine Perkins and Laurie Guy are Language Arts teachers at El Dorado High School in the Placentia-Yorba Linda unified School District in Placentia, CA.]

COPY ME

Cite It? Don't Have to Cite It?

To avoid plagiarism, must you cite your source for this information? Circle your choice.

1. You find the term "cyber-sloth" in a magazine article and decide to use it as the title of your term paper.   *Cite it   Don't have to cite it*
2. You interview your history teacher about his experiences as a soldier in Vietnam and include the interview in your report on the war.
Cite it   Don't have to cite it
3. In a PowerPoint presentation you use the music from Sting's *Desert Rose* for background music.   *Cite it   Don't have to cite it*
4. While doing a paper on the battles of the Spanish-American War, you use the term "Remember the Maine."   *Cite it   Don't have to cite it*
5. Your research for a video documentary turns up a short TV news segment on your topic that you use as part of your introduction.
Cite it   Don't have to cite it
6. You use "stitch in time" in your creative writing assignment to illustrate that your character acts as necessary in a crucial moment.
Cite it   Don't have to cite it
7. You use a magazine picture in your science fair project.
Cite it   Don't have to cite it
8. In writing your paper on the American Revolution you refer to Paul Revere as a patriot from Boston.   *Cite it   Don't have to cite it*
9. After reading a book on your research topic, you summarize it by writing a paragraph about it in your own words.   *Cite it   Don't have to cite it*
10. To show the route settlers used on the Oregon Trail you copy a map from an encyclopedia.   *Cite it   Don't have to cite it*
11. You use a poem you wrote for an English assignment last year to illustrate a point you want to emphasize in a literary analysis.
Cite it   Don't have to cite it
12. You draw a picture of a horse for your report on horse racing in America.   *Cite it   Don't have to cite it*

[Based on an idea from *Using Sources Effectively*, 2nd ed., by Robert Harris (Pyrczak Publishing, 2005).]

COPY ME

Practice for Note Cards, Paraphrasing, Quoting, and Summarizing

For this assignment you need pages from a book, a magazine, a newspaper, and a Web site. Making a class set of copies of each page will make storage easier than if you store class sets of books, magazines, and newspapers.

- From the book, copy the title page and verso with the copyright information, preferably back-to-back to give the students realistic practice in finding the copyright information on the verso. Also copy one page with an interesting paragraph.
- Copy the front cover of the magazine, being sure to show the title, date, and volume number. Copy an interesting article, preferably only one page.
- Copy the front page banner of the newspaper and an interesting article, again preferably all on one page. Be sure the date and page number can be read.
- Copy one interesting page from a Web site and include the Web address.
- Trace five blank note cards onto a sheet of paper and make enough two-sided copies of the note-card page for your class.

Teach the rules for note cards and citations. Students will make a note card for each of the four different items: paraphrase the paragraph from the book, quote from the magazine article, summarize the information from the newspaper article, and make a bibliographic entry for the Web site, each following the style in the student writing handbook.

The graded and corrected pages can be used for reference when students begin their research paper. This also provides a hands-on component to the information in the student writing handbook.

The book, magazine, newspaper, and Web site pages could be color-coded for ease of sorting and distribution, and laminated for use each semester.

Caution: Databases like ProQuest, NewsBank, SIRS, and EBSCO allow you to make multiple copies of magazine and newspaper articles only if you print all of them from the online source. Making multiple copies from the print version, or printing one copy from the online source and then making photocopies, is breaking the copyright law. The author/publisher receives copyright credit only for the number of copies printed from the online source.

COPY ME

Cut-and-Paste Research

Students will demonstrate that they know how to cut and paste from online articles. The teacher will demonstrate a knowledge of how these papers can be assembled. Students then use the same information to create correct citations and a bibliography.

- List three or four questions and let each student select one.
- Identify three online sites for each question.
- Students cut and paste at least one fact from each site to "create" a one-page paper.
- Read the papers to determine whether students know how to cut and paste.
- This shows the students that you understand the cut-and-paste technique, and lets you be sure students understand the technique.
- Discuss why cut-and-paste is not an acceptable research technique.
- Students then rewrite the paper entirely in their own words.
- Finally, students write the paper a third time, supporting their thesis by correctly using and citing at least one of each: direct quote, paraphrase of an idea, summary of an idea.
- Students complete a bibliography in the correct style as directed in the school writing handbook.
- Discuss the process and what has been learned.

COPY ME

Teaching About Plagiarism: Resources

Print Resources

Allen, Camille Ann. *The Multigenre Research Paper: Voice, Passion, and Discovery in Grades 4–6.* Portsmouth, NH: Heinemann, 2001.

Clabaugh, Gary K., and Edward G. Rozycki. *The Plagiarism Book: A Student's Manual.* 2nd ed. Oreland, PA: New Foundations, 2001.

Harris, Robert A. *The Plagiarism Handbook.* Los Angeles: Pyrczak, 2001.

Harris, Robert A. *Using Sources Effectively: Strengthening Your Writing and Avoiding Plagiarism.* 2nd ed. Los Angeles: Pyrczak, 2004.

Nottage, Cindy, and Virginia Morse. *Research in the Real Classroom: The Independent Investigation Method for Primary Students.* Gainesville, FL: Maupin House, 2003.

Romano, Tom. *Blending Genre, Altering Style: Writing Multigenre Papers.* Portsmouth, NH: Heinemann, 2000.

Romano, Tom. *Writing with Passion: Life Stories, Multiple Genres.* New York: Elsevier, Reed, 1995.

Simpson, Carol. *Copyright for Schools.* 4th ed. Worthington, OH: Linworth, 2005.

Online Resources

"About: Lessons on Plagiarism." 712educators.about.com/cs/plagiarism/

Apple Learning Interchange Teaching and Learning. "Plagiarism Advice for Lessons." henson.austin.apple.com/edres/ellesson/elem-writplagerism.shtml, henson.austin.apple.com/edres/mslessons/ms-writplag.shtml

Burwell, Hope, and Allison York. "Kirkwood—Writing Across the Curriculum. Suggestions for Developing Assignments That Minimize Plagiarism Possibilities." www.kirkwood.edu/wac/tips/minimizing_plagiarism.htm

Capital Community College Library. "A Statement on Plagiarism." www.ccc.commnet.edu/mla/plagiarism.shtml

"CD 315: Instructions for Multigenre Research Project (MRP)." www.bayarea-writingproject.org/15/stories/storyReader$24?print-friendly = true

Columbia Gorge Community College. "Alternative Assignments Requiring Library Research." www.cgcc.cc.or.us/Library/alternatives.htm

"CyberSmart! Lesson Plans." www.cybersmartcurriculum.org/lesson_plans

Education World. "Student Guide to Avoiding Plagiarism" + other lessons. www.educationworld.com/a_curr/TM/curr390_guide.shtml

"Educational CyberPlayground." www.edu-cyberpg.com/Teachers/plagiarism.html

"English 121: Research Possibilities—The Multi-Genre and Multi-Media Research Project." www.emunix.emich.edu/~adlerk/multigenre_instructions.htm, www.emunix.emich.edu/~adlerk/multi_genre_research1.htm

Empire State College. "Plagiarism Quiz." www.esc.edu/esconline/across_esc/library.nsf/wholeshortlinks2/Plagiarism+Quiz?opendocument

Frick, Ted. "What is Plagiarism at Indiana University?" education.indiana.edu/~frick/plagiarism/item1.html

Harris, Robert. "Virtual Salt: Anti-Plagiarism Strategies for Research Papers." www.virtualsalt.com/antiplag.htm

"Mrs. Juster's Virtual Classroom: Multi-Genre Writing." www.mrsjustersvirtualclassroom.com/Am%20Htg%20Writing%20MG.htm

"*The New York Times* Learning Network Lesson Plan." www.nytimes.com/learning/teachers/lessons/

OWL (Online Writing Lab, Purdue U. "Avoiding Plagiarism." owl.english.purdue.edu/handouts/research/r_plagiar.html

"PBS Current Events Lesson Plans." www.pbs.org/newshour/extra/teachers/

Plagiarism.org. "Research Resources" (links to Turnitin Research Resources). www.plagiarism.org/research_site/e_home.html

"Plagiarized.com: The Definitive Guide to Internet Plagiarism." www.plagiarized.com

Pyatt, Elizabeth J. "ANGEL Cyberplagiarism Question Bank Randomized." Penn State U. tlt.its.psu.edu/suggestions/cyberplag/angelimportrandom.html

Rudolph, Seri. "Plagiarism Resource Site." Colby College, Bates College, and Bowdoin College. leeds.bates.edu/cbb/media/

Safety Net@2Learn.ca. "On Plagiarism." www.2learn.ca/mapset/safetynet/plagiarism/plagiarism.html

Trivedi, Lisa, and Sharon Williams. "Using Sources." Hamilton College Writing Center. www.hamilton.edu/academics/resource/wc/usingsources.html

"Turnitin Research Resources." www.turnitin.com

U. of Alberta. "Guide to Plagiarism and Cyber-Plagiarism" and "Why Students Plagiarize." www.library.ualberta.ca/guides/plagiarism/

Writing Tutorial Services, Indiana U. "Plagiarism: What It is and How to Recognize and Avoid It." www.indiana.edu/~wts/wts/plagiarism.html

"Your Multigenre Web: Everything you need to know to succeed." www.sheboyganfalls.k12.wi.us/cyberenglish9/multi_genre/multigenre.htm

Media Resources

"Avoiding Plagiarism" (video). "Research Skills for Students" series. Wynnewood, PA: Schlessinger Media, 2004. www.libraryvideo.com/sm/sm_home.asp

---

Part IV

USING TECHNOLOGY
WITH INTEGRITY

CHAPTER ELEVEN

Honesty in Online Education

But it is also advisable to structure multiple opportunities for assessing student learning into a course in addition to—or even in place of—examinations. Depending upon the subject matter of the course, small group projects, case studies, simulations, portfolios, learning contracts, and group discussions can all be appropriate and effective tools for determining how well your students are learning. And all of these activities are readily adaptable to the online settings. (McNett)

Five years ago, *Student Cheating and Plagiarism in the Internet Era: A Wake-Up Call* (Libraries Unlimited, 2000) had less than two pages about distance learning. The subject merits much more attention today.

Many thousands of students around the world are enrolled in online education. The National Center for Education Statistics recently published the first major national survey on the extent of online education in K–12 schools, *Distance Education Courses for Public Elementary and Secondary School Students: 2002–03.* It reports on the rapid growth of online education and ongoing plans for expansion in more than half of the districts surveyed. Selected data are included in this chapter as a COPY ME page.

There are many reasons to welcome this growth; the potential benefits of online education are tremendous. There also is concern about the potential for cheating inherent in the delivery of instruction to students who complete class work and take tests in largely unsupervised settings. The concerns about cheating are valid and are the focus of this chapter.

References

McNett, Mike. "Curbing Academic Dishonesty in Online Courses" (Pointers & Clickers, May/June 2002). http://illinois.online.uillinois.edu/resources/pointersclickers/2002_05/index.asp.

Resources

Article:

Virgil Varvel: "Integrity in Online Education"

COPY ME pages:

Distance Education Courses for Public Elementary and Secondary School Students: 2002–03

Online Learning—Technical Information

See Appendix C for related information in *Student Cheating and Plagiarism in the Internet Era: A Wake-Up Call:* Chapter 2, High-Tech Cheating; Chapter 5: High-Tech Defenses Against Cheating and Plagiarism.

Distance Education Courses for Public Elementary and Secondary School Students: 2002–03

This report was published by the National Center for Education Statistics and is available online at nces.ed.gov/pubsearch/pubsinfo.asp?pubid=2005010. The following statistics are quoted from the Summary section:

- During the 2002–03 12-month school year, about one-third of public school districts (36 percent) had students in the district enrolled in distance education courses.
- A greater proportion of large districts than medium or small districts had students enrolled in distance education courses [and] a greater proportion of districts located in rural areas than in suburban or urban indicated that they had students enrolled in distance education.
- An estimated 8,200 public schools had students enrolled in distance education courses.... approximately 9 percent of all public schools nationwide.
- Overall, 38 percent of public high schools offered distance education courses, compared with 20 percent of combined or ungraded schools, 4 percent of middle or junior high schools, and fewer than 1 percent of elementary schools.
- Among all public schools with students enrolled in distance education, 76 percent were high schools, 15 percent were combined or ungraded schools, 7 percent were middle or junior high schools, and 2 percent were elementary schools.
- More districts reported two-way interactive video (55 percent) or Internet courses using asynchronous computer-based instruction (47 percent) than Internet courses using synchronous computer-based instruction (21 percent), one-way prerecorded video (16 percent), or some other technology (4 percent) as a primary mode of delivery.
- In both urban and suburban districts, Internet courses using asynchronous computer-based instruction was the technology cited most often as a primary delivery instructional delivery mode for distance education courses.
- Fifty-nine percent of districts with students enrolled in distance education courses had students enrolled in online distance education courses (i.e., courses delivered over the Internet) in 2002–03.
- Seventy-two percent of districts with students enrolled in distance education courses planned to expand their distance education courses in the future. (Setzer and Lewis, pp. 4–15)

[Setzer, J. C., and Lewis, L. (2005). Distance Education Courses for Public Elementary and Secondary School Students: 2002–93 (NCES 2005–010) U.S. Department of Education. Washington, DC: National Center for Education Statistics. nces.ed.gov/pubsearch/pubsinfo.asp?pubid=2005010.]

Integrity in Online Education

Virgil Varvel

The explosive growth of the Internet has fundamentally altered the face of distance education. In the short time since graphical user interfaces revolutionized the World Wide Web, the Internet has become the predominant distance education medium, outpacing other distance delivery modes. According to the National Center for Education Statistics (NCES), "During the 1990s, distance education availability, course offerings, and enrollments increased rapidly" (NCES, 2001). Within the state of Illinois for example, dramatic growth trends are evident in online education data gathered by the Illinois Virtual Campus (IVC, 2002) and more recently by the Illinois Virtual High School, according to Matthew Wicks, Director of Virtual Learning (personal communication, September 1, 2004). Online education, or education utilizing networked information technologies as the primary mode of instructional delivery, is a force that almost certainly will continue to grow.

The potential of online education cannot be denied. Students whose needs are not being met by the traditional classroom can achieve a more equitable or complete education at a distance. Home-schooled children can access lessons, seek out experts, interact with other students, and take courses beyond the abilities or time of their parents. Special needs children can attend school without requiring mobility and in an environment where their disability may not even be apparent. Advanced students can more easily take courses not offered at their schools. Online education can include advanced simulations, readings that don't require expensive books and loaded student backpacks, and multimedia distributed via the Web or on digital media through postal mail. Other examples exist, but clearly online education has value.

As online education has grown, so too, unfortunately, has the concern over academic honesty in this new environment. However, a key to successful online programs has been a shift away from traditional teaching methods towards an interactive, student-centered paradigm (Elbaum, 2002; Ko, 2001; White, 2000).

Successful courses develop a sense of community among the students, with everyone contributing to the learning process.

The collaborative nature of online teaching and the use of assignment alternatives such as portfolios, online group work, and discussion exercises have benefits beyond student learning. Students can become more motivated and more involved with the learning process to the extent that participation and learning will outweigh academic honesty issues. While administrators must consider online assessment validity and teachers may remain concerned about student cheating, a properly designed course should reduce these concerns so that more attention may be paid to instruction and student learning.

Despite these thoughts, some resistance to online education continues to be based on a belief (whether true or not) that cheating online is too easy (Rowe, 2004). A teacher cannot know what the students are bringing to the assessment table, whether it is other students, parents, or even paid helpers (Olt, 2002). Students may also bring books, notes, and the entire Internet. All online assessments essentially become open book in nature. But life itself is open book. As a result perhaps of necessity, online education can shift instruction away from the multiple-choice exam and towards more authentic assessments. Knowledge can be explored in a discussion where every student has the opportunity to participate.

When appropriate, though, teachers should not be afraid to use any type of exam, even multiple-choice, in an online course. Computerized testing tools continue to grow in usability and functionality; they can help to make cheating on computerized tests perhaps more difficult than on face-to-face exams in some respects. Advanced testing tools and online course management systems can allow questions to be randomly selected from large question pools, providing each student with a different test. Mathematical values can be randomized among students. Test-taking time can be strictly limited to a specific day or even a specific time of day. Passwords can be used that students are given only immediately prior to the test through a specific e-mail address or even the telephone in an effort to make sure the correct person is taking the exam. Test submissions can be limited so each student only has one opportunity to take the assessment (Rowe, 2004).

On a more technical note, an assignment submission can be tracked by looking at the IP number from which it was submitted. While these numbers may change, they should remain within a relatively small range for a given computer. Without proper safeguards, Olt (2002) argues that it may be possible for students to take the same assessment more than once or even steal poorly protected online assessment documents. However, obtaining answers is equally easy in a classroom when a teacher leaves an answer key out on a desk, or students copy from one another during an exam. Modern course management systems for online education possess good security provided teachers and students maintain password standards. It is more likely that a student will catch a glimpse of an answer in a face-to-face exam than an online one.

When measures must be taken to insure student identity and materials used, several methods can aid in increasing academic honesty. The most common method is to require students to attend a proctored exam session at a local school (ION, 2004; McNett, 2002; Rowe, 2004; Shyles, 2002). So while you can never be absolutely certain the person completing online assignments is the person signed up for the course, it is possible to determine identity at set assessments by using proctors. The likelihood of a student being able to continually acquire help to complete tests and other assessments throughout an online course is low. Another suggestion to make unpermitted help more difficult to obtain is to apply many mini-assessments throughout a course. Eventually a discrepancy will show up in quality or quantity of work/participation, alerting a teacher to a possible problem.

A more realistic conception about online education is that the potential for cheating online is probably no different than that in face-to-face education (Grijalva, 2003; Kaczmarczyk, 2001). Kaczmarczyk found that students and faculty originally believed that it was easier to cheat through online education; having experienced online education, they were equally divided (2001).

In fact, the distance separating online students may actually reduce peer-to-peer cheating from a practical standpoint. Sharing answers with other students online requires more than a glance over one's shoulder. Students may be unwilling to request unpermitted assistance or answers from a student they do not know personally. They may fear being reported to the teacher by other students, especially if they signed some form of honor code at the beginning of the class (Shyles, 2002). It takes time to determine who the best students are when there is no prior knowledge of classmates, so students do not know who to cheat from at first. By the time they do know, they have already worked hard enough to complete previous assignments successfully and may no longer feel an academic need to cheat during the rest of the course.

Independent of whether cheating is any easier or harder in an online environment, is it actually occurring? Unfortunately, we know that cheating overall is increasing for all modes of delivery in both face-to-face and online classrooms (Rowe, 2004; Stephens, 2004). Furthermore, the likelihood of students using the Internet for assignment completion or other cheating is no different in online courses than in face-to-face courses for any assignment that students may complete on their own time (Grijalva, 2003).

There does not appear to be anything specific to online education that enables or encourages students to cheat any more than in a face-to-face classroom. Neither does online education give students new reasons to cheat. The reasons for cheating (and perhaps not cheating) appear to be mostly the same between traditional education and face-to-face education (McMurtry, 2001; Slobogin, 2002; Stephens, 2004).

As the saying goes, an ounce of prevention is worth a pound of cure. Promoting integrity is more effective than policing it. The first measure of honesty preservation in an online course (and perhaps any course) is educating the students about cheating and plagiarism issues.

Sometimes students cheat without realizing that what they are doing is wrong. This problem may be exacerbated in an online course when many students and even the teachers are unfamiliar with online copyright issues or when copying from the Web wrong; they must learn when and how to use a proper method for citing electronic resources. The asynchronous nature of online education means that you do not have to take up class time in order to inform students about these issues. The information can be presented in an online orientation prior to or at the beginning of a class or education program. Unlike the limits of a printed pamphlet, students can access online examples at any time and an expert is available to help when questions arise.

Techniques used to prevent dishonesty in the traditional classroom can be equally effective in the online classroom. Interestingly, some preventions can be used in an online course that may not be as easily available in a traditional classroom. In addition to features of the testing programs already discussed, online education provides teachers with the opportunity to get to know the students well through constant written discourse. Experienced teachers know one key to recognizing cheating or plagiarism is to become familiar with a student's writing style. A paper or test that is far above the student's usual ability level alerts the teacher to possible dishonesty. The fact that all assignments are submitted in digital format also facilitates the use of online plagiarism detection services.

Online teachers do not have to limit their interaction with the students to written text. Audio technology has advanced to a usable stage on the Internet, and many programs are now available for recording and transmitting audio. Students in an online course can be required to complete all or part of an exam or assessment orally and then send the file in some manner to the teacher. The assessment can be directly tied to the student's voice. This can be improved even more when appropriate time limits are used in online assessments. As discussed with online tests, test-taking time can be strictly limited to a specific day or even a specific time of day just as in a traditional classroom. These limits can make it difficult for someone to script what the student would need to repeat in the audio in time to complete the exam.

Many if not all of the techniques described in this chapter are made easier through the use of course management systems (CMS), also known as learning management systems. Some of the more commonly used include WebCT (www. webct.com), BlackBoard (www.blackboard.com), and Moodle—a free open-source CMS (www.moodle.org). The Western Cooperative for Educational Telecommunications (2004) has compiled a thorough and useful reference of CMS and their diverse features. Both synchronous and asynchronous discussions can be moderated. Testing and grading can be coordinated and in some cases automated. The exact time of assignment submission can be determined by the date stamp placed on uploaded documents. Even the delivery of content can be controlled by time, achievement, order, and modality. All of these features exist in an easy to navigate and, more importantly, secure online system.

As all teachers know, the most effective means to limit cheating in any learning environment remains that of getting to know your students. Through the open discourse in an online course, teachers learn a great deal about their students and can share much about themselves. The development of community, sharing work when sharing is appropriate, and building on one another's knowledge can all serve to provide an atmosphere of learning where every student feels like a contributor.

In the end, fear not. By taking the necessary precautions and through effective course design, online education can be both conducive to learning and to academic honesty among students.

References

Elbaum, B., McIntyre, C., & Smith, A.. (2002). *Essential elements: Prepare, design, and teach your online course*. Madison, WI: Atwood Publishing.

Grijalva, T. C., Kerkvliet, J., & Nowell, C. (2003). *Academic honesty and online courses*. Retrieved September 1, 2004, from oregonstate.edu/dept/econ/pdf/cheat.online.pap6.pdf

Illinois Online Network (ION). (2004). *Strategies to minimize cheating online*. Retrieved September 19, 2004, from http://illinois.online.uillinois.edu/resources/tutorials/assessment/cheating.asp

Illinois Virtual Campus (IVC). (2002). *Reports and resources*. Retrieved October 18, 2004, from www.ivc.illinois.edu/pubs/enrollment.html?customerid=21877

Kaczmarczyk, L. C. (2001). *Accreditation and student assessment in distance education: Why we all need to pay attention*. Proceedings of the 6th Annual Conference on Innovation and Technology in Computer Science Education. Canterbury, UK, 113–16.

Ko, S., & Rossen, S. (2001). *Teaching online—A practical guide*. Boston, MA: Houghton Mifflin Co.

McMurtry, K. (2001). "E-cheating: Combating a 21st century challenge." *THE Journal Online 29*(4). Retrieved September 1, 2004, from www.thejournal.com/magazine/vault/articleprintversion.cfm?aid=3724

McNett, M. (2002). "Curbing academic dishonesty in online courses." *Pointers and Clickers: ION's Technology Tip of the Month*. Retrieved September 19, 2004, from www.webct.com/service/ViewContent?contentID=2451803

National Center for Education Statistics (NCES). (2001). *A profile of participation in distance education: 1999–2000*. Report. Retrieved September 5, 2004, from nces.ed.gov/das/epubs/2003154/index.aspOlson, B. (n.d.). *IPtoLL*. Retrieved September 1, 2004, from www-unix.mcs.anl.gov/~olson/IPtoLL.html

Olt, M. (2002). "Ethics and distance education: strategies for minimizing academic dishonesty in online assessment." *Online Journal of Distance Learning Administration 5*(3). Retrieved September 1, 2004, from www.westga.edu/~distance/ojdla/fall53/olt53.html

Rowe, N. C. (2004). "Cheating in online student assessment: Beyond plagiarism." *Online Journal of Distance Learning Administration, 7*(2). Retrieved September 5, 2004, from www.westga.edu/~distance/ojdla/summer72/rowe72.html

Shyles, L. (2002). *Authenticating, identifying, and monitoring learners in the virtual classroom: Academic integrity in distance learning*. Paper presented at the 88th Annual Meeting of the National Communication Association. New Orleans, LA, Nov. 21–24, 2002. (ED 472807)

Slobogin, K. (2002). *Survey: Many students say cheating's OK.* Retrieved September 1, 2004, from www.cnn.com/2002/fyi/teachers.ednews/04/05/high-school.cheating/

Stephens, J. (2004). *Justice or just us? What to do about cheating.* Retrieved September 1, 2004, from www.carnegiefoundation.org/perspectives/perspectives2004.May.htm

Western Cooperative for Educational Telecommunications (WCET). (2004). *Course management systems: Edutools.* Retrieved October 18, from www.edutools.info/course/index.jsp

White, K.E., & Weight, B.H. (2000). *The online teaching guide: A handbook of attitudes, strategies, and techniques for the virtual classroom.* Boston, MA: Allyn & Bacon.

Note to readers in search of more technical information:

- Rowe discusses the design of a large pool from which random test questions can be drawn, ways that students may attempt to circumvent password protections and other security features of online classroom management systems, and other techniques used to maintain testing integrity.
- Shyles examines a variety of biometric approaches to identify students enrolled in online classes.
- Western Cooperative for Educational Telecommunications (WCET) evaluates Course Management Systems.

Information at Illinois Online Network (ION)
www.webct.com/service/ViewContent?contentID=245180

- Pointers & Clickers www.webct.com/service/ViewContent?contentID=2451803
- Online Education Resources www.webct.com/service/ViewContent?contentID=2451803
- Student Assessment in Online Courses
- Quizzing, Testing, and Homework on the Internet
- Strategies to Minimize Cheating Online
- Curbing Academic Dishonesty in Online Courses

[Virgil Varvel is the Computer Assisted Instruction Specialist at Illinois Virtual Campus, Illinois Online Network, University of Illinois at www.ion.illinois.edu. Vvarvel@uillinois.edu]

Online Learning—Technical Information

Virgil Varvel

Rowe discusses the design of a large pool from which random test questions can be drawn, ways that students may attempt to circumvent password protections, and other security features of online classroom management systems.

Rowe, N.C. "Cheating in Online Student Assessment: Beyond Plagiarism." *Online Journal of Distance Learning Administration, 7*(2), 2004. www. westga.edu/~distance/ojdla/summer72/rowe72.html

Shyles examines a variety of biometric approaches to identify students in online classes.

Shyles, L. "Authenticating, Identifying, and Monitoring Learners in the Virtual Classroom: Academic Integrity in Distance Learning. 2002. (ED 472807)

Western Cooperative for Educational Telecommunications (WCET) evaluates Course Management Systems.

Western Cooperative for Educational Telecommunications (WCET). *Course Management Systems: Edutools.* 2004. www.edutools.info/course/index.jsp

A selection of Course Management Systems (CMS)

- WebCT www.webct.com
- BlackBoard www.blackboard.com
- Moodle www.moodle.org—a free open-source CMS

Information at Illinois Online Network (ION) (www.webct.com/service/Vie wContent?contentID=2451803)

- Pointers & Clickers (www.webct.com/service/ViewContent?contentID =2451803)
- Online Education Resources (www.webct.com/service/ViewContent? contentID=2451803)
- Student Assessment in Online Courses
- Quizzing, Testing, and Homework on the Internet
- Strategies to Minimize Cheating Online
- Curbing Academic Dishonesty in Online Courses

[Virgil Varvel is the Computer Assisted Instruction Specialist at Illinois Virtual Campus, Illinois Online Network, University of Illinois at www.ion.illinois.edu.Vvarvel@uillinois. edu]

CHAPTER TWELVE

Keeping Technology Honest

Jacquie Henry

When a kid finishes his test, he takes a picture with his cell phone of the test and the answers. His friend takes the phone into the test a later period and uses picture on phone for answers. Can get any answers they don't know in time between tests. Students also copy the test with picture phone and put the test online for everyone. 11th grade boy

With a cell phone, you can take a picture of the test page with your answers and send it to a friend. Take your cell phone to the restroom to send test or to get answers to questions. Use text messaging phone to phone to ask for answers to questions. 7th grade girl

Students use their cell phones for text messaging with the phone out of sight under the desk. Everybody has a phone. 6th grade girl

To deny students all access to technologies is a futile attempt to turn back the clock. We must prepare students for their future, not our past, and their future will increasingly be wireless. (Fryer, par. 6)

The best two devices for stopping cheating are the teacher's eyes and ears. (Ladewig)

These quotes point out the dilemma facing today's teachers. Our students have seamlessly integrated the power of computers, the Internet, and wireless technology into their everyday lives. Some of them will use the technology to cheat, just as they have been using low-tech cheating methods for centuries.

How can we, as teachers, discourage high-tech cheating, while still supporting high-tech creativity and productivity? First, it is important to avoid engaging in a tech war with students. Instead, as we become more familiar with the new technology and use it in our classrooms, we will realize that many of the techniques used to prevent "traditional" cheating work just as well to prevent high-tech cheating. In the end, teaching our students to listen to their conscience continues to be the most powerful preventative measure.

Part I: Technology the Students are Using

PWDs (Portable Wireless Devices)

Small handheld computers such as PDAs and Blackberries are equipped with personal information management (PIM) software, SMS (Short Messaging Service), and an infrared transmitter that allows users to send and receive text files or applications. A newer technology, known as Bluetooth or WPAN (Wireless Personal Area Network) uses wireless radio frequency to connect computer peripherals and handheld devices to each other and/or to the Internet (Bluetooth, par. 4). Many handheld computers have built-in digital cameras. Watches come with both PDA and camera capability. Language translator PWDs can translate numerous languages but generally are more limited in other functions.

How this technology can be used to cheat or plagiarize: Students store large amounts of information to access during a test. They communicate with others inside or outside the testing area via infrared transmitters or use Bluetooth technology to connect to the Internet via a cell phone. Devices with built-in digital cameras let students take digital pictures of a test and share it with friends. Language translators can be used to cheat on foreign language tests and homework.

Programmable Calculators (Graphic Calculators)

A portable, handheld calculator can handle a broad range of mathematical or scientific applications from algebra through calculus, including interactive geometry, symbolic manipulation, statistics, and 3D graphing. It also can display text, and the newest models have enough memory to load software and a USB port to connect to a PC (Kantor, par. 9–10). "The graphic calculators also allow students to use statistical applications in many non-traditional ways" (Nau). The T1-Navigator is a wireless device that allows a teacher to communicate with all the graphic calculators in the classroom (Joyner, par. 23). This device also could be used to detect other calculators being used in a testing situation.

How this technology can be used to cheat or plagiarize: The graphic calculator is useful for cheating in any class where tests ask for dates, formulas, lists of any type, or other data that students were expected to memorize. Students can enter the test questions and answers into their own calculator to share with students in later classes. Two or more students sharing a calculator during a test can leave answers visible for each other. Students can also transmit information to each other during tests via infrared technology.

Cell Phones / Camera Phones / Pagers

Many cell phones provide information storage, text messaging, calendars, calculators, e-mail, games, Internet access, cameras, and other related services. Pagers can be used to send questions and receive numeric or full-text messages.

How this technology can be used to cheat or plagiarize: Students can send and receive text messages to and from someone inside or outside the testing area. Camera phones can be used to distribute a digital picture of the test to other students. Students can bring cell phones or other handheld devices to the restroom during tests to look up answers on the Internet, solve equations, share test questions, or phone a friend for answers. Cell phones with calculators can be used during math tests (State, par. 10). Students can preprogram their pagers with all the information needed during the test and share information during the exam.

CD and MP3 Players / Portable Data Storage Devices / Cassette Tape Players

CD & MP3 players such as Walkmans and iPods are used primarily to save and listen to music. CD players can play both commercial and home-recorded CDs. MP3 players have very large storage capacity and can be used as a sort of portable hard drive, allowing students to record voice messages, store photos, keep an appointment calendar, or play audio books or games. Information needed for a test can be recorded onto a cassette tape.

Portable Data Storage Devices (flash drives, digital pen scanners, memory sticks, eye monitor glasses, etc.) are designed to allow large amounts of computer data to be moved from one computer to another. The data is not transmitted wirelessly. Instead, these devices are connected directly to a computer, laptop, or handheld device (What, par. 1). With 20 gigabytes or more of memory, these devices can store large amounts of all kinds of data.

How this technology can be used to cheat or plagiarize: Students can use these devices to record all the information they need for a test as text, an audio recording, or even a photo. Small earphones concealed by a scarf or long hair can be used to access any audio information. Eye monitor glasses are "immediately connectable to any device with a video composite output.... Your video cable has just to be connected, no particular setting is required. You can now read any media-information while walking down the street" (Eye, par. 8). Pen scanners can be used to copy a test for students who will take it later in the day.

E-mail / Instant Messaging (IM) / Chat Rooms / Faxes and Scanners

With its ability to send text and also attach files and photos, e-mail has become one of the most frequently used forms of communication at all age levels, for business, educational, and personal use. Instant Messaging allows teenagers to communicate in real time by creating a "buddy list." Teenagers also use IM to create chat rooms where they can chat with each other in real time.

Scanners are used to transfer images and text into a computer. These photos and text can then be altered as desired. The scanned files can be printed, used on Web pages, and e-mailed from one computing device to another. Fax machines are used to send copies of documents over phone lines. Many computers and printers come equipped with both faxing and scanning capabilities.

How this technology can be used to cheat or plagiarize: Students use e-mail, instant messaging, chat rooms, scanners, and faxes to share research papers and homework. Faxes and scanners are useful for sharing handwritten assignments such as math problems or drawings. Students who borrow research papers from friends instead of purchasing one from an online "paper mill" not only save money, but are less likely to get caught. It is harder for a teacher to spot a plagiarized paper that is written at a student level.

Blogs

A world of information is now open to the Internet-connected classroom. Blogs (Web logs) are online journals usually written by a single individual. Blogging software allows students to create and post their blogs with little or no knowledge of html. "The tools that most bloggers use make it incredibly easy to add entries any time they feel like it" (Brain, par. 6). Blogs are very popular with teenagers as well as educators, journalists, and people in every walk of life. A classroom blog that is managed according to guidelines set by the teacher can be a valuable study aid.

Examples of blogs with educational purposes:
School Blogs. www.schoolblogs.com/
Weblogg-ed. www.weblogg-ed.com/
BlogPulse (a search engine for blogs). www.blogpulse.com/

How this technology can be used to cheat or plagiarize: Students use their blogs to share homework or other assignments, answer questions for one another, and post copies of old tests with answers.

School Computer Networks / Wireless Networks

Networks allow school computers and peripherals to communicate with each other and allow large numbers of users to share programs and files efficiently. Wireless networks allow computers and handheld computers to be moved anywhere in the building and still be able to access applications, files, and the Internet.

How this technology can be used to cheat or plagiarize: Students who will be taking tests on desktop or laptop computers can save their notes to their student network files. As they are taking the test, they simply open these files to read or, if they are really bold, to copy and paste information into their test. They also can connect to the Internet, online encyclopedias, and research databases to locate answers. Students can use free translation programs on the Internet to do their homework in foreign language classes or to cheat on foreign language tests. A wireless Internet connection will allow students to tap into the Internet using their PDAs and other handheld devices. Hackers may gain access to a teacher's electronic grade book to change grades or obtain an advance copy of a test. Wireless networks that are not properly secured become easy prey to viruses planted by disgruntled students.

Part II: Discouraging Cheating on Tests

Prohibit the use of *all* electronic devices during testing. They must be in a backpack, purse, or on the teacher's desk. Announce that *any* electronic device seen in the room during testing, whether being used or not, will be confiscated and held for a parent conference, and a failing grade will be assigned for that test. This policy should be in writing in the district or school Academic Integrity Policy, included in the class syllabus, and printed on the first page of each major test.

Control access to technology devices

- Limit calculator use during a test to only those calculators that belong to a classroom set. Remove batteries to be sure the memories have been erased in case students entered test answers, formulas, and so on, when they had access to the calculators before the test.
- Ask students to remove their watches and leave them with the teacher while in the testing area.
- Allow only school-owned pens to be used.
- Locate and monitor any Web sites, chat rooms, or blogs being used by your students to share class information and assignments; be sure tests are not posted at the site.
- Disconnect all computers being used for testing from access to the school network or Internet.
- Arrange to temporarily block network drives so students do not have access to their files. Test files can then be saved onto disks to be collected by the teacher.

Keep tests secure

- Be scrupulous about maintaining test security, keeping tests away from prying eyes or cameras, especially when the same test will be given to later classes.

- Guard your passwords and change them frequently. Never leave a computer unattended without logging out first. To stop hackers, schools can do away with passwords completely by installing biometric devices (fingerprint recognition devices).

What to watch for during testing

- Constantly patrol the classroom during a test, alert for high-tech cheating and also for cheat sheets or other traditional cheating methods.
- Students who frequently check their pockets, purses, or laps, or who fumble with baggy clothing, may be using an electronic device (or reading a more traditional cheat sheet).
- Notice students who may be "pointing" a calculator or other device at another student to send or receive information electronically.
- Students using headsets or earphones may have taped their notes or other information for the test. New earphones are very small and easy to conceal, especially for students with long hair or who wear a cap, scarf, or other head covering.
- Students who check their watches frequently may be using a PDA/pager/camera watch.
- Students using a digital pen scanner may be copying the test for other students.
- Look for eye monitor glasses, ones with a relatively large device mounted on one side.
- Look for portable data storage devices that are plugged into USB ports. USB or flash drives are small enough to fit on a key chain and also come built into watches and even Swiss Army knives. Also check CD and floppy drives (Gadgets, par. 1).
- Listen for "tapping fingers and electronic beeps" (Shaw, par. 7).
- Watch for screen distortions on computer monitors, an indication that a cell phone is being used in the room (Chapman, par. 2).
- Students with several program windows open at the same time may be reading their notes or checking a Web site or online encyclopedia. Never allow more than one open program window at a time.

A teacher's anti-cheating toolbox

"Academic Dishonesty Prevention and Detection Strategies" at www.iub. edu/~teaching/cheating.shtml provides many techniques for recognizing and preventing cheating on tests and homework.

ExamSoft Worldwide at www.examsoft.com "provides academic examination software solutions for all levels of learning...encompassing all elements of the examination process examination software solutions ranging from the traditional single classroom examination format to secure Internet examination systems for Distance Learning Programs."

For multiple-choice tests, use Scantron PDA quiz program (Schools, par. 20). www.scantron.com/products/wizard/

Electronic bug detectors and cell phone jammers can be used to detect the use of handheld devices, cell phones, or similar devices in a classroom (Crowley). This equipment can be very expensive.

The T1-Navigator is a wireless device that allows a teacher to communicate with all the graphic calculators in the classroom (Joyner, par. 23). This device could also be used to detect calculators being used in a testing area.

"Scrutiny" and similar software programs can analyze tests and produce reports that indicate suspicious similarities (Cizek 67–69).

Biometric devices are being developed that can check student identity. www.digitalpersona.com and techupdate.zdnet.com/techupdate/stories/main/0,14179,2818323,00.html

Author's note: Also see Chapters 9 and 10 for information on electronic plagiarism and its prevention. See Appendix C for related information in *Student Cheating and Plagiarism in the Internet Era: A Wake-Up Call:* Chapter 2, High-Tech Cheating; Chapter 3, Electronic Plagiarism; Chapter 5, High-Tech Defenses Against Cheating and Plagiarism.

Works Cited

"Bluetooth." *Fact Index.com.* Wikipedia.com. www.fact-index.com/b/bl/blue tooth.html

Brain, Marshall. "How Blogs Work." *HowStuffWorks.com.* computers.how stuffworks.com/blog.htm

Chapman, Claire. "Cheats Who Phone a Friend Caught On Screen." *Times Higher Education Supplement.* 21 May 2004: www.thes.co.uk/search/search_results. aspx?search=cheats+who+phone+a+friend+caught+on+screen&mode=both& searchYear=&searchMonth=

Cizek, Gregory J. *Detecting and Preventing Classroom Cheating.* Thousand Oaks, CA: Corwin Press, Inc, 2003.

Crowley, Robert, Manager of Spy Outlet, Henrietta, NY. Personal interview. 13 July 2004.

"Eye Monitor Glasses." *4 Hidden Spy Cameras.* www.4hiddenspycameras.com/ eyeglmo.html

Fryer, Wesley A. "The Opportunities and Challenges of Wireless Computing." *tech.Learning.* 1 January 2003. www.techlearning.com/db_area/archives/ WCE/archives/weswire.html

"Gadgets: Geek Tools." ThinkGeek. c.2004. www.thinkgeek.com/gadgets/tools

Joyner, Amy. "A Foothold for Handhelds." *asbj.com*. September 2003. American School Board Journal. www.asbj.com/specialreports/0903SpecialReports/S3.html

Kantor, Andrew. "CyberSpeak: Cheating Goes High-Tech With Commonplace Tools". *USA Today*. 5/21/2004. www.usatoday.com/tech/columnist/andrew kantor/2004–05–21-kantor_x.htm

Ladewig, Joanne. "Catching Cheaters." 6 July 2004. E-mail to John Henry. 14 July 2004.

Nau, Lori. Personal interview. 10 September 2004.

"Schools Rule On Classroom Gadgets." *Wired News*. 21 September 2003. Associated Press. www.wired.com/news/culture/0,1284,60527,00.html

Shaw, Rob. "Cheating Students Go High-Tech." Rense.com. 11 June 2004. www.rense.com/general53/cheat.htm

"State May Ban Electronic Devices During M-CAS Testing." *Boston Globe*. 15 June 2004. Associated Press. www.boston.com/business/articles/2004/06/15/

"What Is Portable Data Storage?" *Becta ICT Advice For Teachers*. 2004. www.ictadvice.org.uk/index.php?section=te&catcode=as_ds_02&rid=667

[Jacquie Henry, MLS, Ruben A. Cirillo High School, Gananda Central School District, Walworth, New York. She is the author of "The Tangled Web—Holding the MP3 Generation Accountable" (*Library Media Connection,* March 2004) and "Schools & The Internet: The Good, The Bad, And The Ugly," an online and expanded version of the material included in this book. This online article and her faculty workshop on Plagiarism and Cheating are available at www.gananda.org/library/mshslibrary/plagiarism.htm. Her library home page is www.gananda.org/library/mshslibrary/indexgcl.htm.]

Part V

APPENDICES

APPENDIX A

National Surveys on Student Cheating and Plagiarism

Josephson Institute of Ethics: "Report Card 2004: The Ethics of American Youth"

Donald McCabe: "Cheating: Why Students Do It and How We Can Make Them Stop"

Report Card 2004:
The Ethics of American Youth

Josephson Institute of Ethics

"Though the *Report Card on the Integrity of American Youth* continues to contain failing grades, there is reason for hope. For the first time in 12 years the cheating and theft rates have actually dipped downward and the stated devotion to ethics is the strongest we've seen. While this results in a troubling inconsistency between words and actions, character education efforts should be able to build on the fundamental appreciation of ethics, character and trust to achieve continuing improvements in conduct. Still, it can't be comforting to know that the majority of the next generation of police officers, politicians, accountants, lawyers, doctors, nuclear inspectors and journalists are entering the workforce as unrepentant cheaters."

This comment by Michael Josephson is from *Report Card 2004: The Ethics of American Youth.** The Josephson Institute of Ethics surveys high school students and publishes the resulting *Report Card* every two years. The 2004 results are based on responses from 24,763 high school students in 85 U.S. high schools.

My parents/guardians would rather I cheat than get bad grades.
Strongly Agree/Agree   91%   Disagree/Strongly Disagree   9%

My parents/guardians always want me to do the ethically right thing, no matter what the cost.
Strongly Agree/Agree   6%   Disagree/Strongly Disagree   94%

Copied an Internet document for a classroom assignment [in the past year].
At Least Once   35%   Two or More Times   18%

Cheated during a test at school [in the past year].
At Least Once   62%   Two or More Times   38%

Cheated or "bent the rules" to win in sports [in the past year].
At Least Once   23%   Two or More Times   12%

**Complete survey data for this 2004 report, the 2002 and 2000 reports, and other earlier reports are online at http://josephsoninstitute.org/Survey2004/*

[Michael Josephson is founder and President/CEO of the Josephson Institute of Ethics, sponsor of **CHARACTER COUNTS!** online at www.charactercounts.org and www.josephsoninstitute.org.]

Cheating: Why Students Do It and How We Can Help Them Stop

(abridged, see below for complete article online)

Donald McCabe

School cheating is not news. Parents and teachers have been worrying about it for generations. Unfortunately, there is evidence that cheating has increased in the last few decades, and the Internet is likely to intensify the problem. It's also unfortunate that the people who worry about cheating often contribute to it. Well-intentioned parents who want their children to be successful in school can place so much pressure on the kids that they resort to cheating. Students believe that many teachers who see cheating look the other way, sending the message that cheating is acceptable. To which a teacher might reply, with considerable justice, that School Boards, superintendents, and principals often fail to back them up when they are faced with angry parents whose child has been accused of cheating. And almost daily, the media give big play to all kinds of cheating carried out by adults in positions of authority: politicians, lawyers, business people, clergy, and educators. As a high school junior recently observed: "Cheating is the American way. Businessmen do it, politicians do it. Why not students?" Indeed, the student who does not cheat now seems to be the exception in many schools.

This past year, I surveyed 2,294 high school juniors at 25 schools across the country—14 public schools and 11 private schools. The results were discouraging. Many students told me they know cheating is wrong, and they are not proud of their behavior. However, they feel they have to cheat to get the grades they need. On the other hand, student comments led me to believe that many students who are self-confessed cheaters would be willing partners in any reasonable strategy to deal with the most serious kinds of cheating.

The prevalence of cheating

Whatever we might want to believe, the evidence is unequivocal. The problem starts early and increases as students move through school. It has also increased significantly at almost every level of our educational system in the last few decades. My recent survey of 2,294 high school juniors confirms earlier findings and indicates that high levels of cheating are a nationwide phenomenon. Table 1 presents some of my basic findings.

Table 1: Common Forms of Cheating Among High School Juniors

% indicates number of students self-reporting one or more incidents of this behavior

Copied from another on test/exam	63%
Used crib notes on test/exam	39%
Got questions/answers from someone who had taken test	77%
Helped someone cheat on test/exam	60%
Copied almost word for word from a source and submitted as own work	34%
Turned in work copied from another	68%
Turned in assignment done by parents	20%
Worked on an assignment with other when asked not to	76%
Copied a few sentences without citation	60%
Let another copy homework	86%
Turned in paper obtained in large part from a term-paper mill or Web site	16%
Copied a few sentences from a Web site without footnoting them	52%

Why are they cheating?

There are a number of possible explanations for the rise in cheating between elementary school and high school. Increasing pressure from parents as students prepare to apply to college is one; the increasing difficulty of the material being taught is another. I believe that the growing influence of peers—and declining influence of parents and teachers—is even more important. Unfortunately, it appears that many parents and teachers are doing little to combat this trend. Forty-seven percent of the respondents reported that teachers in their school sometimes ignore cheating. The most frequent explanation for such behavior, mentioned by 26 percent of students, was that teachers often don't want to accuse a student of cheating because of the bureaucratic procedures involved in pursuing such allegations.

Other explanations offered by students include the belief that teachers don't care about cheating (11 percent); the student is an athlete or a student the teacher likes (8 percent); or the teacher feels sorry for the student and doesn't want to cause him or her additional trouble (6 percent). Parents may send a similar message, not only by putting too much pressure on their children, but also by failing to emphasize the importance of academic honesty. Some parents even look the other way when they think their child may have cheated, or they blindly defend their child if a teacher accuses the youngster of academic dishonesty. And of course the 20 percent of students who say they have turned in assignments on which their parents did most of the work are receiving a clear message that cheating is sometimes acceptable.

Enter the Internet

The Internet has raised new and significant problems for both students and teachers. Younger students, for whom the Internet is such a common form of communication, seem to have difficulty understanding its proper use as an academic tool. And many high school students believe—or say they believe—that if information is on the Internet, it is public knowledge and does not need to be footnoted—even if it's quoted verbatim. Table 2 shows what my survey of high school juniors in public and private schools discovered about the impact of such thinking on students' attitudes and behavior.

Many high school students find Internet plagiarism so easy and consider it so unlikely to be detected that it is almost too tempting to resist. Although the advent of services that check for Internet plagiarism may have altered the situation, high school students who participated in these focus groups said that teachers were not as Internet-savvy as their students and were unlikely to detect Internet plagiarism. Students also felt that the quality of material available on the Net was usually more than adequate for their needs.

The fact that high school students do not take very seriously what we might call Internet "cut and paste" plagiarism is a cause for concern. High school students may be under the impression that lifting information from the Internet, even verbatim, is good research practice rather than cheating. Are we raising a genera-

Table 2: Plagiarism and the Internet

	Students reporting behavior	Students say behavior is serious
Plagiarism from written sources		
Copied almost word for word and submitted as own work	34%	70%
Copied a few sentences without citation	60%	39%
Internet plagiarism		
Turned in paper obtained in large part from paper mill or Web site	16%	74%
Copied a few sentences from a Web site without footnoting them	52%	46%

tion of students who view scholarship as "borrowing" thoughts from a variety of different sources and simply assembling them into a final product?

What can we do?

Some people believe that greater vigilance and more severe punishments are the solutions to student cheating. These tactics are likely to reduce cheating—and that is certainly a worthwhile goal—but they won't touch the attitudes that lead to cheating. To do that, schools need to change the culture that accepts cheating as a matter of course and replace it with one that places a higher value on academic honesty. The Center for Academic Integrity, a consortium of over 250 colleges based at Duke University, recommends several steps to help create this culture:

- Develop standards that are communicated to all members of the school community (including parents).
- Create a process for handling alleged violations.
- Get a commitment, especially from the school administration, to adhere to and enforce these standards.

But these steps will lead nowhere unless the school also sponsors programs that *promote* academic integrity—for instance, schoolwide discussions that grapple with questions about what encourages cheating and how to promote academic honesty.

Many teachers do not work in schools or school districts willing to devise such standards and programs or even to support teachers who discipline students for cheating. And if teachers don't realize the effect of a failure to react to incidents of cheating, they may be tempted to give the issue a pass. Unfortunately, as noted earlier, students often take this as a license to cheat. However, there are things teachers can do on their own to establish an atmosphere that supports academic honesty. At the very least, they need to lead frank and open discussions that deal with questions like why students cheat, how it harms them in the long run, academically and otherwise, and how it harms other students as well.

It is also important for teachers to clarify their expectations for students. For example, many teachers fail to explain what level of collaboration is permissible on assignments. When they don't, students must decide for themselves, and, more often than not, they conclude that whatever has not been specifically prohibited is acceptable. Any teacher who penalizes a student for collaboration when the teacher has not clarified his or her expectations is probably on very weak ground.

The most significant contextual factor in a student's decision to cheat or not to cheat is peer influence. Students look to other students to determine what is acceptable behavior, and acceptability depends to a large extent on the culture in their school. If the school has achieved some level of consensus that cheating is wrong—as can happen, for example, in schools that adopt honor codes—students may hesitate to cheat for fear that peers will disapprove or even report them to the teacher.

In the absence of such a culture, cheating can even create a feeling of solidarity. Students may come to view cheating from a "we" vs. "they" perspective. "We" students need to stick together to overcome the obstacles our teachers and/or the administration keep placing in our way. In this situation, rules on collaboration, plagiarism, and other forms of cheating are viewed as just another hassle by students, and bending the rules a little to overcome such obstacles is acceptable.

Students find teachers' failings—real or supposed—useful in justifying cheating. The relevance and fairness of assessments are issues students often raise. The question here is not the difficulty of the tests or the course material. Everyone has heard students talk with pride about courses they have taken where, despite the difficulty of the course, they simply would not cheat. However, students speak angrily about teachers who give tests that cover material not discussed in class or highlighted in homework assignments, and they may find it relatively easy to justify cheating in such cases. Whatever the truth in individual student complaints, there is no question that cheating can be used to express disrespect for a teacher and defiance of the teacher's authority.

Although promoting academic integrity is superior to policing students, teachers should do what they can to reduce the opportunities for classroom cheating. At the very least, this sends a message to students that academic honesty is considered important. Some useful techniques—none of them new and most, unfortunately, involving additional work for the teacher—include using multiple versions of a test, basing tests on essay questions rather than short-answer questions, and giving different tests for different sections of the same course. Giving open-book exams, where possible, or allowing students to bring notes with them to the exam room also discourages cheating, although such tests require a special kind of preparation if students are to do well on them. Barbara Gross Davis, at the University of California at Berkeley, offers an excellent compilation of classroom strategies to reduce cheating (www.uga.berkeley.edu/sled/bgd/prevent.html) and the Because We Care Education Society of Alberta, Canada, offers some very useful ideas for combating plagiarism (www.2learn.ca/mapset/safetynet/plagiarism/plagiarismframes.html).

Finally, as discussed at length earlier, the increasing use of the Internet by students is creating a serious problem. Students talk about the ease with which papers can be downloaded from the Internet and submitted with little fear of detection. Even if the Internet does not attract new cheaters, data from my high school study suggest it will lead to an increased incidence of cheating among existing cheaters because of its ease of use, convenience, and potential anonymity. Thus, teachers would be foolish if they did not develop assignments that are less vulnerable to cheating on the Internet—for example, assigning papers that are as current and out-of-the-ordinary as possible and requiring students to interpret the information they gather.

Appropriately, the Internet itself can provide much advice both in how to help students use the Internet and to detect material plagiarized from the Internet. For example, a recent search using *www.google.com* and the keywords "student plagiarism" + "Internet" yielded over 800 hits. The sites varied in their quality and usefulness, but many included helpful tips on avoiding and detecting Internet plagiarism.

Conclusion

It is far easier to document the prevalence of cheating than to give useful suggestions about how to reduce the incidence of cheating. In the long run, the key is to convince students that academic integrity is something to be valued. The first step is to talk with students about why academic integrity is a worthwhile goal. For example, teachers and parents should emphasize how little students learn when they cheat—how, in fact, cheating will only lead to serious problems later on when cheaters lack the foundation to succeed in advanced courses. Given the messages students get every day from their peers and the larger society, this discussion is unlikely to meet with immediate success. It will meet with even less success, however, if teachers are not prepared to address cheating that occurs in their classrooms and if parents do not support these teachers. Messages on the value of integrity carry little weight if a teacher looks the other way when cheating occurs or if parents don't seem to consider it as important as good grades. Of course, taking a stronger anti-cheating stance will be difficult in schools or districts where the administration does not support teachers or where community pressures for student success are extreme.

The good news is that many students who cheat seem genuine in their distaste for what they are doing. As I discovered in carrying out my survey, many would be willing, and even prefer, to do their work honestly, but they are not willing to be placed at a disadvantage by their honesty. Students are looking to their teachers and schools to take the lead. Teachers and schools, in turn, must convince parents that teaching our future generation to be honest, to take pride in the work they do because it is their own, is at least as important as any academic skill youngsters learn—and certainly far more important than any grade they get.

[Excerpt reprinted with permission of the author and the publisher from the Winter 2001 issue of the *American Educator,* the quarterly journal of the American Federation of Teachers, AFL-CIO. The entire article is online at www.aft.org/pubs-reports/american_educator/winter2001/Cheating.html.

American Federation of Teachers, AFL•CIO—555 New Jersey Avenue, NW—Washington, DC 20001. Copyright by the American Federation of Teachers, AFL•CIO. All rights reserved. Photographs and illustrations, as well as text, cannot be used without permission from the AFT.

Donald McCabe is professor of Organization Management at Rutgers Business School, Rutgers University, Newark, NJ, and founding president of the Center for Academic Integrity at Duke University.]

APPENDIX B

Survey Forms

All surveys in Appendix B may be copied for use in classrooms and may be adapted to meet the individual needs of the teachers using them. It is important to have written permission from your principal or other appropriate administrator before conducting a student survey.

Do NOT put your name on this survey

We are writing a book about cheating in schools today. We want your honest opinion about why you personally decide to cheat or not to cheat. All replies will be anonymous.

Thank you for your important contribution to our book.

Kathy Foss and Ann Lathrop

YOU are: male   female   GRADE level: 6   7   8   9   10   11   12

Please choose ONE question to write about. Circle the question you choose: 1   2   3   4

1. If you cheat in all or most all of your classes, why do you cheat?
2. Describe one time when you could have cheated in school but you didn't. Why did you decide not to cheat?
3. Why would you never cheat, even when other students are cheating?
4. If you cheat in some classes, but there is one class you absolutely would never cheat in, why don't you cheat in that class?

3-Minute Survey

Thanks for answering these quick questions. Make comments if you want to.

Do NOT put your name on this paper

How many of YOUR teachers have discussed *cheating* on tests and assignments in one or more of your classes this year?

   1   2   3   4   5   6   none

How many of YOUR teachers have discussed *plagiarism* in one or more of your classes this year?

   1   2   3   4   5   6   none

Have your parents talked with you about why you shouldn't cheat at school?

   yes, often   yes, a few times   not this school year

If you copied a paper or part of a paper from the Internet, did your parents know about it?

   yes   no

   What would they say about it?

   it's OK   don't do it

Do you know what your Student Handbook says about cheating and plagiarism?

   yes, I've read it   no idea, never read it

Do your parents know what the Student Handbook says?

   yes   no   I don't know

THANKS!
PLEASE PUT YOUR SURVEY IN ONE
OF THE LIBRARY SURVEY BOXES

Do NOT Put Your Name on This Survey

Thanks for answering these quick questions. Make comments if you want to.

1. Have you observed students cheating on tests or quizzes?   *yes   no*

2. Do you think they cheated because the teacher wasn't paying attention?
   yes   no   probably   other

   Other reasons why students cheat:

   - *didn't study, didn't know answers, afraid to fail*
   - *wanted a better grade*
   - *like to outsmart teachers*
   - *had nothing to lose*
   - *it's a hard subject*

3. Have you ever cheated on a test?   *yes   no*

3a. Was it because you didn't study?   *yes   no   maybe*

3b. Were you under a lot of pressure to get a good grade?
    yes   no   sometimes

3c. Did you do it because everyone does it?   *yes   no   sometimes*

4. Have you ever taken a paper off the Internet and turned it in as your own
   work?   *yes   no   parts of a paper*

5. Have you every bought a paper off the Internet?   *yes   no*

6. Do you think you understand what the term plagiarism means?
   yes   no   not sure

THANK YOU FOR YOUR TIME

Author's note: We received a number of indignant responses to question 3c and probably will drop it from our next survey. Comments ranged from "No, do you think I'm stupid?" to "Of course not, I have my reasons."

APPENDIX C

Student Cheating and Plagiarism in the Internet Era: A Wake-Up Call

Ann Lathrop and Kathleen Foss
Libraries Unlimited, 2000

Annotated Table of Contents

Chapter 1: Overview

We know students are cheating more often today, their cheating techniques are increasingly sophisticated, and many express guilt or remorse only if they are caught. Why do they cheat? The bottom line seems to be (a) it's easy, especially with new technologies, (b) fewer than 10 percent are caught, and (c) most of those who are caught get off without serious penalty. The byword appears to have changed from *Don't cheat* to *Don't get caught.*

Chapter 2: High-Tech Cheating

Small hand-held computers, electronic calculators, pagers, Web sites, and computer networks all can be used legitimately to enhance students' work. They also give some students an unfair advantage when used for cheating. *COPY ME page:* High-Tech Devices Used for Cheating.

Chapter 3: Electronic Plagiarism

Students copy papers from a variety of Internet sites: online "paper mills," reviews of films and plays, electronic journals, and legitimate research sites created to share scientific and scholarly papers. Electronic research services prepare "original" papers for a fee; one even asks for a writing sample from the student in order to produce the appropriate level and style of writing. The types of papers available online and the simple steps of downloading a paper are explained. Students are warned against plagiarizing online graphics or other materials to create their own Web sites; these are protected by copyright. *Chapter topics:* What's Available on the Internet? Plagiarizing 1–2-3; Plagiarizing from Electronic Encyclopedias. *COPY ME page:* Online Sites for Reports and Research Papers. *Article reprint:* "Downloadable Term Papers: What's a Prof to Do?" by Tom Rocklin.

Chapter 4: Why We Are Alarmed

Statistical data from regional and national surveys summarized here indicate a steady increase in cheating behaviors. Student attitudes in a number of interviews show a general acceptance of cheating as "no big deal" and document an almost universal reluctance to "rat" on classmates who cheat. During interviews students brag about their cheating, criticize teachers for not catching them, and scoff at the likelihood of any serious penalty. *Chapter topics:* Things Are Bad and Getting Worse; Are Elementary School Students Cheating? Student and Teacher Attitudes Toward Cheating; What the Students Say; 3 National Surveys on Cheating; Research Highlights on Cheating in Colleges and Universities. *COPY ME pages:* Cheating and Succeeding; Research Highlights. *Article reprint:* "Schooling Without Learning: Thirty Years of Cheating in High School" by Fred Schab.

Chapter 5: High-Tech Defenses Against Cheating and Plagiarism

Possibly the best defense against high-tech cheating is information. Explore the hardware and software in computer stores and read instructional technology journals. Attend technology workshops. Explore online paper mills and learn to download and edit a paper. Ask students to explain how technology tools in their classrooms can be used for cheating. Students may be less likely to cheat when they know their teachers and parents are informed. *Chapter topics:* Information As a First Line of Defense; High-Tech Defenses Against Cheating Technologies; Blocking, Filtering and Rating Systems; Using Technology to Identify Plagiarism; Web Sites with Resources for Countering Plagiarism; Searching the Internet for the Originals of Plagiarized Papers. *Article reprint:* "Student Plagiarism in an Online World" by Julie Ryan.

Chapter 6: Parents: Vigilant, Informed, Involved

Parents have the most important role in limiting cheating and plagiarism. They set the moral tone in the home and model ethical behavior for their children. Active involvement in a variety of school activities can open important lines of communication with their children's teachers. It is especially important that parents deal ethically and fairly with any instances of cheating or plagiarism by their own children. *Chapter topics:* Be Informed About Technology in Your Schools and Involved in School Activities; Be a Model of Ethical Behavior; Be Ethical in Dealing with Student Cheating or Plagiarism. *COPY ME pages:* Help, But Not Too Much; Practical Suggestions to Support Students at Home and School; Willful Blindness About Cheating. *Article reprint:* "Honoring Tomorrow's Leaders Today" by Paul Krouse.

Chapter 7: Integrity, Ethics, and Character Education

Students should receive the following clear and consistent message from adults they respect at school and at home: *Honesty and integrity are the hallmarks of good character and are expected from everyone. Dishonesty in any form, including cheating and plagiarism, is wrong and will not be tolerated.* Educators and parents who send this message, and who model honesty and integrity in their own behavior, *will* make a difference in students' lives. *Chapter topics:* Character Education at Teacher-Training Institutions; The Power of Story; Institutes, Centers and Resources that Support Ethics, Integrity, and Character Education; Student Discussions of Integrity and Ethical Character. *COPY ME pages:* Does Cheating Harm Your Career? Are These Valid Reasons to Cheat or Plagiarize? *Article reprint:* "The Six E's of Character Education" by Kevin Ryan.

Chapter 8: Academic Integrity Policies

We cannot let students make cheating and plagiarizing into a game where *whoever cheats the most is the winner.* One positive approach is the development of an Academic Integrity Policy. It is important that all administrators, Board members, faculty, students, and parents—in effect, the entire school community—participate in the development of the policy. It should define cheating and plagiarism explicitly, prohibit any use of technology for illicit purposes, and establish appropriate procedures and penalties for violations. This policy should be adopted by the Board of Education, publicized throughout the district, and implemented fairly and consistently by all teachers and administrators. *Chapter topics:* Initiating an Action Plan; Gathering Local Statistical Data; Honor Code or Integrity Policy? School Board, Administrative, and Faculty Leadership; Student Leadership; Acceptable Use Policies; Fair Enforcement and an Ethical School Culture; Publicizing the Academic Integrity Policy; One High School's Academic Honesty Code. *COPY ME pages:* How to Develop a Strong Program for Academic Integrity; Ten Principles of Academic Integrity for Faculty; One Principal's Commitment to Ethics. *Article reprint:* "Honor Codes: Teaching Integrity and Interdependence" by Lewis Cobbs.

Chapter 9: Defining Cheating and Plagiarism for Students

Students must have a clear understanding of cheating or plagiarism: *If you had any help that you don't want your teacher or parents to know about, you probably cheated. If you didn't think of it and write it all on your own, and you didn't cite (or write down) the sources where you found the ideas or the words, it's probably plagiarism. Chapter topics:* Learning to Recognize Cheating and Plagiarism; Permissible Collaboration; Ethical Use of Writing Centers and Private

Tutors; Copyright Issues; Explaining Collaboration and Plagiarism to Students from Other Cultures. *COPY ME pages:* When Is Collaboration OK? Are Any of These Cheating? Are Any of These Plagiarizing? *Article reprint:* "But I Changed Three Words! Plagiarism in the ESL Classroom" by Lenora Thompson and Portia Williams.

Chapter 10: Dealing with Student Dishonesty

Cheating and plagiarism are unpleasant realities for teachers. The best preparation for dealing with these problems is to become familiar with the district's or school's Academic Integrity Policy, or to help establish a policy if there is none. The Academic Integrity Policy defines illicit actions, outlines procedures for dealing with violations, and specifies penalties. Make sure students and parents understand the policy and know that it will be enforced. *Chapter topics:* "Why Shouldn't I Cheat? Dealing With Suspected Cheating or Plagiarism; Suggestions for Informing Parents; Fair and Effective Penalties; Concern for Privacy Rights; Requiring That an Assignment or Test Be Completed Fairly. *COPY ME page:* A Case of High School Plagiarism. *Article reprint:* "Notes on Cheating for the Busy Classroom Teacher" by Berk Moss.

Chapter 11: Reducing Cheating on Tests and Assignments

We can reduce cheating when we (1) convince students that all of the teachers are committed to creating an honest and ethical school environment, (2) develop an Academic Integrity Policy that is enforced fairly and consistently, and (3) involve parents in our efforts. Testing procedures are less susceptible to cheating when tests are designed to focus on interpretation and critical thinking, security precautions are in place, and students are closely monitored. Without these efforts the students' grades may be so contaminated by cheating that they no longer represent a fair evaluation of work accomplished. *Chapter topics:* "Smart People" Tests; Teachers Who Care About Cheating; Reducing Cheating on Tests, Assignments, Homework, Lab Reports, etc.

Chapter 12: The Librarian-Teacher Team

The librarian plays an important role in the research process, collaborating with the teacher in designing and implementing projects to build information literacy. Librarians offer faculty workshops, student orientation sessions, and individual assistance to teachers and students in locating and evaluating appropriate research materials online and in print. *Chapter topics:* The Librarian as Team Teacher; Real-life Importance of Research; Librarians Are Sources of Information about the Internet; Teachers and Librarians Collaborate on Research Assignments; Librarians Make Research Materials Accessible. *COPY ME page:* Cyber-Plagiarism Faculty Workshop.

Chapter 13: Identifying and Reducing Plagiarism

Experienced teachers may suspect a paper has been plagiarized when it is written well above a student's usual ability level, doesn't quite fit the assignment, has footnotes that are not found in the bibliography, cites a number of college-level references, has no current references, and so on. The sudden appearance of a completed paper may be questioned in cases where the teacher has not observed any work being accomplished in class or in the library. Parents can suspect plagiarism when they have not observed any of the research or writing being done at home or have been put off with excuses when they ask to see a draft of the paper. Unintentional plagiarism may occur when students do not understand the concept clearly or have not learned the necessary research and writing skills. *Chapter topics:* "High-Tech" and "Low-Tech" Plagiarism; Unintentional Plagiarism; Indicators of Possible Plagiarism. *COPY ME pages:* An Electronic Scavenger Hunt; Plagiarism and the Web. *Article reprint:* "Dear Teacher, Johnny Copied" by Jackson, Tway, and Frager.

Chapter 14: Structuring Writing Assignments to Reduce Plagiarism

A student's grade for a research assignment should be based on an evaluation of all steps in the research *process* rather than only on the content and organization of the written report, or *product*. This can reduce plagiarism by requiring outlines, drafts, working bibliographies, or other specific materials not readily available from online sources. A student research portfolio can help to organize and document the research *process. Chapter topics:* Evaluating Both the Research *Process* and the *Product;* Student Writing Handbook; Structuring an Effective Writing Assignment. *COPY ME page:* Research Portfolio Cover Sheet. *Article reprint:* "Teaching Practices that Encourage or Eliminate Student Plagiarism" by Susan Davis.

Chapter 15: Tools for Writing without Plagiarizing

Students who have learned the skills of paraphrasing, summarizing, and quoting selectively, with correct citations, will have a better understanding of plagiarism and how to avoid it. The lesson ideas in this chapter are excerpts from journal articles or reports that suggest ways to teach the skills students need to avoid plagiarism. Complete citations to the original articles are provided for readers who want to explore a lesson in more detail. *Article reprint:* "Anti-Plagiarism Strategies for Research Papers" by Robert Harris.

Chapter 16: Alternatives to Traditional Writing Assignments

It is more difficult for students to locate a paper online or from other sources when an assignment is unusual, requires a particular focus or point of view, lists quotations from one or more specific reference sources that must be included, or is individualized in some other way. Suggested ideas include writing a paper that includes a survey, interview, or other primary research data collected by the student; comparing and contrasting two points of view on a controversial topic; or writing a letter describing a dinner with an historical person, author, or other famous person from the era being studied. *Article reprint:* "A Way to Break Down Writing Research Papers into Steps That Emphasize the Discovery Aspect of Research" by Helena Worthen.

Chapter 17: Online Sites for Reports and Research Papers

Fifty online sites have been identified as representative of those available to students who want to avoid writing their own report. Many have a disclaimer that their papers are to be used for research only and must not be turned in as the student's own work.

Student Cheating and Plagiarism in the Internet Era: A Wake-Up Call, by Ann Lathrop and Kathleen Foss, Libraries Unlimited, 2000.

Author-Title Index

Subject Index

ABOUT THE AUTHORS

ANN LATHROP is a retired professor of school librarianship at California State University, Long Beach, where she was coordinator of the school library credential program. She has been a library consultant, high school librarian, and elementary school teacher. She was the founder, and director for seventeen years, of the California Software Clearinghouse, a national instructional software evaluation project funded by the California Department of Education. She is co-author of *Student Cheating and Plagiarism in the Internet Era: A Wake-up Call* (Libraries Unlimited, 2000). Her other publications include *Courseware in the Classroom, CD-ROM Databases in School Libraries,* and numerous articles on the evaluation of instructional technology. Her Master of Library Service is from Rutgers University and her doctorate in instructional technology is from the University of Oregon.

Since her retirement, Ann has become interested in the study of student cheating and plagiarism. Her first book on the topic, *Student Cheating and Plagiarism in the Internet Era: A Wake-up Call*, is an in-depth exploration of why and how students cheat and plagiarize, and suggests many practical steps toward prevention. This new book explores in detail a number of strategies being implemented to reduce both cheating and plagiarism. Reader's comments are encouraged and appreciated, especially the sharing of success stories. Contact Ann at alathrop@csulb.edu.

KATHLEEN FOSS is library media specialist at Los Alamitos (CA) High School and also has worked in public libraries. She became interested in student plagiarism when an English teacher asked for help in proving a student had copied his paper from the Internet. She and Ann began work on an article that gradually grew into their first book, *Student Cheating and Plagiarism in the Internet Era: A Wake-up Call.*

Kathleen's on-going research on the topic led to their development of this new book. It is a positive, encouraging description of effective programs where students, teachers, librarians, coaches, administrators, and parents are working together to counter the problems of cheating and plagiarism in our schools. Kathy presents conference sessions and workshops for teachers and administrators on plagiarism and the Internet, and on introducing high school students to electronic research. Her Master of Library Science is from the University of Southern California and her B.A. and teaching credential from California State University, Long Beach. Contact Kathleen at k_foss@losal.org.